Silencing Scientists and Scholars in Other Fields: Power, Paradigm Controls, Peer Review, and Scholarly Communication

Contemporary Studies in Information Management, Policy, and Services
(formerly Information Management, Policy, and Services series)

Peter Hernon, series editor

Technology and Library Information Services
Carol Anderson and Robert Hauptman, 1993
Information Policies
Robert H. Burger, 1993
Organizational Decision Making and Information Use
Mairéad Browne, 1993
Seeking Meaning: A Process Approach to Library and Information Services
Carol Collier Kuhlthau, 1993
Meaning and Method in Information Studies
Ian Cornelius, 1996
Library Performance Accountability and Responsiveness Essays in Honor of Ernest R. DeProspo
Charles C. Curran and F. William Summers, 1990
Curriculum Initiative: An Agenda and Strategy for Library Media Programs
Michael B. Eisenberg and Robert E. Berkowitz, 1988
Resource Companion to Curriculum Initiative: An Agenda and Strategy for Library Media Programs
Michael B. Eisenberg and Robert E. Berkowitz, 1988
Information Problem-Solving: The Big Six Skills Approach to Library & Information Skills Instruction
Michael B. Eisenberg and Robert E. Berkowitz, 1990
Deep Information: The Role of Information Policy in Environmental Sustainability
John Felleman, 1997
Database Ownership and Copyright Issues Among Automated Library Networks: An Analysis and Case Study
Janice R. Franklin, 1993
Research for School Library Media Specialists
Kent R. Gustafson and Jane Bandy Smith, 1994
The Role and Importance of Managing Information for Competitive Positions in Economic Development
Keith Harman, 1989

A Practical Guide to Managing Information for Competitive Positioning to
Economic Development
    Keith Harman, 1990
Into the Future: The Foundations of Library and Information Services in the Post-
Industrial Era
    Michael H. Harris and Stan A. Hannah, 1993
Into the Future: The Foundations of Library and Information Services in the Post-
Industrial Era, Second Edition
    Michael H. Harris, Stan A. Hannah and Pamela C. Harris, 1998
Librarianship: The Erosion of a Woman's Profession
    Roma Harris, 1992
Statistics: A Component of the Research Process
    Peter Hernon, 1991
Statistics: A Component of the Research Process, Second Edition
    Peter Hernon, 1994
Research Misconduct: Issues, Implications and Strategies
    Ellen Altman and Peter Hernon, 1997
Service Quality in Academic Libraries
    Peter Hernon and Ellen Altman, 1996
Microcomputer Software for Performing Statistical Analysis: A Handbook for
Supporting Library Decision Making
    Peter Hernon and John V. Richardson (editors), 1988
Evaluation and Library Decision Making
    Peter Hernon and Charles R. McClure, 1990
Public Access to Government Information, Second Edition
    Peter Hernon and Charles R. McClure, 1988
Federal Information Policies in the 1990s: Views and Perspectives
    Peter Hernon, Charles McClure, and Harold C. Relyea, 1996
Statistics for Library Decision Making: A Handbook
    Peter Hernon, et al., 1989
Understanding Information Retrieval Interactions: Theoretical and Practical Implications
    Carol A. Hert, 1997
Reclaiming the American Library Past: Writing the Women In
    Suzanne Hildenbrand (editor), 1996
Libraries: Partners in Adult Literacy
    Deborah Johnson, Jane Robbins, and Douglas L. Zweizig, 1991
The Dissemination of Spatial Data: A North American–European Comparative Study
on the Impact of Government Information Policy
    Xavier Lopez, 1998
The National Research and Education Network (NREN): Research and Policy
Perspectives
    *Charles R. McClure, Ann P. Bishop, Philip Doty and Howard Rosenbaum
    (editors)*, 1991

Library and Information Science Research: Perspective and Strategies for Improvement
    Charles R. McClure and Peter Hernon (editors), 1991
U.S. Government Information Policies: Views and Perspectives
    Charles R. McClure, Peter Hernon, and Harold C. Relyea, 1989
U.S. Scientific and Technical Information Policies: Views and Perspectives
    Charles R. McClure and Peter Hernon, 1989
Silencing Scientists and Scholars in Other Fields: Power, Paradigm Controls, Peer Review, and Scholarly Communication
    Gordon Moran, 1998
Gatekeepers in Ethnolinguistic Communities
    Cheryl Metoyer-Duran, 1993
Knowledge Diffusion in the U.S. Aerospace Industry: Managing Knowledge for Competitive Advantage
    Thomas E. Pinelli, et al., 1997
Basic Research Methods for Librarians, Third Edition
    Ronald R. Powell, 1997
Information of the Image, Second Edition
    Allan Pratt, 1997
Silencing Science: National Security Controls and Scientific Communication
    Harold C. Relyea, 1994
Records Management and the Library: Issues and Practices
    Candy Schwartz and Peter Hernon, 1993
Computer-Supported Decision Making: Meeting the Decision Demands of Modern Organizations
    Charles L. Smith, Sr., 1998
Assessing the Public Library Planning Process
    Annabel K. Stephens, 1996
Depository Library Use of Technology: A Practitioner's Perspective
    Jan Swanbeck and Peter Hernon, 1993
For Information Specialists
    Howard White, Marcia Bates, and Patrick Wilson, 1992
Public Library Youth Services: A Public Policy Approach
    Holly G. Willett, 1995

In Preparation:

The Information Systems of International Inter-Governmental Organizations: A Reference Guide
    Robert Williams

Silencing Scientists and Scholars in Other Fields: Power, Paradigm Controls, Peer Review, and Scholarly Communication

by
Gordon Moran

Ablex Publishing Corporation
Greenwich, Connecticut
London, England

Printed in the United States of America

Library of Congress Cataloging-in-Publication Data

Moran, Gordon.
    Silencing scientists and scholars in other fields : power, paradigm
controls, peer review, and scholarly communication / by Gordon
Moran.
        p. cm. — (Contemporary studies in information management,
policy, and services)
    Includes bibliographical references and index.
    ISBN 1-56750-342-X. — ISBN 1-56750-343-8 (pbk.)
    1. Communication in science. 2. Academic freedom. 3. Science and
state. 4. Censorship. I. Title. II. Series
Q179.94.M67 1998
378.1'21—dc21   97–30773
                                           CIP

Ablex Publishing Corporation   Published in the U.K. and Europe by:
55 Old Post Road #2   JAI Press Ltd.
P.O. Box 5297   38 Tavistock Street
Greenwich, CT 06831   Covent Garden
                             London WC2E 7PB
                             England

P

Dedicated to the life and works of John Swan, a great inspiration for persons who cherish intellectual freedom and academic freedom

Contents

Preface

Many persons have been of invaluable help in making this book possible. Michael Mallory has been, and continues to be, a collaborator in studies relating to the Guido Riccio controversy. Miles Chappell, Alice Wohl, John Agnew, Craig Smyth, Eve Borsook, Giuliano Catoni, Neil MacGregor, Koos Wynia, Rodolfo Bechelloni, and Giorgio Sacchi have provided help in getting ideas published at crucial times in the Guido Riccio debate.

When the Guido Riccio controversy led to problems of peer review, scholarly communication, and academic librarianship, a number of scholars, led by John Swan, helped place the situation within the parameters of academic and intellectual suppression case studies.These scholars include Brian Martin, Serge Lang, Hans Ruesch, Bill Katz, Hazel Bell, Harold Hillman, Ivor Catt, Ralph Eubanks, Herbert Morton, Walter Stewart, Ned Feder, Gaudenz Freuler, Franco Filippini, Federico Di Trocchio, Michiel Tegelaars, Wilfred Cude, Moti Nissani, Juan Miguel Campanario, Dirk Pereboom, Guy Ankerl, Peter Hernon, Ellen Altman, Robert Fugmann, Ilio Calabresi, and especially Robert Hauptman. Jonathan Bush has been a constant support throughout these studies. Many librarians and archivists have given outstanding help and advice.

Introduction

The setting is the dining room of Pierson College at Yale University during the academic year 1956–1957, where the Fellows of Pierson College had lunch together every other Wednesday or so. These Fellows consisted of some of the most famous professors at Yale (if not also in academia at large) from a variety of academic disciplines.

As a freshman "bursary" student, that is, a work-scholarship student, assigned to clearing the tables in the Pierson College dining room, it was possible to listen in on the conversation of the Fellows. In fact, there was a temptation to linger while clearing the tables, taking in as much of their conversation as possible. Their erudition obviously made a strong impression, but the biggest impression of all was made by the civility of discourse during specific discussions in which there was strong disagreement of opinion. As a result of this experience, it became an assumption, if not a belief, that such civility of discourse characterized the behavior of famous scholars whenever they engaged in intellectual debate with their colleagues.

Years later, as an independent scholar who still believed that civility of discourse and debate was a hallmark of the academic world, I had no hesitation to attempt to publish some information and hypotheses that contradicted what was being taught as a paradigm in art history classrooms, and what was written in art history textbooks, monographs, encyclopedias, and so on. The Guido Riccio debate among scholars, thus, formally began in 1977 with a small article in which the traditional attribution to the famous artist Simone Martini for the large equestrian portrait of the mercenary soldier Guido Riccio da Fogliano was contested (Moran, 1977). This large wall painting located in the Palazzo Pubblico museum in Siena, Italy, not only is famous among art historians, but is also a major tourist attraction that is reproduced extensively in Siena and Italy on the covers of guidebooks, posters for tourist agencies, posters for tennis tournaments, plates, ashtrays, lampshades, bathroom tile decoration, and even wine bottle labels.

I did not expect that all other scholars would immediately agree that this famous painting was painted by someone other than Simone Martini, but at the very least I expected that any debate that ensued would proceed with a civility of discourse more or less similar to that of the Pierson College Fellows in 1956–1957. Instead, the Guido Riccio controversy, which is still ongoing, has been characterized by, among other things, insults, censorship, and falsifications, all directed toward silencing the new, unwanted hypotheses. This situation intensified to such a degree that I received a request to write an article on the case from the standpoint of "Resistance to Critical Thinking" (Moran & Mallory, 1991a). More recently, I received another request to write a chapter on the subject for a book entitled *Confronting the Experts* (Mallory & Moran, 1996).

What happened? Was it simply foolishly naive to assume, much less believe, that civility of discourse and debate, based on scholarly critical analysis, extended beyond groups of scholars such as the Pierson College Fellows? Or, was it a case of confusing interdisciplinary collegiality among a small, close-knit group of scholars who lunched together regularly with the reality of debate within a specific academic discipline on an international level? In any case, the reactions of the art history community, in the face of various scholarly evidence, created such a great sense of surprise that I felt that such reactions must be an exception rather than the norm.

At one point, Stewart and Feder, scholars in the field of biomedical research, having heard of censorship attempts in the Guido Riccio case, got in touch with me to compare notes and to seek advice on how to overcome censorship that they were facing at the National Institutes of Health (NIH) and elsewhere in the scientific community. This contact led to a study of some of the "file" studies of Serge Lang (mathematics department, Yale University) dealing with problems of censorship and responsibility among the higher echelons of the scientific community, including the National Academy of Sciences (NAS). At that point, it became obvious that problems encountered in the Guido Riccio debate occurred elsewhere in academia as well, and also that such problems extended beyond the specific subject matter of specific academic disciplines, involving, in effect, larger problems of peer review, scholarly communication, and information management. These larger problems involved the work of information scientists, academic librarians, historians of science and medicine, and sociologists. In several cases, I have compared experiences in the Guido Riccio case with situations in science that relate to problems of peer review and academic librarianship, and these studies were published in *Library Trends* (Moran & Mallory, 1991b), *The Indexer* (Mallory & Moran, 1994), and *The Reference Librarian* (Moran, 1991).

In the midst of these studies of scholarly communication that incorporated the Guido Riccio case with similar cases in the sciences, a book appeared that turned out to be crucial: *Silencing Science* (Relyea, 1994). It contains a thorough and vivid account of how, in the name of national security, attempts were made to withhold certain scientific information from the Soviet Union during the 1980s. Relyea's work shows how power, on the part of individuals and institutions, overcame the principles of academic freedom and intellectual freedom. Throughout his book, Relyea asserted that the censorship and suppression in this case were contrary to traditional scientific communication, which is marked by "open communication and free sharing of information" (p. 6), and he stated that "the practice of openness became institutionalized" (p. 9) from around the second half of the 17th century.

The question arose whether the assertion or belief that "openness became institutionalized" was any different from the assumption or belief that scholars who disagreed with each other in academic debates used the same civility of discourse that the Pierson College Fellows did in 1956–1957 when they disagreed with each other. In other words, was the systematic suppression and censorship of some types of scientific information during the 1980s the exception, or was it business as usual in the sense that those in power who feel inclined to suppress information, for whatever reason, might attempt to do so? This question lingered.

Thus, an expansion on the theme of "silencing" in academia seemed warranted. M. Nissani (personal communication, June 11, 1996) suggested that if research were conducted for "any period in the history of any natural science," a large amount of rejection and suppression of new ideas would be revealed. Obviously such a study is beyond the scope of this book. At the same time, a study of how scholars are silenced, and why scholars are silenced, based to a large extent on selective case studies, can build on Relyea's (1994) work within the context of information management, policy, and services.

In fact, with the use of the term *silencing,* Relyea (1994) seemed to invite, or provoke, discussion of an expansion on some themes in his book. Silencing is a more encompassing term than censorship, suppression, or peer-review rejection. Silencing takes place at various levels: A scholar might be silenced, an idea might be silenced, and the truth might be silenced by a big lie. In some cases, scholars might be able to overcome specific attempts to silence them, but the ideas in their published work might have little or no impact on what is taught in the classroom, what is published in textbooks and reference books, or what becomes public health policy or foreign policy. Thus, despite numerous publications, a scholar's ideas can, in all practicality, be silenced as a result of lack of impact. As I show, when such silencing based on lack of impact results in the silencing of the truth, great harm can be done.

Silence is not only imposed, in some cases, on scholars and ideas, but silence is also employed, by academic leaders and peer review authorities, for instance, as a tactic. Letters are not answered. Requests to present papers at scholarly conferences are not acknowledged (much less taken into consideration). When a pattern of such silence develops, the situation is called *stonewalling.*

Several of the chapters in this book cover material that could easily be expanded into book length, and not all of the pertinent material can be included in this book. There is no intention of giving a history of intellectual suppression, or a full discussion of peer review in all its aspects. Rather, the theme of silencing of scholars is illustrated by means of various case studies from the past as well as the present. Within such a context, this book is also intended as an appeal: one to academic peer-review authorities to live up to the rhetoric of openness, open discussion, open debate, and free exchange of ideas among scholars. It is also intended as an appeal to academic librarians to broaden the concept of "free flow of information" to include information that is the subject matter of both (or all) sides of academic controversies. Within the framework of these appeals, the contents of some of the chapters in this book are overlapping and intertwined. Some of the source material that is referred to and cited in order to illustrate some of the case studies may be hitherto unknown to some readers, even though some of this material was published years ago and has had rather wide distribution. One of the reasons such material might be unknown to readers is that there have been rather successful efforts to silence the material, as far as the mainstream of academic literature is concerned.

In a certain sense, any book about the silencing of scholars at any time in history might be seen against a backdrop in which the "whole picture is one of a power struggle where the odds against innovation are great but the addiction of the innovator to truth is supreme" (de Grazia, 1978, p. 200). The major forces, or factors, against innovation would include paradigm protection, and so-called turf protection. Along this line, in an article in *Science* about controversies in astronomy, Burbidge was quoted as saying, "When we come across things we don't like we cut them off, we referee them to death" (Marshall, 1990, p. 16). For the purposes of this book, terms such as *cut off* or *referee to death* are equivalents of silence. If a new hypothesis is successfully cut off, it is silenced. To the extent that peer-review authorities manage to referee a new idea to death, that idea is silenced as far as the mainstream academic literature and teaching are concerned.

Under such circumstances, it would seem that many scholars who come up with ideas and discoveries that peer-review authorities "don't like" might become resigned to being silenced to some degree regarding such ideas and discoveries, and, as a result, turn their scholarly attention elsewhere. They might rather switch than fight. (They might also be aware that if they fight and lose, they might eventually be forced to switch anyway, as far as a career is concerned.)

However, some scholars resent being silenced and do not give up easily in their attempts to be heard and to make an impact. In the book *Confronting the Experts*, Sharma (1996) asserted that he performed best "when in confrontation with powerful authorities" (p. 173). From a similar standpoint, a book about silencing of scholars amounts to investigations of academic confrontations involving strong vested interests—of a personal or institutional nature—battling against the academic equivalent of what the famous poet Byron referred to as the "Eternal Spirit of the chainless Mind."

1

Silencing of Scholars Within Totalitarian and Democratic Forms of Government

In his book *Heidegger and Nazism*, Farias (1989) stated that under the law only those scholars who completed political indoctrination courses were granted the right to teach in German universities (p. 194). Cude (1987a) referred to Lysenko as "the biologist who arranged the banishment to the gulag of his intellectual rivals during Stalin's time" (p. 61). Hitler was the enemy of Stalin during World War II, but both leaders had a common bond regarding higher education; namely, the policy that the government was in control of who could teach and what could be taught. Scholars who did not conform were silenced. No matter what the political ideology is, in a totalitarian government those who have political power have the power to silence scholars within their academic systems. The government censors and suppresses unwanted information and ideas.

PUNISHMENT OF DISSIDENTS AND THE BIG LIE

In theory and in practice, in totalitarian states scholars *can* write and communicate—in secret—ideas that are banned by the government. They can also try to

5

smuggle them out of the country and have them published under a false name. In this sense, complete silencing is virtually impossible. However, these secret writings do not get into the mainstream scholarly literature of the country and are not taught in the classrooms (where monitors might be stationed to make sure that dissident views are not expressed).

If scholars in a totalitarian state attempt to challenge the system or its leaders openly, these scholars might end up in mental institutions for experiments with drugs that attempt to bring about thought control. Even a passive attitude toward the official government ideology might result in punishment. In a movie that depicted university life under Nazi rule, a professor was lecturing on the composition of human blood. He was asked (by a monitor, either an official monitor, or a self-appointed one) if the blood of Aryans was different than that of non-Aryans. The professor stated that it might be true, but as far as he knew, there was no scientific proof for it. This was enough, according to the script, to have the professor sent to prison and fired from the university. He died shortly thereafter in prison (it was not clear if he was killed from hard labor or was actually executed).

The silencing of scholars in totalitarian regimes is an extension of government control of speech by individuals, control of the press, and control of mass media. Truth is not as important as various forms of expression that will help prop up and strengthen the specific totalitarian form of government. In such a case, the Big Lie technique can replace the search for truth. On an evening radio broadcast in the wake of the dismantling of the Berlin Wall, and during the process of reunification of Germany, it was announced that textbooks in East German schools had to be changed, that much of the content of the present textbooks was untrue and now obsolete. These textbooks might be regarded as part of the Big Lie technique, which is often taken for granted as an integral part of a totalitarian system.

ACADEMIC FREEDOM AND INTELLECTUAL FREEDOM

By contrast, in democratic societies, academic freedom is a logical extension of freedom of expression and freedom of the press. Academic associations and professional scholarly societies often have their own policy statements of commitment to academic freedom incorporated into their charters, regulations, or other documents. The same is true for specific institutions of higher learning.

Within the library profession, the concepts of First Amendment freedom of speech, and of academic freedom in universities, find equivalents in terms such as intellectual freedom, free flow of information, and the "freedom to read" ideal (Cornog & Perper, 1992, p. 12). Some librarians take an activist attitude and role in intellectual freedom activities (often associated with anticensorship activity).

The underlying principle of these various concepts of freedom of expression is that the government does not have the right to interfere with or curtail freedom of expression of individuals, private groups, or institutions. If the principles of the First

Amendment, academic freedom, intellectual freedom, freedom to read, and the free flow of information were all combined in practice, it would seem impossible to silence scholars. Not only would scholars be free to write and teach whatever they want to, but their ideas would be included in the free flow of information.

SILENCING SCHOLARS BY LAWS AND LAWSUITS

In practice and in reality, however, there are various ways to silence scholars in democratic societies. Some of these are legalistic. In *Silencing Science*, Relyea's (1994) excellent discussion of "national security" shows that the term can be used in various ways, ranging from a narrow definition to a very broad, encompassing one. Some scientific and technological information, and scholars who discuss this information, can be silenced in the name of national security, which allegedly has priority over academic freedom if there is a conflict between them. The broader the definition, the greater the possibility legally to restrict ideas and information and to deny access to some scholarly material, all of which can result in silencing scholars to one degree or another.

Although, as Relyea (1994) pointed out, there has been much disagreement about how far the definition of national security should be extended, there is general agreement about the logical necessity, particularly in wartime, for legal restrictions and secrecy based on national security concerns. The contents of such restrictions can have silencing effects on scholars, particularly scientists. The greater the sense of urgency or emergency, the more likely scholars are inclined to sacrifice their academic freedom on a temporary basis in the interests of national security. Problems begin, however, as Relyea (1994) pointed out, when there are attempts to silence scholars in the name of national security when it is not clear that such urgency or emergency exists. At that point, scholars might feel that the term *national security* is being used as an excuse for censorship and suppression.

National security, however, is not the only form of restriction based on law. Libel and defamation laws also play a role in the silencing of scholars. The government utilizes national security controls, but individuals and institutions can utilize libel and defamation laws to try to silence scholars. Like national security, *libel* and *defamation* are terms that can be quite elastic and subject to varying interpretations. Not all libel laws are exactly the same, and not all judges interpret them in exactly the same manner. Even the mere threat of a libel or defamation suit might scare some scholars, and even editors of scholarly publications, into silence, not necessarily because of the likely outcome (winning or losing), but merely because of the large sums of money and long hours of time and effort that might be required to fight a lawsuit.

A few recent examples can demonstrate how such lawsuits, whether they are followed through to a legal judgment, or whether they are withdrawn long before a legal judgment would have been made, can silence scholars and editors. A rather scary story—scary from the standpoint of academic freedom—is told in the first person by

Beck (1993) in *Art Restoration: The Culture, the Business and the Scandal*. Beck was chair of the art history department at Columbia University in New York City. His main field of study is Italian Renaissance art, and his specialty is the art of Jacopo della Quercia, a 15th-century sculptor from Siena. Beck is regarded as a leading expert on Jacopo della Quercia, and on Quercia's masterpiece, the sculptural portrait known as Ilaria, located in the Tuscan town of Lucca.

The sculpture of Ilaria was recently restored. As Beck (1993) told it, an artist who saw the restored work was taken back by how different it looked after the restoration. Beck was asked to look at the restored work, which he eventually did, and he, too, was surprised by the result of the restoration. He disapproved of how the work of art now looks, and in his role as a specialist in the field of study, he gave a negative judgment about the restoration, and he called for an open debate and discussion about it. His remarks were reported in various newspapers and on television, perhaps not only because he was a leading expert on the subject, but also because he had previously harshly criticized the restoration of the famous Sistine Chapel paintings in the Vatican, setting off a bitter controversy.

In the wake of the newspaper and television coverage, the person who restored the Ilaria sculpture sued Beck for defamation in courts in Torino, Livorno, and Firenze (i.e., the cities where the press had reported his negative criticisms). Of the three suits, the most dramatic one took place in Firenze, because, as Beck (1993) recounted it, the judge decided, even before the evidence was presented, that he would be convicted. By pure chance, according to Beck, a person overheard the judge making the conviction comment to the restorer's lawyer in a hallway near the courtroom. It was reported to Beck's lawyer, and eventually to Beck himself and protest was made to the judicial body that oversees the judiciary.

If he had been convicted, Beck would have become a silenced scholar, and the upshot and ramifications of the case might well have caused many other scholars to become silent, out of fear that they, too, might be convicted before the evidence was heard in court. Such fear could silence many important critical scholarly judgments that otherwise might have been expressed in specialized fields of study. This situation would seem to represent one of the greatest chilling factors in academia.

As it turned out, Beck won the lawsuit, and, as a result, he has become more vociferous. Among other things, he founded an organization called ArtWatch International, Inc., dedicated to the protection of works of art, similar to organizations dedicated to the protection of human rights or protection of the environment. Obviously, one of the purposes of Beck's organization is to protect works of art from bad restorations. Furthermore, before major restorations are made on works that are masterpieces and considered to be part of the artistic patrimony belonging to all mankind, Beck (1993) proposed open debate and discussion among specialists, scholars, and other interested persons, relating to the necessity of the restoration and to the type of restoration that will be made.

There have been further attempts to silence Beck now that he is engaged in ArtWatch activity. One of these attempts to silence him has led to a paradoxical twist, as it is Beck who has taken legal action against a famous art historian after this art historian wrote very negative judgments about Beck, and after these strongly negative comments got into the Italian news media. Beck (1996) wrote in an ArtWatch letter, "I was accused of being 'presumptuous' and 'ignorant' by a distinguished art historian.... The language used was so extraordinary that I have filed a court petition" (p. 2). All of this is a far cry from the civility of debate that marked the disagreements among the Pierson College Fellows, and it seems very strange that debates about art restoration techniques can take place in courtrooms instead of at cordial luncheons, scholarly conferences, or in scholarly publications.

Not all scholars fare as well as Beck did in court in relation to the Ilaria restoration case, however, and it seems that the outcome for Beck himself would have been much different if someone had not overheard, by chance, the indiscreet words of a judge. The case of Hans Ruesch may break all records (or come close to breaking all records) in terms of the number of legal actions taken against a scholar and the scholar's organization. Ruesch is a scholar of the history of medicine, although many persons may regard him as being famous for his skill as a racing car driver, or for his ability as a writer of best-selling novels.

Much of Ruesch's scholarly work is directed toward demonstrating that animal experimentation in medical research can be unreliable, misleading, and very dangerous when results based on such experimentation are used as models for humans. (Some of his studies and ideas are discussed in other chapters of this book.) He reported that between1989 and early 1996, more than 70 legal actions were taken against him by persons connected with the medical and pharmaceutical establishment. In one of his recent publications, *International Foundation Report*, Ruesch (1993) related that, as a result of these legal actions, some publication plans of the Centre d'Information Vivisectionniste International Scientifique (CIVIS) have been held up (and, thus, silenced, at least for a period of time): "CIVIS had planned an important publication program which lay within our possibilities three years ago. Uninterrupted legal actions conducted against Hans Ruesch through the Swiss courts ... prevented the realization of our program" (p. 16).

Although he has not been completely silenced, much of Ruesch's time, energy, and financial resources have been taken up by the legal actions against him. The sheer number of such actions seems to imply that they function as harassment. As a scholar, Ruesch is being silenced to the extent that time, energy, and financial burdens required to fight the legal actions prevent him from writing, publishing, and giving lectures on his scholarly material.

ROLLING STONE, AIDS RESEARCH, AND A LAWSUIT

Another interesting and revealing attempt to silence scholarly discussion is found in the case involving Tom Curtis, *Rolling Stone* magazine, and Hilary Koprowski. Koprowski, formerly head of Wistar Institute, developed a polio vaccine that was used on a massive experimental basis in Africa (in the region of the former Belgian Congo) in the 1950s. The production of this vaccine involved the use of kidneys from monkeys. Some scholars formulated the hypothesis that the so-called HIV virus, because of its similarity to some simian viruses, was transmitted to humans from monkeys. There were also hypotheses made that the virus jumped the species gap from monkey to man as a result of the polio vaccine experiments in Africa in the 1950s.

Curtis (1992) a freelance investigative journalist, recounted these hypotheses in an article in *Rolling Stone*. Obviously, these hypotheses were very upsetting to many persons in the medical research establishment, and particularly to Koprowski. As a result, Koprowski sued both Curtis and *Rolling Stone*.

Based on principles of truth, falsehood, and malice that are inherent in libel cases in the United States, it did not seem that Curtis would lose the case. Hypotheses were presented as hypotheses, as far as can be determined, and the hypotheses discussed in the article were not inventions of Curtis, but were formulated by other scholars. Besides, another scholar—Louis Pascal—had independently formulated similar hypotheses, and Pascal's (1991) work was published as part of a series of studies by the University of Wollongong. I predicted (G. Moran, personal communication, June 10, 1993; personal communication, November 5, 1993; personal communication, November 18, 1993) that Koprowski would not win his lawsuit, and that the settlement reached would be claimed as a victory for Koprowski. That is what happened.

The lawsuit itself might have created a dampening effect (or chilling effect, to use a common buzzword in academia) on subsequent studies about the relation of polio vaccines to the HIV virus, although there have been some attempts to discuss the issues in various forums. Scholars have been silenced to the extent that the lawsuit has discouraged scholarly discussion and more profound scientific investigations of the subject.

SLAPP SUITS

Some lawsuits that are made primarily to silence criticism are known as *SLAPP suits*. In one case, Yeshiva University sued Leonard Minsky. In an article (Greenberg, 1990) that discusses this lawsuit, Minsky claimed that Yeshiva's action was a "legalistic ploy to silence criticism, otherwise known as a SLAPP suit, for 'Strategic Lawsuit Against Public Participation'" (p. 6). From the standpoint of silencing scholars, it seems significant and revealing that this type of lawsuit has attained a formal name and designation. It is possible that the suits against Beck, Ruesch, and Curtis (as well as against many others attempting to get involved in scholarly discussions or investigations) are of this nature. When such types of lawsuits are used to silence scholars, they become a SLAPP in the face to academic freedom.

LOGISTICAL FACTORS

In addition to legal restraints on academic freedom and the free flow of information, there are also logistical restraints of a practical nature. One of the most obvious is the problem of selectivity. Individual libraries are not able to acquire and process everything that has been written, nor can scholars read and study everything that has been published. Scholars cannot teach, in a single course, everything that has been published on the subject matter of the course, nor can students be expected to read all of the pertinent material as outside reading.

Before the age of electronic publishing, selectivity was already a major problem for peer-review authorities and librarians. Electronic publishing has compounded these problems. Selectivity can also be an excuse for suppression. Although it is true that all papers that have been submitted for a scholarly conference might not be able to be on the program of the conference because of lack of time to read all of them within the time limit of the conference, who knows how many times papers (or manuscripts for articles) have been rejected for "reasons" of time or space when, in fact, the real reason for rejection was that peer-review authorities did not approve of the subject matter.

Also, in some cases, nonselection of a scholarly work might not be the result of deliberate suppression, but instead, the result of a lack of understanding or comprehension of the significance of a work. Whatever the reasons for nonselection, the logistical necessity for selectivity is a major factor in the silencing of scholars. To the extent that scholars' works are not selected, the ideas of these scholars are silenced.

BUREAUCRATIC IMPEDIMENTS

In totalitarian states, centralized governments control the flow of information. In democracies, academic freedom and the free flow of information are, in theory, free of government control. To be completely free of government control, academic freedom and the free flow of information would be in the private realm. In reality, however, much research and scholarship is funded and subsidized by governments, and permission is needed from government agencies to begin and carry out such research. This is particularly true in the field of archaeology, for example. Excavations require a lot of bureaucratic paperwork before the actual research can get underway. If permission is denied, potential important discoveries might not be made. In such cases, denial of permission would create a silence barrier for specific subject matter. Thus, even in democracies there can be a large amount of government control of research and scholarship, based on funding policies and bureaucratic procedures.

Likewise, scientific research sponsored by governments might reflect certain biases, preferences, or priorities of government leaders, who in turn implement bureaucratic procedures to carry out specific research programs. President Richard M. Nixon announced a "war" against cancer. At present, AIDS research is a top priority in some countries.

Such research programs, however, often have certain restraints on the type of research that will be subsidized, to the extent that there is a monolithic rather than open approach to the subject matter. To the extent that scholars' research remains outside of the approach dictated by the bureaucracy, the scholars' ideas might be silenced (examples are discussed in subsequent chapters).

ACADEMIC POLITICS, CAREERS, PARADIGMS, AND "TURF"

The top career positions in an academic discipline include, for instance, head of department (chairs), dean, officers of professional societies and learned societies, editors (and advisors) and peer-review referees of scholarly publications, officials of grant-approving organizations, editors and consultants (advisors) of scholarly reference works, directors and officers of research centers, and directors and organizers of scholarly conferences. There are fewer such positions than there are career-minded scholars competing for these positions. These positions, and the academic, bureaucratic, and financial power that go with them, represent the "turf" of the scholars who have attained and hold such positions. In general, there are several factors that determine, to one degree or another, whether a scholar will attain one or more of these prestigious academic positions. These include productivity (publication of books, articles, and papers given at scholarly conferences), reputation (as teacher, lecturer, or researcher), and academic politics.

The prestige associated with these various positions conveys an aura of authority and implies that the scholars who hold these positions are among the leading experts in their fields of study. The concepts of authority and expertise, in this case, are based on knowledge that has become a body of paradigms within a given academic discipline. It would follow that if new discoveries, findings, ideas, and hypotheses demonstrate—or even indicate—that paradigms believed to be true (and taught as if they were the truth) were, in fact, false, then the aforementioned authority and expertise are placed in doubt. As Schneider (1989) pointed out, "If the knowledge expounded by recognized scholars to their students should prove to be of dubious reliability, then their authority is open to question. Thus, scientific progress and changing theories are natural enemies of authoritarian tradition" (p. 137).

Paradigm busting, or even the mere serious challenge to an entrenched paradigm, can thus create unsure footing for specific academic turf, or place the turf on slippery grounds, as the case may be. At the very least, paradigm-busting ideas prove to be uncomfortable for those scholars who possess the turf. Along this line, Schneider (1989) observed that the "rise and fall of empirical and rational science is mirrored by the rise and fall of scholars and experts who represent that science" (p. 147). As a result, there is a tendency for those who enjoy a reputation of authority and expertise to discourage the publication and discussion of scholarly material that might undermine such authority and expertise. Such discouragement can take place at various levels: awarding of degrees (particularly the PhD), promotion, tenure, peer-review rejection or acceptance of publication of books and articles, participation in scholarly conferences, awarding of research grants, and collegial acceptance or ostracism on the part of colleagues. To the extent that scholars have had paradigm-busting ideas rejected from publication or discussion, and to the extent that scholars have not expressed such ideas out of fear of consequences for their careers, these scholars have been silenced.

SILENCING OF SCHOLARS WHO ATTEMPT TO CORRECT ERROR

In the field of biomedical research, Margot O'Toole detected what she believed was a serious error in a published article (for which she had been involved in the basic research). She felt it was her duty as a scientist to correct the error. In an article, Lang (1993) published her testimony describing a meeting with a high university official: "He told me to charge fraud or drop the matter entirely" (p. 8). In the same article, Lang reproduced part of a letter from David Baltimore to Edward Rall, a high official of the NIH. Baltimore did not approve of NIH scholars Walter Stewart and Ned Feder being involved with the correction of the alleged error that O'Toole detected. Baltimore suggested a commission ("a couple of immunologists") to review the data, and asserted that Stewart and Feder must accept the commission's conclusions: "They must agree to abide by whatever decisions are reached. This means they must promise to cease all discussions of this issue" (p. 15). All scholars involved in the correction of scholarly error who, on the advice or instructions of academic authorities, decide to "drop the matter entirely," or to "cease all discussion" are being silenced. It seems clear that such advice and instructions are contrary to principles of openness and the free exchange of ideas among scholars.

If a situation boils down to a choice between career enhancement or speaking out, scholars might decide on silence instead of speaking out, particularly if they are in the categories somewhere between PhD candidates and professors seeking tenure. Even when tenure and career enhancement have been achieved, however, scholars might be tempted to maintain silence in order to avoid endangering bonds of collegiality with colleagues. If they propose, or even support, paradigm-busting ideas, or if they support someone like O'Toole in the correction of error, their actions might be considered betrayal of their colleagues' authority and expertise.

In *Confronting the Experts*, Hillman (1996) wrote:

There are so many academics, doctors, teachers, and publishers who have a vested interest in current views ... in Britain at least—where academic tenure has been virtually abolished—it is unlikely that anyone who raised the fundamental questions or came to the same conclusions publicly as Mr. Sartory and I have, would ever be appointed to a lectureship, be awarded a large grant for research, or enjoy a successful career in science. (p. 125)

Hillman (1991) added that it "is not surprising that the grant-giving bodies, the research councils and scientific advisory committees, are composed of academics and research directors who support conventional beliefs" (p. 261).

SILENCING OF DISSIDENT SCHOLARS AND UNORTHODOX RESEARCH

After achieving success and esteem in his career in biomedical research, Duesberg (1996) raised some serious questions about orthodox AIDS research. Not long thereafter, "the AIDS establishment directed its power toward isolating and neutralizing Duesberg within scientific circles" (p. 396). Isolating and neutralizing individuals are part of the silencing process, as far as scholarly ideas are concerned.

Lang described some "strong forces which inhibit criticism" in academia:

> One of these forces is "collegiality." … There are other forces of intimidation of various kinds … some influential academics are giving priority to protecting their tribe; they close ranks behind each other; they give priority to "collegiality"; and they obstruct, in so far as they can, criticism of "their own" … there are pressures to shut people up: social pressures, use of bylaws, use of the pecking order, intimidation, etc. (Falcone, 1991, p. 38)

In effect, these forces and pressures that Lang alluded to are some of the many mechanisms and tactics that can be employed in democratic societies to silence scholars and their ideas. One paradoxical tactic that can be employed is to abandon—rather than uphold—the principles of academic freedom when a scholar is under attack for saying or writing things that upset others in the academic's discipline. The Beck trial, described earlier, provides an example. Dunn (1993) wrote that Beck's "fearless stand for free speech did not endear him to the mandarins of art history. Indeed, the editor of *The Burlington Magazine*, an elevated forum for artistic debate … observed privately during the trial that Beck was going to lose so there was not much point in supporting him" (p. 18). Such an attitude would seem to imply that what Beck said or wrote was somehow out of bounds, and the right of freedom of expression must stay within those bounds. As seen later, such bounds are not necessarily strictly legalistic ones, at least in the opinions of some scholars. There are also bounds determined by orthodoxy.

2

Intellectual Freedom, Intellectual Suppression, the Big Lie, and the Freedom to Lie

"Sticks and stones can break my bones, but names will never hurt me." This widespread saying among generations of children might be regarded as something of a childhood preparation and orientation toward intellectual freedom and academic freedom. One implication is that physical violence is forbidden, but verbal violence (or at least verbal impropriety) can be tolerated. However, according to Franklin (1989) in the Foreword to *The Freedom to Lie* (Swan & Peattie, 1989), such a situation might not be valid in the future:

> As humanity enters the cusp of a millennium ... the freedom to lie, to create or deny, to propound or reserve, will predictably ever more be feverishly tested. ... The "socially responsible" ... *will* win some far away day. ... I see the libertarian's cause as a ... postponement ... of the inevitable chill. (pp. xv, xxi)

With these thoughts, Franklin seemed to envision an increasing tendency toward censorship. If he is correct, it can be imagined that scholars will be among the persons against whom censorship (and therefore silence on certain subjects) is imposed.

Peattie (Swan & Peattie, 1989) added to Franklin's ideas:

> I am suggesting that the librarian does have a responsibility ... to help the community ... to distinguish truth from falsehood, allowable opinion from bigoted manipulation ... a library association is not obliged, in the name of intellectual freedom, to offer space and time to a person who proposes to defend racist falsehoods. (pp. 53, 94–95)

It would seem that for both Franklin and Peattie the free speech movement developed at Berkeley some years ago is completely invalid.

In 1988, the activities of the American Library Association (ALA) included a debate entitled "Two Views of Intellectual Freedom." This debate became the basis for a book, with the title changed to *The Freedom to Lie: A Debate About Democracy* (Swan & Peattie, 1989), and the text of the ALA debate was expanded with the inclusion of more material.

This book seems very important for a discussion of silencing of scholars for more than one reason. First, although the ALA and other library associations have been regarded as among the strongest proponents of intellectual freedom within democracies, recently a specific section of the ALA, known by the name of Social Responsibilities, has been formally activated. As the 1988 debate—and the book it spawned—testify, the traditional concepts of intellectual freedom have been questioned and challenged. Furthermore, the scope of the Social Responsibilities' philosophy and activities within the ALA seems to go beyond the phenomenon, on many campuses, known as political correctness (which, as discussed in chapter 11, can be faddish, trendy, and inconsistent).

According to Peattie (and perhaps to many other social responsibilities advocates), evils such as racism and sexism are results of dangerous lies that, as they spread and become believed, become Big Lies. Along this line, Peattie described antisemitism and the Holocaust in terms of "activities of those who got a racist Big Lie in their teeth and ran with it" (Swan & Peattie, 1989, p. 68). In Peattie's view, such activities included conferences "with scholars brought in by train and plane from countries under German occupation," and he cited the "participation of anthropologists, psychologists, and other social scientists" (p. 71). Big Lies should be suppressed, and it would seem to follow that the dangerous lies that comprise the subject matter of the Big Lies should be suppressed before they increase to Big Lie status.

LICENSE FOR A GENERAL SILENCE?

Swan, who debated Peattie at the 1988 ALA conference (and in *The Freedom to Lie*), takes a libertarian stance that would allow all voices, even those proposing Big Lies, to be heard. Swan stated that Peattie wanted "to cast words uttered in the service of the Big Lie out of the environs of free discourse" and observed that "to decide that silencing the offenders is proper recourse ... is to give license for a general silence" (Swan & Peattie, 1989, pp. 109, 111).

Both Swan and Peattie denounce the Big Lie and affirm the necessity of truth to overcome it. It seems that Peattie would ban the Big Lie, whereas Swan would allow it to be uttered, but would combat it, debate it, and expose it as a lie from the time it germinates. The ALA members present at the 1988 debate in New Orleans voted Swan the winner of the debate, but Franklin (1989) stated that "there can be no winner in this debate. ... What there must be is never-ending contention" (p. xx). Franklin's use of the word *contention* in this context might be interpreted to mean attempts to silence persons, including scholars.

From one point of view, it would seem that an important lesson of the Swan–Peattie debate (both at the ALA conference and in the book) is that social responsibilities depends on intellectual freedom. There were no social responsibilities forces to combat the Big Lie because there was no real intellectual freedom within which to operate. From the standpoint of academic freedom, social responsibilities advocates might do better to embrace and support a libertarian version of intellectual freedom, rather than try to place restrictions on it.

This last statement is based on the fact that the concepts of social responsibilities, intellectual freedom, intellectual suppression, academic freedom, political correctness, national security, and peer review are intertwined, to one degree or another, and, as concepts, they are elusive in nature because they can be broadly or narrowly defined. Varying definitions might depend on the mood, atmosphere, and political proclivities at different times in different countries. The elusive nature of these concepts and the elasticity of possible definitions for them can be the cause of disagreement, conflict, and confusion among scholars and academic administrators, and, as the 1988 debate showed, among academic librarians.

Within the framework of the intertwining nature and elusive definition of these concepts, a social responsibilities scenario similar to the following can be envisioned: Racism is evil. Racism is based on a Big Lie. Racists are evil because they propose and perpetuate a Big Lie. It would seem that up to this point social responsibilities proponents would be in general agreement. However, suppose the scenario continues thusly: Racists should not be allowed to teach racist material. Racists should not be allowed to teach at all, because they cannot be trusted to refrain from teaching racist propaganda. Social responsibilities advocates might agree about these points also (although exceptions might be made for some very famous scholars who are suspected of harboring racist feelings).

Now suppose the scenario proceeds further: Scholars who advocate segregation (by race or sex) in education, or who propose the abolition of welfare payments, are racists or sexists. They should not be allowed to teach, and their ideas should neither be published nor discussed at scholarly conferences. If social responsibilities proponents held sway, if there were no intellectual freedom in place to allow debate on these issues, their ideas about segregation and welfare might become official policy. In the face of this scenario, the United Negro College Fund has given support to more than 40 segregated colleges and universities in the United States. Donors to this fund, and administrators and officers of the fund, believe that the colleges and universities that they support have given, and continue to give, valuable educational opportunities. Likewise, there is also a school of thought that sees abolition of welfare not as a racial backlash or an act of injustice, but as a positive step toward greater economic opportunity and enhanced self-esteem, and regards the "culture" of welfare as demeaning to self-esteem and as economic entrapment at a near-poverty level. And so on.

As a concept, social responsibilities seems better equipped to develop and flourish if the concept itself is nourished and protected by intellectual freedom, rather than being in conflict with it. In the various Big Lie situations Peattie referred to, social responsibilities lacked intellectual freedom, the most effective weapon against the Big Lie.

BIG LIES

The classic example (or definition) of the Big Lie is a lie that is repeated often enough, widely enough, and loud enough to drown out all opposing views; thus, it becomes accepted as true. No serious, prolonged, or persistent attempts to contest it are allowed. Some Big Lies are bigger and more dangerous than others. In some cases, the Big Lie is not a deliberate attempt to deceive, but something that is sincerely believed to be true, both by those who proposed it and those who repeat it. In such cases, the Big Lie might be more accurately described as a Big Falsehood. (The book *The Freedom to Lie,* in fact, uses the word *lie* to mean falsehood as well as deliberate lie.)

Big Lies exist and have existed for long periods of time in academia. It is not always possible to know if they originated and grew as a result of deliberate deception or of sincere belief that a falsehood or error was, in fact, true rather than false. In academia, Big Lies are often found in the form of false paradigms. Intellectual history, the history of medicine, and the history of science are filled with examples of false paradigms being accepted as true for long periods of time before being corrected.

The academic equivalent of the concept of "freedom to lie" in the Swan–Peattie debate and book is the freedom to make errors, to propose hypotheses that turn out to be false, and to err in the trial-and-error process, all in the pursuit of the truth. In fact, in the *Cell*-Baltimore case, in which a Congressional committee led by Representative John Dingell was involved in investigations, it was claimed that "politics was seeking to deprive science of the valuable right to make mistakes in seeking the truth" (Greenberg, 1989, p. 4). However, as seen in chapter 1, and as documented later in this book, Baltimore and others tried to silence and obstruct discussion relating to the correction of perceived error.

SOCIAL RESPONSIBILITIES AND ACADEMIC RESPONSIBILITIES

Whether the freedom to lie is used in the context of the Swan–Peattie debate, with social responsibilities attempting to prevent, combat, and destroy Big Lies, or, in the academic context of "right to make mistakes," in either case there is the implied freedom (if not the responsibility) to expose the lie (e.g., Big Lie, mistake, error, or false paradigm) and have it replaced with the truth. If social responsibilities librarians have a role in exposing and defeating Big Lies of a political and social nature, it might follow, in a logical manner, that academic librarians could, and should, have an academic responsibilities role in helping to expose lies (errors, mistakes, and false paradigms) in the scholarly literature, and have the truth overcome these lies.

Much of academic rhetoric affirms the importance of the scholarly search for the truth, and the importance of the correction of error. In fact, it would seem that phrases such as "science is self-correcting" would emphasize such importance.

In the case of social responsibilities and intellectual freedom activities within library associations, there is usually general agreement that Big Lies such as racism are bad. Librarians and other persons are usually aware of racist spoken language or written material when they come across them. Sometimes there might be hidden messages or subtle symbols, but, for the most part, because of its very nature, racist material (considered by Peattie and others to be dangerous lies) is often blatant and easily identifiable.

AMBIGUITY AND INTERPRETATION

Problems might arise about whether or not some material is intentionally racist or, instead, subject to ambiguous interpretation. Problems begin, from the standpoint of social responsibilities and intellectual freedom, at the levels of ambiguous interpretation, or of spoken remarks or writings that were never intended to be racist, but were nevertheless considered to be so by other persons. At that point, the label of *racist* can be applied to a wide range of expression. Something similar occurred during phases of the Cold War with concepts such as Communist, subversive, or anti-American. In fact, the ALA has taken an official stand against the use of labeling in such cases.

If the academic equivalent to what social responsibilities librarians consider to be "dangerous lies" (or a Big Lie) is falsehood or error in the scholarly literature, it becomes obvious that an academic librarian will not be able to identify these errors and falsehoods as readily as social responsibilities librarians identify material that is racist or sexist. If specialist scholars who are experts and authorities in the field are unable to spot and identify the errors, how can academic librarians be expected to do so?

It is generally agreed by both social responsibilities librarians and academic librarians that dangerous lies and Big Lies are bad and should be corrected. In the case of errors and falsehoods in the scholarly literature, academic freedom is invoked and exercised as a means of helping to detect and expose the errors, allowing them to be corrected. (At least that is how the situation is supposed to be according to the rhetoric.) It is generally regarded that the correction of such errors is the responsibility of the scholars who made them or the colleagues of these scholars. Likewise, correction of the errors made in the past would be the responsibility of the scholars who have succeeded their predecessors as authorities in a field of study.

At the same time, as discussed in chapter 13, some academic librarians are coming to the conclusion that they, too, have an important role and responsibility in the correction of error in the scholarly literature. The term *intellectual freedom* is a broad term that generally applies to the public at large. The term *academic freedom* might be considered a part of intellectual freedom that applies specifically to scholars. For academic librarians, the equivalent of social responsibilities might be called academic responsibilities.

In any case, in terms of silencing of scholars, terms such as intellectual freedom and academic freedom should be considered from the standpoint of rhetoric and reality. The rhetoric that is used when these and similar terms are invoked does not necessarily match the reality of what actually takes place. Rhetoric versus reality gaps can be a major factor in the silencing of scientists and other scholars.

3

Rhetoric Versus Reality in Academia

The rhetoric relating to the nature of academia and science in the United States and other democracies is well known both in academia and throughout large segments of the general public. Colleges and universities often have their own renditions of the rhetoric in their regulations, handbooks, promotional material, and other publications. Academic professional societies can also have their own versions that apply specifically to their own specialized academic and scientific disciplines. Scholarly journals and specialized reference works (e.g., encyclopedias and lexicons) might also have passages explaining their editorial policies, which reflect and repeat some of the academic rhetoric.

The substance of this rhetoric goes along the following lines: Scholars are committed and devoted to seeking the truth; scholars enjoy academic freedom in their pursuit of truth; scholarly research and communication are characterized by openness, free exchange of ideas, and open debate that involves critical inquiry, analysis, and evaluation; science is self-correcting; peer review fosters quality control and integrity in research grants and publications; science and scholarly research and communication are based on trust; and so forth, with some variations.

An acknowledgment of one aspect of this rhetoric—openness—is found in Relyea's (1994) *Silencing Science*:

The advancement of knowledge ... is the basic function of the scientific community. This is accomplished ... through a high degree of open communication and free sharing of information. Indeed, the open character of science has proven to be essential for the advancement of knowledge and, concurrently, vital for the detection and elimination of error. (Relyea, 1994, p. 6)

In fact, one of Reylea's themes is that the silencing of science is contrary to "traditional" scientific communication.

A concise synthesis of the content of the rhetoric of academia can be found in a recent six-page Action Plan issued by Concordia University in Montreal, Canada (n.d.): "a climate of mutual trust and collegiality," and "openness, fairness, dialog, and integrity" (Concordia University, pp. 4, 6). This Action Plan was formulated in the wake of a series of turbulent events on campus that culminated in 1992 with a tragic act in which a professor of engineering shot several members of the department. Several specific investigations of this situation were conducted, followed up by written reports. Copies of these reports were requested from the university as research material for this book. The complete reports, and additional material as well, were sent by return mail. The specific subject matter of the reports is not flattering for the University. In such a case, the willingness on the part of university officials to send all this sensitive material promptly to someone not affiliated with the university and not Canadian represents an exemplary, if not extraordinary, act of "openness". If Concordia University can achieve similar standards for "fairness, dialog, and integrity," it should enjoy a front-rank position among institutions of higher learning of the highest quality.

OPENNESS AND FREE EXCHANGE OF IDEAS

For the purposes of the theme of silencing scholars, the question of "openness" is the most important aspect of the academic rhetoric described earlier. As long as there is a true sense of openness in debate, critical analysis, peer review, and so on, scholars will not be silenced. On the contrary, they will be active participants in the search for truth. To the extent that the rhetoric is not matched by reality, the rhetoric becomes a lie (falsehood). No individual or institution is perfect, so there are bound to be some violations of the academic rhetoric. After all, as it is often observed, scholars are human. Such violations might be regarded as occasional exceptions to the rule—a sort of "little white lie" in relation to the rhetoric—and it might be assumed, or expected, that these violations might occur among the lower ranks of academia, including insecure graduate students, untenured scholars, or junior researchers.

On the other hand, if there is a wide rhetoric versus reality gap in academia, if there are systematic violations within academia, or if there are, within specific disciplines, "knee-jerk" responses on a scale that amount to systematic violations, then the academic rhetoric or portions of it might be regarded as something of a Big Lie. The Big Lie concept is reinforced if systematic and blatant violations occur within the highest echelons of academia that formulate, profess, and publish the rhetoric (e.g., university administrations, leaders of academic professional societies and learned societies, editors and editorial boards of scholarly publications, and peer-review authorities).

Openness and trust (particularly mutual trust) are important components of the academic rhetoric. Secrecy and distrust are opposites. If secrecy and distrust are systematic in academia relating to research and publication, they would create a Big Lie situation, as far as academic rhetoric is concerned.

REALITY IN PEER REVIEW

Academic research projects of various types often require financing that extends beyond the personal financial resources of the scholars conducting the research, and beyond the internal funds generated by the institutions where the research is conducted. Grants and subsidies for such research are provided by government agencies, foundations (and various other types of institutions or associations), and industry and commerce. Without such financing, much important research could not be conducted.

To a large degree, peer-review decisions determine which research will be financed and which research results will be published. Some requests for funding are accepted and other requests are rejected. Some manuscripts submitted for publication are accepted and some are rejected. The same is true for requests to present papers at scholarly conferences. In some cases, scholars might pay for their own research and publish in their own private publications, thus bypassing the peer-review process. For the most part, however, a very large percentage of academic research and publication depends on peer-review acceptance.

Do peer-review activities adhere to the principles of the academic rhetoric as far as openness and mutual trust are concerned, or do they reveal a rhetoric versus reality gap? For example, is there openness or secrecy, and is there mutual trust or distrust when editors decide which referees will be chosen, and when referees write their recommendations? Anyone who has made even a casual study of peer review, or who has submitted material to a variety of scholarly journals for publication, will soon realize that a dominant feature of peer review is secrecy instead of openness. This concept of secrecy is so engrained and imbedded in some parts of academia that Judith Serebnick, a specialist in the field of the ethics of scholarly publishing (Serebnick, 1991), is on record as stating that editors have no ethical obligation to tell authors what peer-review referees have recommended (Moran & Mallory, 1991b).

It should be noted that peer review does not have to be secret. In fact, some editors and peer-review referees operate in the open. Authors of manuscripts know who the referees are, referees know the identities of the authors, and editors send copies of the referees' reports to authors. However, as far as can be determined, only a small minority of editors and referees conduct peer review in this manner. It seems that in the vast majority of cases, peer review operates with the provision that the names of referees are kept secret from the authors. Moreover, sometimes the secrecy is doubled, in the sense that not only do authors not know who the referees are, but the names of the authors are also kept secret from the referees. In the latter case, however, referees are often able to determine who the authors are based on the specific subject matter and based on the citations used (Fisher, Friedman, & Strauss, 1994).

To the extent that peer review is systematically marked by secrecy instead of openness, the academic rhetoric about openness and free exchange of ideas becomes something of an academic Big Lie. (The use of terms such as anonymity, masking, blinding, or double blind does not change the secrecy involved.)

MOTIVATIONS FOR SECRECY

At this point, being aware that "openness" is an integral part of the academic rhetoric, and secrecy would amount to a violation of this rhetoric, the question arises: Why is secrecy involved at all in peer review? In fact, this question has been brought up and discussed in studies of peer review. The reasons given to justify secrecy vary in their wording, but the underlying reason, based on the various wording, is a rather surprising one. In fact, distrust among scholars pervades the peer-review process. In effect, referees are not trusted to give candid and honest opinions if their identities are known: "Anonymous review was viewed by editors as a means of obtaining an honest opinion" (Weller, 1990, p. 1345). Likewise, authors of manuscripts are not trusted to refrain from retaliation if they do not like what refrees say or recommend: "Anonymous review was viewed by editors as a means of ... protecting the reviewer from potentially unpleasant interactions with the author" (Weller, 1990, p. 1345).

If mutual trust were prevalent in academia on a large enough scale to give proof that the rhetoric about mutual trust is actually true, editors would trust referees to give honest opinions whether or not their identities were known to authors, and editors and referees would trust authors to refrain from retaliation whenever unfavorable opinions and recommendations were given. It would seem logical that in every specific case where secrecy is imposed in the peer-review process, it would represent an example of one scholar (or perhaps an administrative official, in the case of government agencies) not trusting another, or of scholars feeling that they cannot trust each other. Otherwise, if it is true that the purpose of peer review is to foster the advancement of knowledge, and if it is also true, as Relyea (1994) affirmed, that "open communication and free sharing of information" are "essential for the advancement of knowledge" (p. 6), then peer review would be characterized by openness and sharing of information rather than by secrecy.

DISTRUST AND ITS EFFECT ON CRITICAL EVALUATIONS

The concept of distrust goes even further, and distrust is involved with the concept of silencing of scholars. According to the rhetoric of peer review relating to quality control, advancement of knowledge, pursuit of truth, and so on, scholars are chosen by editors to be peer-review referees based on their proven, alleged, or reputed expertise in a specific subject or field of study. Because of their reputations as experts, some scholars are called on to referee many manuscripts over a period of time. The subject matter of these manuscripts is, to one degree or another, the same as that in which the referees or experts have published in order to establish their reputations as experts in the first place. If editors cannot really trust these referees to give candid and honest opinions regarding the subject matter of the manuscripts if their identities are known, can editors, or any other scholars for that matter, really trust these referees or experts any more or less so in relation to their published works in the same field of study in which their identities are known? In other words, would the contents of these published works be different if they had been published anonymously?

For example, if a referee, whose identity remains secret, recommends rejection of an article (but would not necessarily have recommended rejection without the protective cover of anonymity), would the same referee comment differently on the contents of the same article if the contents were subsequently published in another journal? In a similar hypothetical situation, suppose an expert is chosen as a referee for the manuscript of a book submitted to an academic publisher such as a university press. The expert, whose identity remains secret, recommends rejection (but would not have recommended rejection without the protection of anonymity). The book is subsequently published by another academic publisher. Then suppose that the same expert who had earlier rejected the work (but only because of the protection of anonymity) in manuscript form is commissioned to write a book review for the same work now that it is published. In this case, the expert's identity would be known. Would the published review be the same, or similar, to the earlier secret review, or would it be different? If it would be the same, or similar, why would there really be any need for secrecy in the first place? If it would be quite different, as a result of the lack of secrecy, would it represent candid and honest judgments? It would seem that a different review (different from the secret review) would be an example of a rhetoric versus reality gap in relation to mutual trust and scholarly research and publication, because it would seem that either one or the other of the reviews would not contain candid and honest judgments. To the extent that scholars fail to give honest and candid judgments, their judgments are silenced. Which judgment can be trusted to be the honest and candid one in the case of opposite judgment by the same scholar for the same work? If it is the secret judgment, it remains silenced as long as it remains secret.

Dalton (1995) commented that secrecy "protects the referee from endless arguments with disappointed authors" (p. 236), and she cited "a survey of referees" that shows "that referees feel strongly that all reasonable means should be taken to conceal their identity" (p. 236). This survey itself would tend to reveal a rhetoric versus reality gap regarding openness and free exchange of ideas. As Commoner observed, "The present, very limited, one-sided structure of the peer review process aborts the open dialogue that is so essential to the progress of science" (Dalton, 1995, p. 235).

To the extent that this one-sided situation actually "aborts the open dialogue," those scholars who are consequently shut out of the dialogue are silenced.

A STARTLING RHETORIC VERSUS REALITY GAP AT YALE

Sometimes the nature and the degree of the rhetoric versus reality gap can be rather startling. The rhetoric about academic freedom and the free exchange of ideas is intertwined with the concept of freedom of expression. Benno Schmidt built a reputation as an expert on the First Amendment before becoming president of Yale University. In his inaugural address, which received widespread media coverage, Schmidt gave a ringing endorsement of academic freedom and freedom of expression on campus:

> To stifle expression because it is obnoxious, erroneous, embarrassing, not instrumental to some political or ideological end is—quite apart from the grotesque invasion of the rights of others—a disastrous reflection on ourselves. ... There is no speech so horrendous in content that it does not in principle serve our purposes. (Fiske, 1986, p. 40)

In this inaugural speech, Schmidt did not confine his criticism to the Reagan administration; he extended his criticism to political leaders of both major parties in the United States, who, in Schmidt's view, have little regard for academic freedom (Fiske, 1986).

Not very long before Schmidt was chosen to be Yale's president, the question of freedom of expression on campus at Yale had been the subject of much discussion. The conclusions of this discussion were drawn up in the *Report of the Committee on Freedom of Speech at Yale* (Woodward, 1975). C. Vann Woodward was chairman of this committee. Hentoff (1986b), a famous advocate of freedom of expression, wrote, "The 'Woodward Report,' incorporated in Yale's Undergraduate Regulations, is the most compelling argument for free speech on campus—even at the cost of civility and deeply wounded feelings—that I have ever seen" (p. 29). In fact, Woodward explained to Hentoff, "The 'Woodward Report' does not guarantee that the speech has to be acceptable or pleasant or even correct. It simply guarantees the right to all to exercise their speech. ... After all, it's the unpopular speakers that need protection" (Hentoff, 1986b, p. 29).

It seems clear that the main thrust of Schmidt's speech amounted to something of an echo and repetition of the Woodward Report, and of Yale's written regulations for undergraduates. Thus, the specific rhetoric about freedom of expression on campus in this case has at least three documented sources: the Woodward Report, Yale's printed regulations, and Schmidt's inaugural address. The reality is that, in the face of this rhetoric, a Yale student was punished by the Yale College Executive Committee, without opportunity for appeal, because the student created and displayed on campus a satire in the form of a poster that contained speech that powerful Yale authorities did not like. Furthermore, the student was suffering the punishment at the very time that

Schmidt was delivering the inaugural address (and also at the same time that university regulations allowed freedom of speech on campus).

A letter was written to Schmidt, asking if he thought that this student enjoyed the freedom of expression that the President advocated so fervently in his inaugural address. Schmidt replied that the situation was not a "pressing" matter, and that it had been "resolved" by A. Bartlett Giamatti (who preceded Schmidt as president). Giamatti "resolved" the case by telling the student that there was no appeal allowed, except to the very committee that punished him in the first place. Hentoff (1986a) commented on this situation in "How Yale Punishes Bad Thoughts":

> Found guilty by Yale College's Court of the Star Chamber—also known as the Executive Committee ... And there is no appeal unless the Executive Committee itself decides to grant one. In the outside world ... these procedures would be scorned and scrapped as an outrageous violation of due process. (p. 27)

Hentoff also speculated that other students might have been likewise punished in secret for saying things that Yale authorities did not like, but that these students might have been too scared, too embarrassed, or too intimidated to protest.

A similar rhetoric versus reality gap also took place at Yale recently, this time involving another Yale president, Richard Levin. In a letter dated May 12, 1995, to members of the Class of 1960, Jim Taylor and Tim Ritchie wrote, "Our sense is that this new administration is eager to engage in an active two way exchange with its alumni. We urge you to express your concerns and ideas to the administration." A short time later, a publication for the Class of 1960 included the following:

> The inaugural Class Leadership Workshop held this fall at the Yale Club of New York was designed to enhance communication between the highest levels of administration (i.e., President Rick Levin ... and Alvin Puryear) and you. ... They are open and encouraging about alumni feedback. ... Please let us know your thoughts and feelings regarding Yale. (Schaller & Schaller, 1995, p. 68)

(Alvin Puryear is a member of the Class of 1960, who in 1995 was also a Fellow of the Yale Corporation, the university's highest administrative body.)

Despite this rhetoric, two specific letters to Levin, directly related to his own speeches and to Yale activity, remained unanswered and unacknowledged. Taking the advice of Class of 1960 officials, Yale Corporation Fellow Puryear (a professor of Management at Baruch College of the City University of New York) was contacted, with an appeal to have a short open letter published in the Alumni Notes of the *Yale Alumni Magazine*. What followed is best described as a bureaucratic runaround, followed by stonewalling. At first, Puryear replied (a few months after the letter was written) with thanks for the material that was sent to him: "Thank you for the materials which show your interest in Yale and alumni affairs." However, when further inquiries were made to him regarding the runaround (or bureaucratic mix-up, as the case may be), for some reason Puryear retreated into silence. Thus, both the university president and one of the members of its highest administrative body decided to be silent—by means of stonewalling—in the midst of a flurry of rhetoric that the new administration was keenly interested in maintaining openness in terms of communication with alumni. Whatever the reasons might be for such a lack of communication, this situation indicates that rhetoric versus reality gaps in universities can occur not only at the level of the office of the president, the executive committee, and of other university governing bodies, but also at levels of alumni class officers and Alumni Notes sections of alumni publications.

SOME RHETORIC VERSUS REALITY AT NIH

Another aspect of academic rhetoric relates to the interrelated issues of pursuit of truth and the correction of error. If scholars pursue truth, they correct errors once errors are detected. If there is uncertainty about whether material is truthful or erroneous, investigations and discussions are carried out, based on critical analysis and evaluation of the material. The rhetoric states that science is self-correcting. Obviously, science can be self-correcting only if scholars have the volition and opportunity to correct errors, or at least have the opportunity to participate in critical discussions that might lead to eventual correction of errors.

As in the case of the Woodward Report and Benno Schmidt—with their rhetoric in favor of protection of obnoxious, embarrassing, and horrendous speech—and the student who was nevertheless punished for creating and displaying a satirical poster, problems associated with the correction of error can turn up some rather startling rhetoric versus reality gaps. In a very early phase of the *Cell*–Baltimore controversy in biomedical research, Stewart and Feder, scientists at the NIH, were trying to expose what they perceived to be serious errors in the disputed *Cell* article. Letters were sent (not by Stewart and Feder, in this instance) to the Director of NIH, James Wyngaarden, and to another NIH official, J. E. Rall, asking them if NIH would stifle or suppress material that contested and challenged the published results of research that was funded by NIH. Another official of NIH, Mary Miers, replied (after about 3 months) on behalf of Wyngaarden: "I cannot envision a situation in which NIH would seek to suppress a rebuttal article." Likewise, Rall answered as follows: "It is clearly not NIH policy to discourage or indeed otherwise suppress publication of discussions and corrections of errors" (Moran & Mallory, 1991b, p. 344). These replies were written on September 25, 1987, and December 15, 1986. Such replies would conform with the rhetoric about the correction of error and the self-correcting nature of science, to the extent that rebuttal articles are not suppressed.

If those replies are examples of NIH rhetoric, the reality in the specific case was quite different. Stewart and Feder had, in fact, written an extensive rebuttal article, exposing alleged serious errors in the *Cell* article that was co-authored by David Baltimore. Under NIH regulations, they had to have approval from an NIH authority (or more than one) before they could submit their article to a scholarly journal for publication. When they sought approval, it was denied. Rall signed a memorandum (of which Miers received a copy), sent to Stewart and Feder, in which he wrote, "I am withholding approval of your manuscript for publication." Rall then wrote to Baltimore, co-author of the article, which by then had already become controversial, "I have told Feder and Stewart that their manuscript cannot be submitted to a journal" (Moran & Mallory, 1991b, p. 344).

It would seem that such withholding of approval results in the silencing of scientists, impedes the free exchange of ideas, denies academic freedom, and stifles the self-correcting process of science. The rhetoric versus reality gap seems quite wide when one considers that an NIH official wrote "I cannot envision a situation in which NIH would seek to suppress a rebuttal article," when the official received a memorandum that specifically suppressed a rebuttal article (Moran & Mallory, 1991b).

Lang (1993) noted other instances of a rhetoric versus reality gap in the *Cell*–Baltimore case. Lang's article in *Ethics and Behavior* contains a subsection entitled "The rhetoric and the reality. Speaking out—when? Publishing—when?" (p. 33). Lang stated:

The reality has been the opposite of the rhetoric especially when questions have been raised about eminent figures in the establishment. The discrepancy between the rhetoric and the reality is partly documented by scientific journals refusing to publish an article critical of the Baltimore paper, and is further documented in the way *Nature's* editor John Maddox described first hand Baltimore's reaction. (p. 33)

Along a similar line, Lang (1993) wrote:

Baltimore and Lewin's position goes against the open discussion of claimed scientific results. ... The National Academy of Sciences' *Issues in Science and Technology* published only Baltimore's point of view. ... It did not publish an opposite point of view, for instance Margot O'Toole's testimony ... nowhere do the two *Nature* editorials consider the fundamental problem of scientists not answering scientific criticisms of their work, not allowing publication of criticisms. (pp. 19, 32, 38)

REFERENCE WORKS AND RHETORIC VERSUS REALITY

Examples of rhetoric versus reality gaps can also be found in specialized and academic reference works. One factor that might tend to widen the gap is the self-flattering promotional material that is printed in order to augment sales of the work. A rather clamorous case recently occurred with the *Lexicon of the Middle Ages* (Avella-Widham, Lutz, & Mattejiet, 1977–1997).

This case involves the rhetoric of one of the lexicon's scholars and advisors, Walter Ruegg (1986), who wrote (in an issue of *Minerva* dedicated to academic ethics), "the absolute commandment of respect for truth is fundamental to the exercise of scientific and scholarly professions" (p. 408). This rhetorical thrust is given some elaboration in the lexicon's explanatory and promotional material, which refers to "absolutely reliable information ... all the available knowledge ... results of the latest research," all of which imply a "respect for truth." What is more, the material states, "In the case of controversial problems and theories the Lexicon also gives the protagonists of opposing positions a chance to express their views. ... What is disputed must be described as controversial or uncertain" (Moran, 1991, p. 163). This last item seems particularly significant, because not all reference works describe controversies. In fact, some describe Harvey's observations about the circulation of blood as a break-through discovery of a heroic nature, without describing or even mentioning the pro-longed bitter controversy that his observations provoked (and that Harvey himself had predicted would take place).

Details of the *Lexicon Of The Middle Ages* case are documented in an article in *The Reference Librarian* (Moran, 1991, pp. 159–172). A brief summary can illustrate problems relating to rhetoric and reality. The lexicon sent a request to a scholar to write an entry for the lexicon in the field of art history. The scholar, not being a spe-cialist for that particular entry, and having read the item about "controversial problems and theories," asked permission to write an entry on the Guido Riccio controversy in art history. There is much material describing the controversy, and some key items were cited, including

> At the center of attention in a controversy that has shaken the art history world ... the "case of the century." ... The controversy has exploded ... one of the great art historical questions of the century ... one of the most intense and acrimonious battles in the annals of art history. (pp. 164–165)

It is difficult to imagine an academic controversy being described in a more direct manner to indicate that a major controversy has broken out.

Despite the evidence for the existence of a major controversy, and despite the rhetoric of the reference work, permission for "a chance" to express views was denied. An editorial board member cited essentially three reasons for the denial: (a) there was not enough room in the lexicon for the dissenting views; (b) the traditional view was the prevalent view in the mainstream art historical literature; and (c) the con-troversy specifically concerned art history, whereas the lexicon dealt with all aspects of the Middle Ages.

Permission was also requested to write an entry on the controversy involving Beato Ambrogio (of Siena) in the field of religious history of the Middle Ages. This request was met with silence and, thus, denial. Therefore, as things stand, references to at least two controversies have been silenced in the pages of the lexicon. Many other controversies have likely been dealt with in a similar manner, with the result that scholarly material pertinent to an academic controversy has been silenced.

If there is not room for dissenting views, or if only prevailing orthodox views are published, why does the lexicon rhetorically claim that in the case of controversies "the protagonists of opposing sides" are given "a chance to express their views"?

Furthermore, the scholar was originally asked to write an entry that was specifically in the field of art history, yet one of the specific reasons the request to write an entry on Guido Riccio was rejected was precisely because it was in the field of art history. (Perhaps the Beato Ambrogio item was also rejected because it dealt specifically with religious history of the Middle Ages.) Ruegg was asked if the "academic commandment" of respect for the truth applied to the editorial policy and contents of the lexicon (Moran, 1991). In his correspondence on the subject, he supported the reasons for rejection, thus adding to the rhetoric versus reality gap at the lexicon.

Obviously, scholarly points of view were silenced in the pages of the lexicon, despite the rhetoric that opposing views would be presented. How many other cases, presently unknown, of silencing of scholars have taken place in this lexicon, and possibly also in the many other specialized academic reference works that are on the shelves of academic libraries throughout the world?

A WIDESPREAD PROBLEM

The examples described so far in this chapter indicate that the rhetoric of academia does not always coincide with reality. Many other documented examples exist, and some are brought up in other chapters. In fact, much of the content of some of the other chapters of this book might be described as variations on the theme of an academic gap between rhetoric and reality that results in the silencing of scholars by one means or another.

A justification for a rhetoric versus reality gap might be that academics are "human" and the rhetoric is too idealistic. In fact, this type of thinking was discussed by Hillman (1997), who described reactions to his studies of "parafraud": "An extremely common reaction was that ... research workers are no more or less honest than salesmen, politicians and spies. They seek to advance themselves by whatever mechanism society allows them ... one should expect no more of scientists than of the population at large" (p. 133). Certainly this argument has some validity, but at the same time it might be that this human element itself is part of the cause of the problem. In fact, the human element in academia consists of social and professional relationships in various institutions and organizations. If these relationships remain within the halls of academia, they are often marked by so-called collegiality. However, if they extend to government agencies and private industry (as is becoming increasingly the case, based on current practices involving funding of research), these relationships can lead to conflicts of interest and vested interests, thus, creating divided loyalties. Conflicts of interest and vested interests can, in turn, lead to the perceived need for cover up and suppression of the truth. It might be that in many cases scholars do not deliberately create rhetoric versus reality gaps as much as they get caught up within them.

Specific problems of this nature have been studied recently by Fox and Braxton (1994). They observed that "the majority of research universities have policies and procedures for investigating allegations ... but their surveillance and investigation are open to question ... universities are subject to. ... conflicts of interest. ... Whether universities can manage such conflicting interests has been questioned in meetings, reports, and publications" (p. 375).

There have been comments and observations by various scholars regarding rhetoric and reality in academia. In *Intellectual Suppression*, Martin (1986b) wrote:

> Rhetoric and reality of professional freedom do not always match. During the cold-war period, university officials at Harvard and Yale collaborated with the FBI [Federal Bureau of Investigation] in vetting applicants for positions. But the officials, perhaps aware of the discrepancy between this complicity and the professional norms publicly espoused by the university, opposed revealing this connection both at the time and indeed ever since. (p. 193)

Diamond (1992) described this type of rhetoric versus reality activity by use of the term "Public Masks, Private Faces" (p. 111). Because of the unwillingness of universities to reveal such material, it is impossible to determine the extent of rhetoric versus reality gaps in academia.

In "On Influential Books and Journal Articles Initially Rejected Because of Negative Referees Evaluations," Campanario (1995) documented many cases of peer-review rejection of works that later turned out to be accepted as cases of important discoveries, including rejections of studies that later won Nobel prizes. At one point he observed, "This type of incident shows how the stereotype of scientists as open-minded people clashes frequently with reality" (p. 318). Along a similar line, Hillman (1996) considered the rhetoric about science being self-correcting to be "just wishful thinking" (p. 102). In fact, the situation involving the rhetoric about self-correction in the face of reluctance to admit error and to allow error to be corrected constitutes one of the major problems in academia and science involving rhetoric versus reality, and one of the major problems involving silencing of scholars.

At the same time, even though there is ample documentation to show discrepancies between academic rhetoric and reality, the rhetoric still has much influence. Nissani (1995) wrote, "We have all been raised with the stereotype of the scientist as 'the open-minded man' ... we tend to view any allegation or evidence to the contrary with incredulity" (p. 177).

RHETORIC VERSUS REALITY AND SOCIODYNAMICS

In any case, if the rhetoric does not always match the reality in academia, what is the reality? It is perhaps sometimes a combination of power and the pursuit of truth. Perhaps it is sometimes a situation in which truth is pitted against power. If this is true, maybe one of the best descriptions of academic reality is found in a page written by Lang (1992), entitled "The Three Laws of Sociodynamics." Lang, a mathematics professor at Yale, as well as a member of the NAS, has waged several battles (some still ongoing)—using a a very effective methodology that he calls "file" studies—relating to issues of scientific and peer-review responsibilities. These battles have been taking place within the highest echelons of academia, including the NAS, NIH, American Association of University Professors (AAUP), and the American Association for the Advancement of Science (AAAS), and give valuable insights into many aspects of academic reality as practiced by those in power. (His file studies would seem to be of greatest interest and importance to scholars of peer review, scholarly communication, information ethics, higher education, and academic librarianship. A complete publication of them would be very useful.)

It seems that these three laws of sociodynamics were formulated after—and as a result of—encounters with many of the high authorities in academia and related government agencies. At any rate, the first law has two parts: the first is (a) "the power structure does what they want, when they want; then they try to find reasons to justify it." The second part is (b) "if this does not work, they do what they want, when they want, and then stonewall." The second law is as follows: "An establishment will close ranks behind a member until a point is reached when closing ranks is about to bring down the entire establishment; then the establishment will jettison that member with the least action it deems necessary to preserve the establishment." (Lang distributed these laws in unpublished form to a group of scholars as part of his "file" studies relating to scientific responsibility.) These "laws" should be kept in mind throughout the following chapters, which, to a large extent, show that it is ultimately power that is a primary force in the silencing of scholars.

4

Paradigm Dependency in Academia and Its Effect on Peer Review

---

Our very belief that we have found out most of the answers ... could be considered a superstition as great as any hope entertained by a simple tribesman that dancing will bring rain in the dry season. Equally primitive is the idea that we are prepared to tolerate radically new ideas. (Brookesmith, 1984, p. 6)

How dare you question me? Who are you to question me? Just who do you think you are to question me?

The ideas expressed in the second item partly summarize the title of this chapter. The first item, from *Thinking the Unthinkable: Ideas Which Have Upset Conventional Thought*, is a reflection on the phenomenon described as paradigm dependency.

The "How dare you..." item approximates the exact words of former Yale President A.Whitney Griswold, in three separate replies to a student who questioned him three times. The setting was the dining room of Calhoun College on the Yale campus. Griswold had called a special meeting of Calhoun students in the wake of a campus disturbance that had marred Yale's reputation somewhat (in the wake of some negative media coverage), and that had strained relations with some elements of the New Haven community (so-called "town-gown" relations, which have historically been a cause of some friction). Griswold blamed the students and scolded them verbally. On three separate occasions, a student questioned Griswold. Rather than engage in dialogue, Griswold stated that the student should not be asking any of these questions in the first place. The student walked out of the room. (The student's identity is unknown to the author. It is not even certain if the student was a resident of Calhoun.)

At first glance, Griswold's replies should have been a revelation and a stark warning that the erudite, open discussions of the Fellows of Pierson College (described at the beginning of this book) in 1956–1957 were not necessarily the rule at Yale, nor throughout academia.However, because Griswold was not speaking as a scholar, but rather as a high administrative official involved in a sensitive administrative problem, his reaction was more or less written off as a ploy of a powerful official pulling rank on a hapless student.

Looking back, however, and reflecting on the situation many years later, Griswold's behavior might well be seen as a characteristic academic action within a bigger academic picture. Griswold most likely did not speak off the cuff. Given the sensitive nature of the situation, he most likely had given careful consideration to what he would say, and believed that what he decided to say was appropriate, right, and correct—so much so that he would not allow alternative thoughts or questioning of his position. His reaction was essentially a reaction of power to suppress unwanted ideas. On a larger scale, this situation essentially resembles that involving peer-review authorities when they are presented with intellectual ideas, hypotheses, and evidence that question academic paradigms.

PARADIGMS IN ACADEMIA

Various scholars have discussed, in different contexts, the nature of paradigms and the difficulty involved in changing the paradigms when evidence shows they are false. Kuhn's (1970) *The Structure of Scientific Revolutions* has come to be regarded as a classic. He observed that academics are educated and trained within the confines of paradigms of a specific discipline. This training might begin in secondary school or undergraduate years in college, and might solidify during study for a graduate degree, with continued reinforcement as academic careers progress. As scholars attain tenure, and as they continue career enhancement, they become part of a group of peers who have been trained in a paradigm and who collectively teach the paradigm to their own students.

The process of being introduced to a paradigm, being brought up—academically speaking—within it, and then repeating (teaching) it to others, has similarities to the Big Lie technique, in the sense that something is repeated often enough, without question or rebuttal, until it is believed to be true. Once it becomes engrained as truth, evidence that comes forth indicating it is false is not easily accepted. In this sense, academic rhetoric—or at least part of it—has attained what amounts to paradigm status, based on Nissani's (1995) observation, "We have all been raised with the stereotype of the scientist as 'the open-minded man' ... and we tend to view any allegation or evidence to the contrary with incredulity" (p. 177).

The histories of science, medicine, and other academic disciplines are filled with examples of revolutions; that is, situations in which paradigms turned out to be false and were eventually overturned and replaced with new ones. In many of these cases—if not the vast majority of them—there was long-term, fierce resistance to the new paradigm, and bitter controversy before the false paradigm was abandoned. In this case, how can anyone really have been raised with the stereotype of the scientist as an open-minded person?

Kuhn (1970) provided what appears to be at least a partial answer. First of all, he observed that textbooks have to be "rewritten in the aftermath of each scientific revolution" (p. 137). (The same would be true for reference works and classroom lectures.) Then Kuhn stated that the revised texts do not tell the full story:

> Textbooks ... once rewritten ... inevitably disguise not only the role but the very existence of the revolutions that produced them. ... Textbooks then begin by truncating the scientist's sense of his discipline's history and then proceed to supply a substitute for what they have eliminated. ... The depreciation of historical fact is deeply, and probably functionally, engrained in the ideology of the scientific profession. (pp. 137–138)

Persons who read textbooks that "disguise not only the role but the very existence of the revolutions that produced them" might well develop a sense of the stereotype of scientists as being open minded. This stereotype might be further reinforced by hearing or reading other ideas such as the following: "It is extremely rare for any scientist to publish an epoch-making discovery and have it ignored. As a rule, the knowledge of the discovery spreads rapidly and the scientist is honored promptly and copiously" (Nissani, 1995, p. 166). Or, in a similar vein, "Scientists ... are sensitive to history. Their reaction has been to become exceedingly receptive to new ideas" (p. 166).

Would a person who reads the revised textbooks get the same impression, as far as scientists being open minded is concerned, as a person who reads the actual source material? It is a rather widely known fact that William Harvey is regarded as having made an important discovery relating to the circulation of blood, and as a result he is regarded as a hero and a gigantic figure in the history of medicine and science. This seems to be something of a revised textbook version of events, rather than a description of what actually took place. One account states that "William Harvey 'was subjected to derision and abuse and his practice suffered badly. Only after a struggle of over twenty years did the circulation of the blood become generally accepted'" (Nissani, 1995, p. 173). Harvey himself seemed to have been quite aware that his discovery would meet strong disapproval and resistance from his fellow scientist peers, as evidenced by his own alleged premonitions:

> But what remains to be said about the quantity and source of the blood which thus pass-
> es, is of so novel and unheard-of character that I not only fear injury to myself from the
> envy of a few, but I tremble lest I have mankind at large for my enemies, so much doth
> wont and custom, that become as another nature, and doctrine once sown and that hath
> struck deep root, and respect for antiquity, influence all men. (Nissani, 1995, p. 168)

PARADIGMS AND PEER-REVIEW REFEREES

Campanario published studies involving resistance to new ideas, one of which is
"Have Referees Rejected Some of the Most-Cited Papers of All Times?" (1996b). He
listed many examples, including about a dozen cases where new findings that received
harsh peer-review rejection were later honored with Nobel prizes. Excerpts from this
article include:

> The scientific community often finds it difficult to accept new ideas. ... The greatest and
> most harmful source of resistance from scientists to scientific discovery comes precise-
> ly from those peers whose mission is to preserve the quality of scientific work. ... Some
> papers were rejected because the referees felt the findings ... clashed with existing ideas
> or methods ... article on alpha and beta receptors was initially resisted and ignored
> because the concepts developed in that paper did not fit with ideas developed since 1980.
> (pp. 302, 306)

In another article, Campanario (1995) wrote that, "in other instances referees' and
editors' negative evaluations demonstrate that they did fail to appreciate the importance of a potentially influential manuscript. Sometimes authors are 'guilty' of chal-
lenging in their papers the current views or paradigms of a given discipline" (p. 320).

Horrobin (1990), in "The Philosophical Basis of Peer Review and the Suppression
of Innovation," lists 18 cases of exclusion of innovative ideas from journals, scholarly conferences, and grants. He stated that this is "by no means a complete list"
(p. 1441). Horrobin added that:

> Examples of the total suppression of an innovation ... are by definition nonexistent.
> How can one know about them if they have been suppressed? ... Editors must be con-
> scious that, despite public protestations to the contrary, many scientists-reviewers are
> against innovation unless it is *their* innovation. Innovation from others may be a threat
> because it diminishes the importance of the scientist's own work. (pp. 1440–1441)

Cude (1987a), who discussed the themes of "by definition nonexistent" and "How
can one know about them if they have been suppressed?," observed that the tendency
toward suppression of innovation (by default, so to speak) is part of graduate students'
experiences: "Representative of many other topics requiring originality that are avoided like the plague by doctoral candidates. ... Collegiality and tenure have combined
to ensure a conspiracy of silence among our academics on the delicate topic of vari-
ant methodologies" (pp. 89, 124). Thus, in order to get their PhD degrees, according

to Cude, students must pretty much restrict their research to subject matter and conclusions within accepted paradigms.

Catt (1978) also believed it is possible to cite many instances in which scientific institutions have suppressed innovative ideas. He asserted that referees are censors who operate within "a system of censorship, the censor having no training in how to differentiate between 'wrong' and 'heretical'" (p. 138). And, in line with Kuhn's ideas, Catt added, "What is *not* permissible is to write or say something which contradicts the shared paradigm, and expect it to be tolerated by the accepted journals, conferences and faculties" (pp. 138–139).

HOW MANY GENERATIONS OF SCHOLARS DOES IT TAKE TO CHANGE A PARADIGM?

The suppression of new ideas has also been seen in terms of refusing to admit errors that are embarrassing to those who enjoy academic fame and power. Along this line, Ruesch (1978/1991) described some studies of Vesalius that contested a paradigm that had been followed and adhered to since the time of Galen, and Ruesch observed that in this case "the university teachers would not admit that they had perpetuated a millenarian error" (p. 154). According to Ruesch (1993), after Vesalius showed that Galen had been badly mistaken, it took another two centuries "before the textbooks were corrected" (p. 1).

From the standpoint of silencing scholars within the framework of resistance to paradigm changes, an interesting situation has developed recently in the Guido Riccio controversy. In this case, it seems that a rather subtle use of, or appeal to, Kuhn's observations has been made as a reason, excuse, or justification for not doing further research on the Guido Riccio problem. It sometimes take generations after paradigms are discovered to be false before these false paradigms are replaced by true ones. Why not let another generation resolve the Guido Riccio problem?

In fact, Falcone (1991) wrote an honors thesis, *Is Knowledge Constituted by Power? The Politics of Knowledge in the Art History Community: A Case Study of "The Guidoriccio Controversy."* He placed this specific academic controversy within Kuhn's ideas of paradigms:

> I will utilize Thomas S. Kuhn's book *The Structure of Scientific Revolutions* ... in this thesis, drawing similarities. ... The Guidoriccio debate serves as my case study, illustrating how the normative model for the art history community limits the art historians in it, and when their modes of debate fail to resolve a dispute, political power ultimately equals knowledge. (p. 3)

At various points in his thesis, Falcone quoted and cited Kuhn and related his ideas to specific situations in the Guido Riccio controversy.

A part of Falcone's work is based on a taped interview with Professor Samuel Edgerton (Williams College, Graduate Program in the History of Art), a famous scholar of Italian Renaissance art, particularly on the relation of science to art. Perhaps due to his strong interest in science, Edgerton suggested that Falcone write his thesis from the standpoint of Kuhn. As Falcone (1991) himself stated, "In fact, it was Professor Edgerton who first gave me the idea to put Kuhn's conception of the paradigm, as it pertains to anomaly in the normative science community, together with the idea that the Guidoriccio case represents a parallel, as an anomaly being resisted by 'normal' art historians" (p. 47).

More specifically, regarding the importance of the traditional view about the Guido Riccio painting for art history specialists, Edgerton is quoted as follows: "This issue is central to their scholarship. ... All these art historians have their intellectual life. It has been based on accepting this and working in it ... they would have to sit and write something else to get themselves out of their holes" (Falcone, 1991, p. 48).

Having placed the Guido Riccio problem within a paradigm setting, Edgerton then related how he would approach the problem: "Like I would do with it; shrug my shoulders and say, O.K., let someone else handle it in another generation. Let's put it aside..." (Falcone, 1991, p. 49). Later Edgerton (personal communication, January 30, 1992) asserted that "the truth about Guido Riccio will be revealed" but he repeated the "another generation" aspect, claiming that the Guido Riccio problem is "an issue which may well need a couple of generations to finally work itself out. ... Other advocates ... need *time* to salve their own egos. It's my opinion that things might move faster if you would just—pardon my bluntness—*shut up*."

At this point, this question might be asked: On what grounds, or on what basis, should a scholar let scholars of a future generation handle a paradigm-busting issue, rather than tackle the issue head on (perhaps with an intensive graduate program seminar, or more than one seminar, devoted to it)? It would seem that there might be two possible answers. Either the present generation of scholars lacks the necessary critical ability (in the case of art historians this would mean connoisseurship, stylistic analysis, critical analysis, historical analysis, etc.), or else there is a specific volition not to allow the new evidence to be discussed and published during the present generation.

Having a scholar shut up is one of the most effective ways of silencing a scholar. If in the near future Edgerton were to be chosen as an anonymous referee for a paper on Guido Riccio that contained additional paradigm-busting evidence, would he suggest to the editor that discussion should be put off until a future generation can look into it? If he were chosen as a referee for an article that tried to shore up the traditional establishment view, would he suggest the topic should be left for discussion by a future generation? What would editors think of such a recommendation?

FALSE PARADIGMS CAN BE HARMFUL AND DANGEROUS

Duesberg (1996b) wrote that during 1914 the pellagra epidemic "reached the two-hundred thousand-victim mark" (p. 51). During the epidemic, official research was conducted along the lines that the disease was infectious, based on the so-called germ theory. At one point, Joseph Goldberger was named by the Public Health Service to head the government's pellagra research effort. He discovered that the disease was not infectious and that it was caused by a nutritional deficiency. His ideas contrasted sharply with the official establishment hypothesis of an infectious agent. In fact, research relating to infectious agents had become a paradigm in pellagra studies. As a result, Goldberger "stirred up intense anger and controversy," and he was harshly dealt with in medical journals and newspapers. (Duesberg, 1996b, pp. 51–52) Goldberger was right, but there was much suffering and and death taking place during the time he was being mistreated in the newspapers and medical journals.

Philip Semmelweis confronted a similar situation when he found the cause of childbirth fever and proposed the precautions to prevent it. In the midst of the anger, embarrassment, and controversy that Goldberger and Semmelweis (and who knows how many other medical researchers like them throughout the history of medicine) provoked, should they and their colleagues and adversaries have let another generation try to solve the scholarly problems involved?

In the case of pellagra, and of childbirth fever, to mention just two documented examples, clinging to a false paradigm in the face of evidence that the paradigm is wrong led to much death and suffering. Sometimes the harm to health as a result of scholars perpetuating false paradigms can last for centuries, as in the case of research into the cause of scurvy, for instance.

If scholars involved in the Guido Riccio case "need *time* to salve their own egos," it would seem that scholars who were clamorously wrong in the pellagra and childbirth fever cases would also have needed time to salve their egos. It is true that research relating to disease, with all of the suffering, death, and grief that are involved in the subject matter, has a greater urgency than vexing problems of attribution in art history. However, if search for the truth is part of the academic mission and the academic rhetoric, there is no reason why the truth should be purposely delayed and, thus, withheld from a generation or two of fellow scholars, from students whose families pay tuition, from tourists who pay admission fees to museums, buy guidebooks, and pay for audio–video explanations, and so on.

One of the most extraordinary cases of challenge to academic paradigms in recent times involves the studies of Immanuel Velikovsky. This case is exceptional both for the breadth of the nature of his studies and the number of paradigms that were simultaneously challenged, and for the intensity and viciousness of the reactions of scholars who were angered by his ideas. The totality of Velikovsky's interdisciplinary studies "ravages established doctrines in disciplines from astronomy to psychology" (de Grazia, 1978, p. 19). In *The Velikovsky Affair*, which gives a vivid account of the reactions against Velikovsky, de Grazia (1978) wrote that "the uproar against Velikovsky resulted from his trying to relate ... historical memories and documents to astronomical and physical research" (de Grazia, 1978, p. 158). From groups ranging from scholars at Harvard and editors at the American Philosophical Society (APS) to officials at the AAAS, Velikovsky faced censorship and verbal attacks. Velikovsky

(1978) himself was well aware that his startling ideas would not be accepted by the contemporary academic establishment, when he wrote, "it is almost impossible to change views acquired in the course of decades of reading, writing, and teaching" (p. 6), and also when he observed that scholars "will express their disbelief that a truth could have remained undiscovered so long" (pp. 6–7).

THE HIV–AIDS PARADIGM

Some paradigms have been around for centuries, whereas others are relatively new. There are also nearly instant paradigms. One example of the latter is the hypothesis that a virus called HIV is the cause of what has variously (i.e., changing with time) been defined as AIDS. If the Velikovsky case is an example of a widespread interdisciplinary reaction of perhaps unprecedented fury in an attempt to prevent several paradigms from being proven false and overturned in one fell swoop, the HIV–AIDS hypothesis, and the challenges to it, seem to represent an excellent case study of how an increasingly monolithic institutionalization of research can make a challenge to a paradigm very difficult and problematic (Lang, 1994, 1995).

The HIV–AIDS hypothesis gained virtually instant paradigm status in the wake of a 1984 press conference. Apparently about 100,000 articles have been written on the subject since then, all of them based on this paradigm. Many scholars have doubts about the HIV–AIDS hypothesis, however, despite the fact that it is official establishment dogma. One of the most outspoken and persistent of them is Duesberg, who has worked and written extensively on the subject. If Duesberg is right, his book *Inventing the AIDS Virus* (Duesberg, 1996b) might well become one of the all-time classics in the history of medicine and science.

In a review of Duesberg's work, Horton (1996) asked, "How could so many scientists have gotten it all so badly wrong?" (p. 15). Such a question might be called an appeal to the paradigm. However, the fact is that history shows that many establishment scientists have been "so badly wrong" on many occasions in the past on many subjects, and for various reasons. Horton's question in this case might have been formulated better by not asking "How could they...?" but by asking, instead, "Have they done it again?"

In fact, Duesberg (1996b) traced several cases, from centuries ago to the present century, in which so many scientists did, in effect, get it all so badly wrong in trying to establish an infectious cause for diseases such as scurvy, beriberi, pellagra, SMON, and kuru. If Duesberg is right, the fact that scientists might have gotten it all so badly wrong in this case would not be as much of a very exceptional event as it would be just one more example that constitutes part of a centuries-old pattern. Along this line, Di Trocchio (1997) described many cases in which the scientific establishment was not able to understand revolutionary ideas, much less accept them. For example, in 1901, when Marconi attempted to send a transmission from Great Britain to Canada, the invention of the radio was impossible in the establishment's view. Likewise, at a meeting of the Royal Society of London in 1878, it was declared that Edison's idea of electric illumination was idiotic ("idiota") and that the problems Edison faced were impossible to resolve from a technical standpoint. Shortly before the Wright Brothers made their brief historic first airplane flight, the scientific establishment believed that it was mathematically impossible for an airplane to fly. Di Trocchio also related how, from about 1917 to 1937, leaders of the physics establishment were on record, at the British Association for the Advancement of Science and elsewhere, with their beliefs that the atom could not be split and that nuclear energy could not be harnessed.

Thus, the establishment has been very wrong in the past. In the case of the current HIV–AIDS hypothesis, even persons without training in biomedicine who have been following the controversy even casually might end up with some doubts about the official (or orthodox) view that HIV is the cause of what has been defined at various times as AIDS. Decades before AIDS was known or given an official name, a young man in Manchester, England, died from what was considered a strange malady. The case seemed so unusual that it was reported in *Lancet*, a leading medical journal (of which Richard Horton is editor). When AIDS was defined and given a name, another item appeared in *Lancet*, suggesting that the Manchester patient was an early AIDS victim, if not the first known victim. Later, it was claimed that HIV was found in his body (which had been preserved, in part, for future medical research). The announcement of this claim made a big hit in the medical research establishment, because it would nullify the theory that HIV jumped the species gap from monkeys to humans as a result of the polio vaccine experiments in Africa in the 1950s. (The Manchester patient would have been infected before those experiments took place.)

At that point, two scientists who specialized in the mutations of the HIV virus requested samples of the batch of virus found in the Manchester patient, as they did not have any samples of HIV from that early date. When they received the samples, they determined that the HIV was from the early 1990s and not from the 1950s. It seemed obvious that either the HIV had been contaminated with later samples, or else HIV from the 1990s had been used. The specialists then sought samples directly from the preserved tissues of the Manchester patient. They received the tissue samples, but not a trace of HIV was found (events were reported in this manner in various newspaper articles; Connor, 1995, p. 1).

If it is true that the Manchester patient did not have HIV, it is obvious that something other than HIV was the cause of AIDS in this case. In other words, HIV would not be necessary to cause the weakening of the immune system to the extent that one or more of the 29 or so AIDS-defining opportunistic diseases took hold in the patient. Nevertheless, in his review of Duesberg's published AIDS research, Horton (1996) wrote, "HIV has been shown to be a necessary factor for the occurrence of AIDS" (p. 16). Even though the journal of which he is editor, *Lancet*, was a protagonist in the events that allegedly show that HIV is not necessary to cause AIDS, Horton continued to take the official view on this topic. His attitude would seem to be a further reflection of how deeply the HIV–AIDS paradigm has taken hold in just a dozen years or so. In fact, now many in the mass media often refer to HIV as the virus that causes AIDS.

Some paradigms consolidate, survive, and become entrenched for long periods of time partly, if not entirely, because of a lack of serious intellectual challenge. Duesberg (1996b) attempted to demonstrate how the recent HIV–AIDS paradigm quickly became entrenched as a result of a monolithic government-controlled peer-review grant system that does not tolerate challenges. In this case, it does not seem to be the accumulation of evidence that consolidates the paradigm as much as the bureaucratic, administrative, and commercial interests that have been built up around the paradigm, and, in some cases, have become dependent on it. Excerpts from Duesberg's observations include:

> No medical scientist could even hope to make a career without a research grant from the NIH. Grant allocation selects and rewards conformism with the establishment view. Non-conformists are eliminated. ... The growing number of researchers creates a herd effect, drowning out the voice of the lone scientist who questions official wisdom. ... Through peer review the federal government has attained a near-monopoly on science. ... By declaring the virus the cause of AIDS at a press conference sponsored by the Department of Health and Human Services, NIH researcher Robert Gallo swung the entire medical establishment, and even the rest of the world, behind his hypothesis. Once such a definitive statement is made, the difficulty of retracting it only increases with time. (pp. 452–454)

(In these passages, words like "eliminated" and "drowning out" are direct references to silencing of scholars and their ideas.)

DIFFICULTIES IN DISLODGING FALSE PARADIGMS

A common theme of discussion of paradigms involves the difficulty in overturning them and dislodging them in the face of evidence that they are false. Why should this be so in academia, where the mission includes the correction of error in the pursuit of truth? Some scholars try to explain this difficulty in terms of psychology or human nature. Nissani (1989) defined one psychological aspect as "conceptual conservatism," whether it includes child development or history of science: "Although we are all indisputably capable of changing our beliefs, everyday experience suggests that such changes are hard to make: we often cling to old and familiar conceptions of reality, disregarding or explaining away contradictory evidence" (p. 19).

Experimental psychology provides evidence for conceptual conservatism, according to Nissani (1994): "Experimental psychology strongly supports the notion of conceptual conservatism—the human tendency to cling to strongly-held beliefs long after these beliefs have been decisively discredited" (p. 307).

Margolis (1993) discussed the issue in terms of mental habits, in *Paradigms and*

Barriers: How Habits of Mind Govern Scientific Beliefs: "It is the robustness of the habits of mind that block the path to the new idea" (p. 31). In other words, mental habits affect thinking in a manner similar to the effects of physical habits on behavior. Just as persons, including scholars, are subject to physical chemical dependencies (e.g., tobacco, alcohol, recreational drugs, and pharmaceuticals), it would appear that scholars are subject to paradigm dependencies (mentally and intellectually). Such paradigm dependency might be seen as a reflexive, "knee-jerk," negative reaction to ideas that challenge academic paradigms.

If a paradigm that was believed to be true turns out to be false, the situation would be a case of what is commonly called *honest error.* (No matter how clamorous the error, if it was made unwittingly it would be considered honest error.) In such cases, scholars sincerely believed they were adhering to the truth. This honest error concept would also extend to the reflexive action (or knee-jerk reaction) of assuming that specific evidence to the contrary is not sufficient to invalidate the paradigm that is being challenged. In such cases, scholars were brought up, intellectually, to believe the false paradigm to be true (in which case the paradigm might be considered an unwitting Big Lie).

PARADIGM DEPENDENCY AND PARADIGM PROTECTION

Within academia, particularly in light of recent research fraud investigations, there have been attempts to distinguish among honest error, misconduct, and fraud. These three terms are elastic in the sense that they can be interpreted in different ways, meaning different things to different persons and institutions. Besides, what might seem to some scholars to be a case of obvious intellectual fraud might not be regarded as such by administrators in government agencies and universities, and it might not constitute fraud in the sense of legal terminology and the courts.

One common way to judge the difference between honest error and cheating (e.g., misconduct and fraud) is to view the situation from the standpoint of intent. As long as scholars seek the truth and strive for accuracy, the errors they commit are considered honest errors. Only when there is deliberate intent to deceive does the situation involve fraud or misconduct, according to one point of view. Of course, only the specific scholars themselves knew at the outset if there was intent to deceive, and if there was such intent, there might be a strong tendency not to admit it.

The notion of intent to deceive is important for the discussion of academic paradigms and the silencing of scholars. Obviously, if scholars teach their students false paradigms they believe to be true, there is no intent to deceive, even though students end up being deceived. Even when contrary evidence that contests the validity of the paradigm is presented for the first time, the initial knee-jerk incredulity concerning the new evidence can be understood in terms of sincere belief, based on an inherent paradigm dependency.

At certain points, however, in the face of persistent paradigm challenges that are marked by increasing evidence that shows the paradigm to be false, peer-review authorities begin to suspect, fear, or even realize that the paradigm might be false. At this point, if there is further resistance to critical inquiry, paradigm dependency is no longer entirely based on honest error, conceptual conservatism, or mental habits, but rather on vested interests of one type or another. It would seem that at certain points, adhering to a false paradigm becomes more a case of deliberate paradigm protection instead of inherent, basic paradigm dependency. Peer review and academic rhetoric are then put to severe tests and scholars, their ideas, and the truth are all silenced to the extent that critical analysis and debate are not allowed in regular academic forums (e.g., scholarly publications, conferences, and workshops) to test whether the paradigm is true or not. At a certain point, suppression of evidence for the purpose of paradigm protection amounts to an intent to deceive.

Aside from the fact that, in general, no one likes to be proven clamorously wrong, there is a basic vested interest that scholars have in terms of reputation, expertise, and authority. Schneider (1989) alluded to this vested interest when he wrote, "If the knowledge expounded by recognized scholars to their students should prove to be of dubious reliability, then their authority is open to question. Thus, scientific progress and changing theories are natural enemies of authoritarian tradition" (p. 137). As a result of this basic intellectual vested interest, paradigm protection might be seen as a predictable follow-up to, or extension of, paradigm dependency. Schneider further observed that during the controversy that Lavoisier's ideas provoked in the field of chemistry, "Those who were not only involved in research, but who also taught chemistry and needed to instruct their students and answer questions, were put into a difficult position" (pp. 141–142). At a certain point during a persistent challenge to a false paradigm, paradigm dependency and paradigm-protection are no longer identical. As embarrassing as it may be, authoritative scholars and experts can admit error and inform their students that a major breakthrough in the advancement of knowledge has possibly been made. In fact, Lavoisier's startling discovery about combustion is now taught in high school chemistry classes without the paradigm-related problems that the academic chemistry establishment faced in the 18th century.

Although Schneider's observations were made in relation to Lavoisier and studies in chemistry of the 18th century, vested interests in academia relating to authority were strong from well before the 18th century, and continue to the present time. Meanwhile, vested interests of a commercial, industrial, and financial nature have increased greatly since the era of Lavoisier's research in chemistry. Horton (1996) referred to the "gravy train that has become AIDS, Inc." (p. 19). From their beginnings less than two decades ago, vested interests in the HIV–AIDS hypothesis have mushroomed into a multibillion-dollar affair on an international level, involving diagnostic tests, research, expensive treatments, mass media advertising campaigns, and educational programs in schools. It almost seems as if the momentum of the totality of all this activity on behalf of the HIV–AIDS hypothesis does not even allow enough widespread attention to, or consideration of, the possibility (backed by considerable evidence, as Duesberg and others have shown) that the hypothesis might amount to a false paradigm. It would seem that the larger the vested interests become, the greater the tendency to brush aside, ignore, or suppress and censor evidence that would endanger the vested interests that are based on the HIV–AIDS hypothesis. Under such circumstances, it is easy to imagine how peer-review authorities might be tempted to make decisions that are evasive or deceptive in nature.

According to Strohman (1995), Duesberg's doubts about the HIV–AIDS theory were a follow-through and logical extension of Duesberg's research into retroviruses as a possible cause of cancer. Strohman related that the cancer establishment was "committed to a virus hypothesis" (p. ix), but that Duesberg found serious flaws in the establishment view, and also that Duesberg's "case was a strong one" (p. ix). Strohman added: "I remember discussing it with some of my own friends at the NIH who were quite surprised that someone of Peter's stature would basically declare obsolete one of the mainstream approaches to such an important disease" (p. ix).

The element of being surprised in this specific instance is important from the standpoint of paradigm dependency, paradigm protection, paradigm changes, and possible intent to deceive. If Duesberg's case was in fact a strong one, were the NIH scholars surprised because inherent paradigm dependency obstructed them from making the same paradigm leap that Duesberg made? Or, were they surprised because they really thought Duesberg was wrong and they wondered how so brilliant a scholar could go so far off the track? Or did they realize, or suspect, on the other hand, that Duesberg might be right, based on the merits of his "strong" case? If this were the case, were they surprised because Duesberg engaged in a form of noncollegiality, a form of betrayal of his colleagues by exposing a clamorous error on their part? There seems to be another possibility. Perhaps they were surprised because they felt Duesberg should have been aware of the retaliation that he would face from the establishment. If they, in fact, suspected that Duesberg was right, their surprise—instead of their support and praise—would represent an obstacle to correction of error, if the surprise was motivated by collegiality with the establishment scholars, or by fear of retaliation.

If these friends of Strohman at NIH were chosen to be peer-review referees for manuscripts that included research results that "surprised" them in a similar manner, how could they be expected to react? Whether or not such surprise would lead to rejection or acceptance recommendations on the part of these colleagues of Strohman at NIH, it seems obvious that challenges to paradigms pose serious problems for peer-review authorities, and it seems possible that such problems can lead to double standards in the evaluation of manuscripts.

5

Double Standards and Peer Review Suppression

Ruesch (1989) compiled many scholarly opinions and observations relating to animal experimentation in medical research, including the following:

- "The experiments performed on animals in order to determine the effects of medicaments offer a very insecure basis for drawing conclusions as to the effects on humans ... 1879" (p. 251).
- "Medicants do not function the same way in humans as in animals ... they can not possibly be dosed appropriately for such a function ... 1891" (p. 246).
- "The effect of drugs upon animals is so entirely different from their effect upon man that no safe conclusions can be drawn from such investigations ... 1895" (p. 242).
- "An experiment on an animal gives no certain indication of the result of the same experiment on a human being. 1906" (p. 216).
- "The attempts to establish the effectiveness of antitoxins on humans by means of animals are frankly ludicrous ... 1926" (p. 183).
- "My own conviction is that the study of human physiology by way of experiment on animals is the most grotesque and fantastic error ever committed in the whole range of human intellectual activity ... 1933" (p. 151).
- "We must face the fact that the most careful tests of a new drug's effect on animals

may tell us little of its effects on humans. 1962" (p. 106).
- "The animal and human organs show striking differences in their sensitivity to chemical combinations ... 1978" (p. 80).
- "A drug that is tested on animals will have a completely different effect in man. 1985" (p. 62).
- "There are things that work in mice that do not work in people. 1986" (p. 47).

More recently, Lang (1995) came across a similar opinion that was expressed in 1994: "Dosing mice chronically with compounds does not prove that the same conditions will be found during 'normal' human usage" (p. 18). In an editorial announcing a forthcoming conference on peer review in Prague in 1997, Rennie and Flanagin (1995) wrote that "the only true peer review is the universal assessment that work receives after publication" (p. 987). There has been a continual assessment for more than a century, as the items cited at the beginning of the chapter illustrate, that animal experiments used in testing drugs for medical research are misleading, unreliable, and therefore also dangerous. (The thalidomide disaster, for instance, serves as a reminder.) Ruesch (1989) pointed out that Irwin Bross, former head of research at Sloan-Kettering Institute (one of the world's leading cancer research centers), came to believe that animal experimentation in cancer research was "worse than useless" because it was "consistently misleading" (p. 24). Bross (1994) elaborated on the theme of such unproductive research in *Fifty Years of Folly and Fraud "in the Name of Science."* Henry Bigelow of Harvard University was quoted as going so far as to say, "A day will come when the world will look upon today's vivisection in the name of science the way we look today upon witch hunts in the name of religion" (Ruesch, 1978/1991, unnumbered). Despite such extensive, long-term, negative assessment, animal experimentation for the testing of drugs and for other tests has been a paradigm in medical research for a long time (Ruesch, 1992).

DOUBLE STANDARD FOR REJECTION OF A RESEARCH PROPOSAL

Perhaps there is no more effective and revealing way to document double standards in peer review than to discuss peer review that involves animal experimentation in the testing of drugs. The author of the opinion from 1994 listed earlier that reads "dosing mice chronically with compounds does not prove that the same conditions will be found during 'normal' human usage" is none other than an establishment scholar recommending that Duesberg's proposal for a research grant be rejected. In the midst of this negative judgment—a judgment that repeats many similar opinions of the past about the unreliability of animal experiments—grants for large sums have been awarded often and consistently, both before and after 1994, for drug-testing experiments using mice and other animals.

In this case, the double standard used to deny Duesberg a grant went even further, as Lang (1995) pointed out: "The objection states: 'Twenty-four months is a very large part of the total life span of laboratory mice. Many mice might not survive the experiment'" (p. 17). In the face of this objection, Lang countered that "cancer studies on mice which routinely study mice for periods up to 24 months are routinely funded" (p. 17). In effect, Duesberg's proposal in this case involved research into a form of cancer.

Not long after Duesberg's request for funding was rejected, it was reported that the Food and Drug Administration (FDA) approved a new drug used to combat obesity. Approval was given despite "side effects seen in animal studies." Some experts mentioned "studies in which high doses of the drug caused brain damage in laboratory animals." Then, the comment was made that "there is no proof that people are similarly affected," and it is also reported that the drug has been in use in Europe and that none of the side effects found in the animals have been reported in persons living there who used the drug (Hellmich, 1996, pp. 1A–2A).

Here are two peer-review situations. In one, a negative judgment of Duesberg's research proposal is based on the statement that "dosing mice . . . with compounds does not prove that the same conditions will be found in 'normal' human usage." In the other, peer-review approval is given amidst statements to the effect that "there is no proof that people are similarly affected" (i.e., affected with brain damage and perhaps other side effects), and that in Europe the people who have taken the drug so far have not been reported to have suffered the same effects as the animals have. Thus, in one case, rejection is recommended because humans and animals might not react in the same way to a drug, and in the other case approval is given in the very hope that humans and animals will not react in the same way to a drug. Why was there rejection in one case, but not in the other? If research in one case was accepted, why was the research proposal not likewise accepted in the other case?

DOUBLE STANDARDS IN PEER REVIEW IN THE THALIDOMIDE CASE

The thalidomide tragedy of a few decades ago provides examples of more double standards. The drug, produced by Chemie Grunenthal and hailed as something of a wonder drug after years of experiments with animals in which no birth defects were reported, caused about 10,000 babies to be born with horrible birth defects. Apparently there were also serious nervous system disorders among the women who took the drug. Ruesch (1978/1991) reported that animals used included "dogs, cats, mice, rats, and as many as 150 different strains and substrains of rabbits, with negative results. Only when the white New Zealand rabbit was tested, a few malformed rabbits were obtained" (p. 361). Ruesch described further what took place:

> In December 1970, the longest criminal trial in Germany's judicial history ... ended with the acquittal of Chemie Grunenthal, *after a long line of medical authorities had tes-*

tified that the generally accepted animal tests could never be conclusive for human beings. This was unprecedented, for the testimonies came from an impressive array of individuals whose careers and reputations were practically built on animal experimentation, including the 1945 Nobel laureate biochemist Ernst Boris Chain. ... Even Prof Widukind Lenz ... testified at the trial that "there is no animal test capable of indicating beforehand that human beings, subjected to similar experimental conditions, will react in identical or similar fashion." (pp. 361–362)

Despite the details of this tragic thalidomide story, which comprise a sad chapter in the history of medicine, in 1988, Varaut (1990) presented a paper at a conference that included these ideas:

The tragic thalidomide case, which is still cited, would never have happened if the drug had been administered to other species of animals than rats, which unfortunately were not affected by this product. Thalidomide is the best example of the absolute necessity for some experimentation on animals. (p. 36)

The implicit double standard for peer review in Varaut's (1990) statement becomes obvious with his reference to "other species of animals." The fact is that, as Ruesch (1978/1991) pointed out, many animals were tested for thalidomide (with negative results), whereas in other cases one type of animal might be used: monkeys, rats, dogs, mice, and so on (but not necessarily all in the testing for the same drug). Besides, if all drugs were tested on all species of animals, most likely at least one animal would show severe side effects for large doses of the drug being tested. It is obvious that not all species are tested for each drug. So where would Varaut, or anyone else, draw the line regarding the total number of species used before experiments with a drug are terminated?

The difficulty with Varaut's logic is illustrated by what happened in the case of the drug diethylstilboestrol (DES). Ruesch (1992) described the situation:

DES ... was developed in 1939, tested without adverse effects on animals for years, but then it was suddenly discovered to have caused cancer in girls whose mothers had been prescribed this 'miracle drug' by their doctors during pregnancy. ... After DES had turned out to be the first drug that the medical confraternity itself had recognized as being responsible for creating a new type of cancer in human beings, animal tests with DES were started all over again, and again with no results; the test animals did not develop cancer. (p. 22)

Peer-review double standards for animal experimentation can have disastrous effects. In the case of the disease subacute myelo-optico-neuropathy (SMON), Inuoe claimed that a virus he discovered caused the disease (which had grown to epidemic proportions). Duesberg (1996b) stated that Inuoe "insisted he had caused SMON-like symptoms in mice ... either by injecting the virus into their brains or feeding the virus to other immune-suppressed mice" (p. 25). This type of research and the peer-review acceptance it receives, in the face of other peer-review judgments that point out that results of animal experiments are unreliable when applied to humans, tended to put scholars off the track in relation to the real cause, which turned out to be the "miracle" drug Oxychinol that Ciba-Geigy had developed. Regarding this situation, Ruesch (1992) noted:

> At least a thousand deaths had to be counted in Japan and 30,000 cases of blindness and/or paralysis of the lower limbs before it was realized that heretofore unexplained similar cases of death, blindness, and paralysis in Holland, Denmark, Germany, France, Great Britain, Belgium, Italy, Sweden, etc. had also been caused by Oxychinol-containing drugs. (p. 20)

In this case, Ruesch (1992) related that according to the studies of Hansson, the researchers discovered (but kept secret) severe side effects on the experimental animals "who were seized by violent convulsions and respiratory difficulties as soon as they were made to swallow Oxychinol" (p. 20). The drug was marketed anyway, with a warning, as Ruesch noted, not to give it to "*house pets*." (p. 20) He cites this case as evidence "that the researchers themselves do not believe in the validity of animal tests in respect to human beings" (p. 21).

A double standard in peer review is based on an oscillating viewpoint, as the situation suits the peer-review authorities. On the one hand, results of animal experiments are not applicable to humans (as in the rejection of Duesberg's research grant proposal, and in extensive expert testimony during the thalidomide–Chemie Grunenthal trial in Germany). On the other hand, animals are valid models for humans in drug testing (as evidenced by the large number of peer-review acceptances for grants and publications of such studies using animals as models for humans). It is possible to accept or reject a grant proposal or a manuscript by suddenly and arbitrarily changing the rules (or the criteria, as the case may be).

IDENTIFYING DOUBLE STANDARDS

Distinctions should be made among different standards, different criteria, and double standards. Some journals may have more stringent, stricter (higher) criteria for acceptance than other journals have. Some referees for the same journal may be generally considered harsh and strict in comparison with other referees who are considered more lenient in their judgment. These are subjective differences, but not necessarily double standards. Criteria for hiring, promotion, and tenure at some universities are more stringent than at others. These are different standards, but not necessarily double standards. By contrast, double standards usually involve a sudden, arbitrary shift in judgment or policy that is contrary to usual policy.

The subjective nature involved in different standards and criteria sometimes makes it difficult to identify a double standard. The distinction might be blurred and unclear. The famous study published by Peters and Ceci (1982) can be regarded as a classic case of double standards in peer review. Dalton (1995) summarized what took place:

The authors took 12 published research articles by investigators from prestigious and highly productive American psychological departments in 12 different highly regarded American psychological journals. ... After replacing the authors' original names and institutions with fictitious names and affiliations that had neither reality nor prestige, they resubmitted the articles to the same journals. ... Only 3 of the 12 articles were recognized. The remaining nine proceeded through the refereeing process ... eight of the nine were rejected. Sixteen of the eighteen referees recommended against publication, often on the grounds of serious methodological flaws. (p. 215)

It is obvious that the eight rejected articles were treated completely differently the second time around. If they had the same referees both times, it was obviously a case of double standards. However, the fact that only 3 of the 12 articles were recognized indicates a certain laxity, or a certain policy, on the part of the editors, who seem to have glanced at the papers (rather than read them carefully) and then relied heavily on referee judgments.

It is possible that different referees have sincerely different ideas and standards about methodology, and the embarrassing rejections of the same articles reflect these differences. On the other hand, if the referees and the editors rejected the articles because they were too long or too short in length, or because the format, genre, or style were declared inappropriate and unacceptable, then obvious double standards have been used.

One referee might have actually detected methodological flaws and inaccuracies of various types that slipped by another referee. In that case, sloppy evaluation, rather than deliberate double standards, might have caused the embarrassing discrepancies in peer-review decisions. If this were the case, the rejection recommendation would be the equivalent of a rebuttal article or a letter to the editor pointing out defects in the published article. (For this reason, among others, peer review should not be secret.)

DOUBLE STANDARDS AND BIAS

The issue is further blurred by the concept of *bias*, which is often identified with double standards. Referees who are usually somewhat lenient might become quite harsh in judgment of scholars or ideas they do not like. Or, on the contrary, harsh referees might suddenly become lenient if the referees' personal or professional vested interests are better served by leniency in specific cases. However, the mixture of subjective factors and critical evaluation often makes precise distinctions difficult. For example, a manuscript that was rejected by referees and editors who had a strong bias against the author of the manuscript might also have been rejected by referees and editors who had no bias at all against the author. (As long as referees' identities remain secret, and reasons for rejection remain secret, some clear cases of double standards might escape detection.)

In any case, many scholars seem to feel that they and their ideas are being silenced because of bias against them. Some years ago, the Office of Scholarly

Communication of the American Council of Learned Societies (ACLS) conducted a survey of 5,385 scholars, of whom about 71% responded. Morton and Price (1989) discussed the results, including views about bias:

> About three out of four respondents think the editorial peer review system is biased. ... About 40% think bias is so prevalent in their disciplines that it merits reform. ... The question is, therefore, not whether bias exists in the peer review system, but whether it is prevalent and whether it systematically interferes with the free exchange of information and ideas by discriminating against particular subjects, opinions, and classes of authors. ... The survey shows that suspicions of bias appear to be held by scholars in all types of universities and among all the disciplines sampled ... the unease is pervasive, not an occasional outcropping of discontent. (pp. 7–9)

EXCUSES AND "DIRTY TRICKS"

In addition to being reflections of bias against specific persons and their ideas, double standards in peer review can have other characteristics. Sometimes they are excuses rather than reasons for rejection. A good example is rejection because of length when articles recently published in the same journal were longer and shorter than the rejected article. Another example involves "catch 22" type reasons, such as, on the one hand, rejection for not citing and discussing other publications on the subject, and, on the other hand, rejection for repeating information and ideas that have already been published elsewhere.

In one way or another, double standards might be considered "dirty tricks." Remus (1980) stated that one such trick is to criticize the work negatively "for vices it does not have" (p. 89), and then recommend rejection based on the alleged vices, or defects, as the case may be. It seems something of a dirty trick to recommend rejection of a grant proposal on the basis that animals may not react to drugs the same way humans do at the same time that grants for such animal experimentation are, in fact, an integral part of the research paradigm. (On the other hand, rather than considering the rejection opinion in this case to be a peer-review dirty trick, some scholars might consider it instead to be a forthright peer-review admission—if not confirmation—that the prevailing paradigm is a false one.)

"Almost everyone who has ever submitted anything to a journal has a horror story or two to tell." If this harsh judgment by Leslie (1989, p. 125) is true, it would suggest that double standards abound in the peer-review process. A close scrutiny of referees' files in the editorial offices of journals might give some hint as to what extent Leslie's views are accurate, but Campanario (1995) found that an attempt to engage in such scrutiny "encounters resistance from most editors, even if it is possible to keep referees' names anonymous" (p. 320). In his discussion of peer-review rejections by *Science* and *Nature*, Campanario referred to a double-standard incident at *Nature* in which "one of the reviewers tried to change the requirements he had laid down for acceptance in the first place" (p. 313).

DOUBLE STANDARDS FOR EXCLUSION AND INCLUSION

Such an attempt to "change the requirements" might be considered a form of double standard by means of "changing the rules as you go along." Something quite similar to this situation took place at the editorial offices at *Art Bulletin*, the major publication of the College Art Association, which is is member organization of the ACLS. An article was submitted by Donna Baker for publication. A main part of the subject matter dealt with the Mappamondo, a large map that was painted in the Palazzo Publico in Siena, Italy, where the Guido Riccio fresco is also located. In this article, the author disagreed quite strongly with the establishment point of view on some issues that involved the Mappamondo and its relation to the Guido Riccio controversy. The editor, Richard Brilliant, rejected the article. In his rejection letter to Baker of May 19, 1991, Brilliant stated that he read the article "several times" (there is no indication that he ever sent it to a referee before rejecting it).

In the editor's view, Baker made "allegations" and, according to the editor, such allegations "would require the *Bulletin's* provision of an opportunity to be heard to all the contestants." Provision for this opportunity was based on "fairness,"according to Brilliant. He then expressed reservations about presenting the views of all the contestants because discussion "could well be endless." The article was rejected and that seemed to be the end of the matter.

Then, in the June 1996 issue of *Art Bulletin*, a long article appeared by a different author (Kupfer, 1996) on the same subject (i.e., the Mappamondo in the Siena Palazzo Publico). The hypotheses and conclusions were in sharp disagreement with those of the article that had been rejected. Besides, in the published article the following allegations appear: "But holding the *Mappamondo* hostage to the *Guidoriccio* ... will not help advance understanding of either work ... a desperate attempt at obfuscation for the sake of sustaining an attack on the traditional attribution of the *Guidoriccio* ... interpretation of the ambiguously worded inventory seems gratuitous" (pp. 288–289).

The double standard in this case should be easy for all to grasp. One article was rejected because, in the name of "fairness" all sides of the controversial issue should be heard, particularly because the article contained "allegations." But discussion might be "endless" if all sides are heard. Under these terms, publication was dependent on all sides being heard, not just one side, but that was not practical for reasons of space.

After the article was rejected in this manner, another article on the same subject was published in the same journal. The published article disagreed with the contents of the rejected article, and similar to the rejected article, the published article contained allegations. Apparently the "fairness" reference did not apply to scholars against whom the published allegations were made, or to scholars who disagreed with the contents of the published article. This seems to be a rather ironic double standard case, in which the fairness concept is invoked in a manner that results in the establishment view being published and the dissenting view being silenced and shut out from the pages of the journal. (Usually, fairness is invoked to allow a point of view to be heard, not to suppress it.)

Another glaring example of peer-review double standards regarding inclusion and exclusion took place during the Guido Riccio controversy in 1985, when a conference devoted to the art of Simone Martini was held in Siena. At that time, the controversy was in full swing. Some new evidence that further contested the official attribution came to light, and a request was made to the Organizing Committee (Comitato Scientifico) to be allowed to present the new material in a paper as part of the program of the conference. The request was denied. Inquiries were made to seek the reason for rejection.

What followed is described in *Confronting the Experts*:

> The reason for our rejection was explained by Professor Bellosi ... of the Organizing Committee ... to another member of the Organizing Committee, Professor Miklos Boskovits. ... According to Boskovits, Bellosi stated that by then scholars knew where each side stood on the issue of Guido Riccio, that the subject had been worked over in detail recently, and that there should be a pause for reflection. Boskovits said he agreed with the reasoning behind the decision to exclude us from the program. (Mallory & Moran, 1996, p. 144)

Up to this point, this decision resembled the *Art Bulletin* rejection of the Mappamondo article, in the sense that no discussion on the subject from any side or point of view would be held. So far, no discussion at all, and therefore no double standard, but then the following took place: "After having kept us off the program because Guido Riccio was not to be discussed, the ... Committee included one of their own members ... Torriti, on the program to give a long talk on the Guido Riccio situation in which he attempted to refute our views" (Mallory & Moran, 1996, p. 144).

Such a situation is not an isolated case in the attempt to silence scholars. Velikovsky faced similar treatment after he came forth with evidence and theories that upset authorities and experts: "The ... settings provided for the discussion ... were mostly arranged ... by hostile critics or intimidated moderators. He was excluded from discussion of his own work and his works were not subsequently published" (de Grazia, 1978, p. 173).

THE RIGHT TO REPLY

The right to reply seems to be a major problem involving double standards in peer review.

According to the rhetoric of academia, all scholars have the right to reply, because there is free and open discussion and debate in which all points of view are given a hearing. In reality, however, apparently some scholars have a right to reply, and others do not. As far as can be determined, this right is determined by arbitrary editorial decision. Apparently from a legal standpoint, in many cases at least, editors have the legal power to decide what will be excluded from their journals. In this legal sense, scholars do not have a right to publish a reply in the pages of a journal. Instead, they are granted the opportunity (the privilege, honor, or however it may be described) by the editor. On the other hand, when an editorial official or a scholar refers to a right to reply, the reference is usually to an ethical or moral right based on the rhetoric about free and open discussion and debate, or else based on the ethical concept of fair play, in which scholars who have been verbally "attacked" in the pages of a journal have the right to defend themselves, rebut, explain, and so on.

Perhaps one of the most revealing cases of double standards involving right to reply took place with *Burlington Magazine* and the manner in which it dealt with aspects of the Guido Riccio controversy. In response to an article and also to an editorial published in that source, a letter to the editor was published. It begins, "Sir, this is not the appropriate place for us to discuss the evidence presented in Professor Andrew Martindale's article on the Guido *Riccio* controversy" (Mallory & Moran, 1987, p. 187). In the original submission, the letter began, "Letters to the Editor are customarily brief and therefore not the appropriate place for us to discuss the many ambiguities, discrepancies, and errors that we feel we have detected so far in Professor Andrew Martindale's article," but the text was changed based on the suggestion of the editor in a letter to the authors (N. MacGregor, personal communication, July 2, 1986). The specific intention of this opening to the letter in its original text was to alert scholars who had read Martindale's article that errors had been detected in his article and that these alleged errors would be discussed in publications planned for the future.

The editor, Neil MacGregor, was receptive to the publication of the letter, but he stated in his letter that he considered the reference to "many ambiguities, discrepancies, and errors" as being "unnecessarily discourteous." In this case, an attempt to alert scholars to error was silenced, but the silence would be broken in planned future publications, and there did not seem to be the same urgency as there might have been if the errors had involved medical research, atomic energy, or political science dealing with sensitive issues that might lead to war.

The published letter provoked a reply in the form of a letter to the editor by Piero Torriti, published in the July 1989 issue of *Burlington Magazine* (p. 485). The letter begins, "I should like to take the opportunity to refute once and for all the absurd and defamatory accusations ... contained in the letter published ... in the March 1987 issue" (by the time this letter was published, Caroline Elam had replaced MacGregor as editor). A case could already be made that an obvious double standard has been used, as charges of having made "absurd and defamatory accusations" would seem to be more "discourteous" than charges of "ambiguities, discrepancies, and errors." On the other hand, maybe it was a case of different standards of different editors, rather than a double standard per se.

In any case, a reply seemed warranted to rebut the charges (deemed completely false) of having made "absurd and defamatory accusations." By simple logic, these charges would be false. If an editor would not allow references in a letter to "ambiguities, discrepancies, and errors" because they were "unnecessarily discourteous," would the same editor allow the publication of absurd and defamatory accusations, which are much more discourteous? Besides, publishing "defamatory" material would have placed the journal itself, and those persons who have statutory responsibility for the journal's contents, in potential legal trouble. Therefore, it was unlikely that the editor would have allowed "absurd and defamatory accusations" to be published.

In a desire to rebut the untrue and unfounded charges that absurd and defamatory accusations had been made and published, a letter to the editor was submitted. However, the editor, Caroline Elam, rejected it, stating that she considered *Burlington Magazine's* discussion on the subject closed. Obviously, the editor had the legal power to deny publication of the letter, so the right to reply was not a legal issue. Instead, the question was placed within the framework of fair play; that is, scholars who have been falsely accused in print should have the opportunity to defend themselves and to set the record straight.

Over the course of about a year, Elam wrote several rejection letters, despite appeals to fair play. In the face of the rejections, the appeal was taken to other members of *Burlington Magazine's* leadership, including Sir Brinsely Ford, a trustee, who supported Elam by responding quickly (personal communication, October 23, 1989) with, "You have made accusations to which Professor Torriti had the right to reply, and that, in my opinion, should be the end of the matter as far as the *Burlington* is concerned" (Mallory & Moran, 1996, p. 148).

In Sir Brinsely's response, the issue of right to reply was brought up directly. Torriti had the right to reply but that "should be the end of the matter," even though Torriti made accusations. In this case, the double standard is undeniable. On what basis (legal, fair play, or otherwise) would Torriti have a right to reply to other scholars, but no other scholar would have the right to reply to Torriti, except the basis of power that arbitrarily decides to employ a double standard? By use of power and double standards in peer review, scholars can be silenced. (As it turned out, MacGregor became Chairman of the Board, and at a Board meeting, Elam's rejection decisions were reversed and a reply to Torriti was allowed, and eventually published in the January 1991 issue.)

In addition to taking the appeal, based on fair play within the *Burlington* leadership, various scholars outside of art history who were specialists in scholarly communication, were consulted, and their opinions were requested. One of these scholars is Ralph Eubanks of the University of West Florida. Eubanks (personal communication, February 6, 1990) stated:

> I do indeed believe that scholars who have been charged with having made a "defamatory" statement should be given the chance to reply to such a charge in the pages of the scholarly journal. ... Simply in the interest of justice, one should be allowed the opportunity to refute this kind of allegation.

In the same letter, Eubanks recalled a situation he was confronted with when he was editor of a scholarly journal. In a book review that was to appear in the book review section, the reviewer charged that the author plagiarized. Eubanks gave the author the chance to publish a rebuttal alongside the review itself. In explaining his editorial position, Eubanks affirmed that he "did not regard this editorial decision as an extraordinary one." Instead, he "thought of it as one *dictated* by the standard of fairness." (As far as known, the February 6, 1990 letter by Eubanks has not been published.)

Perhaps the majority, or even the vast majority, of scholarly journals follow the standards of fairness to which Eubanks adhered. The concept of fairness and justice in scholarly communication becomes a component of the rhetoric relating to open discussion, debate, and free exchange of ideas. In light of such standards, the questioning of a scholar's right to reply, statements that a scholar does not have the right to reply, or opinions to the effect that one scholar has the right to reply and "that should be the end of it," should lead to suspicion that the concept of right to reply is being invoked in order to silence scholars. Such invocation usually involves, by its very nature, a double standard.

Velikovsky had difficulty, on several occasions, getting his rebuttals into the scholarly literature. It seems that on one occasion *"The Proceedings of The American Philosophical Society*, which in 1952 carried extensive attacks upon him, would not suffer his reply" (de Grazia, 1978, p. 179). In this regard, Duesberg, with his dissident views on AIDS research, was in the same situation as Velikovsky as far as being refused the right to reply in establishment publications.

Among Lang's file studies, there is one called the "Journalistic Suppression and Manipulation File." In an item from February 19,1996, Lang wrote, "I have documented the way information and certain points of view are currently suppressed by the quartet constituted by *Science, Chemical and Engineering News*, the *Lancet*, and the *New York Times. Nature* is in a class of its own." (There are plans to have some of Lang's recent file studies published in the near future.) Within the context of these instances of suppression, the right to reply is a specific issue. For instance, in a letter dated January 15, 1996, to Duesberg, the editor of *Chemical & Engineering News (C & EN)*, Madeleine Jacobs, wrote, "As I have stated before, you do not have a right to publish a letter in *C & EN*." (After considerable activism at the grass roots level in the scientific community, primarily including the large mailing list for Lang's file study, Duesberg's letter was published in *Chemical & Engineering News* on March 25, 1996, p. 4.)

Duesberg (1996b) described what happened at *Nature*: "The editor, John Maddox, not only refused to publish the letter, but advertised the censorship in a full-page editorial, entitled 'Has Duesberg a Right to Reply?' The answer, according to Maddox, was no" (p. 401). The very fact that such an editorial was published, proclaiming a denial of the right to reply, might in itself place *Nature* "in a class of its own."

DOUBLE STANDARDS SET BY LEARNED SOCIETIES

Double standards that might result in the silencing of scholars can take place on levels other than those of editors' and referees' peer-review decisions. A rather unusual case took place at the NAS. Once again, it is NAS member Lang, in a file study piece entitled "Comments on the Meaning of Membership in the National Academy of Sciences," dated October 7, 1992, who documented and described the situation. (Until the file studies are published, they may be obtained from Lang, care of the Mathematics Department at Yale University.)

According to Lang's account, several years ago, the NAS Council urged a Russian dissident mathematician, Igor Shafarevich, to resign as a member of NAS because Council members did not like the contents of some of the things he published after he gained NAS membership. Lang described this as a "spectacular and unprecedented action of the Academy." The Council claimed that the Russian scholar violated NAS's "principles." Lang's documentation and discussion compare Shafarevich's behavior (which allegedly violated NAS principles) with similar behavior by Yuval Ne'eman and William Shockley, who were treated differently by the NAS Council; that is, their behavior was tolerated and they were not urged to resign. Lang also raised questions about whether or not the famous scholars Samuel Huntington, David Baltimore, and Robert Gallo might also have violated one or more NAS principles, and he observed that "whatever 'principles' the Council of the Academy had in mind were left unspecified, except for the ones which they chose to mention to Shafarevich."

It should be obvious how the violation of unspecified principles and the punishment of NAS members for writing about ideas that violate the principles can lead to the silencing of scholars. Double standards of enforcement of unwritten or unspecified principles only add to the uncertainty that might serve as an inhibiting factor resulting in silence rather than expression.

If Duesberg's (1996b) account is accurate, it seems that the NAS was recently involved in another case of suppression by means of double standards. Supposedly, "Academy members such a Duesberg have an automatic right to publish papers without the standard peer review" (p. 397) in the NAS publication *Proceedings of the National Academy of Sciences*. Duesberg (1996b) related that he submitted a paper but the "editor promptly rejected it. ... Duesberg invoked his rights as an academy member and protested. The new editor took up the issue ... insisting he could not publish it without peer review" (p. 397). After some negative and hostile reviews, the paper finally appeared. Duesberg submitted another paper, and "again the editor promptly rejected the paper, arguing that it was too long" (p. 397). Duesberg redid the work and submitted two shorter articles. One was accepted, the other was rejected after several negative peer-review reports. It was reported that this decision "made Duesberg the second member in the 128-year history of the Academy to have a paper rejected from its journal; apparently, the other had been Linus Pauling, who had argued vitamin C might prevent cancer" (p. 398).

DIFFERENT SETS OF RULES

In a brief chapter, "For the Freedom to Comment by Scientists," in *Intellectual Suppression*, Springell (1986) concluded that "rank and file scientists operate under a different set of rules from the chiefs" (p. 75). He also wrote, "In the meantime, my attention had been drawn to an initiative of the U.S. National Academy of Sciences designed to guarantee the freedom of Inquiry and Expression for scientists" (p. 76). This NAS declaration was from 1976, or so, in the wake of Shafarevich's election to NAS. As a dissident scholar in Russia, Shafarevich battled with the Soviet authorities about the rights of scientists to speak out. The NAS makes an appeal for freedom of inquiry and expression, but then when one of its members says something the NAS Council does not like, attempts are made to punish the member. This double standard resembles somewhat the case at Yale where Schmidt's inaugural address with its fervent pitch for freedom of expression on the nation's campuses was delivered at the same time that a Yale student was being punished for having displayed a satirical poster that Yale authorities did not like.

Another case that seems to involve double standards based on different sets of rules took place at Yeshiva University medical school. (Albert Einstein College of Medicine and its teaching hospital, the Montefiore Medical Center). A researcher, Heidi Weissmann, charged a colleague, Leonard Freeman, with plagiarism. Lawsuits ensued. An article in *Science and Government Report* (Greenberg, 1990) relates that Weissmann had to pay her own legal expenses, but Freeman's were apparently reimbursed by Montefiore Hospital. A district court decision favored Freeman. In the wake of the court ruling, the president of Montefiore was quoted as saying, in a memo to the hospital staff, "The Federal District Court has completely vindicated our colleague, Leonard Freeman ... I know you are all as pleased as I am with the decision" (p. 4).

Then, after Weissmann appealed the case in court, a U.S. Court of Appeals ruled in her favor against Freeman, stating that Freeman had "attempted to pass off the work (by Weissmann) as his own" (Greenberg, 1990, p. 4). Meanwhile, an inquiry panel had been formed at Montefiore to investigate the case. In the wake of this court decision, the panel "expressed indifference to the court findings, stating that 'The committee did not feel bound by the decisions of the Appellate Court or the District Court'" (p. 4). It was reported that the "Court of Appeals decision favoring Weissmann did not inspire" the president of Montfiore "to a similar conclusion on her behalf" (Greenberg, 1990, p. 4) as the lower court decision inspired a conclusion on Freeman's behalf. It does not seem that there was a statement by the president that Weissmann had been "completely vindicated." In fact, it was reported that Weissmann lost her job, and Freeman received a promotion.

As in the Yeshiva case, and other cases discussed later, the use of double standards can lead to the problem of toleration of falsification. This toleration includes attempts to silence scholars who try to expose falsifications. Toleration of falsification within the scientific community is itself something of a double standard, because the rhetoric of science claims that science is self-correcting and that the pursuit of truth is a main part of science's mission.

6

Toleration of Falsification

The hierarchies define ethical practices. ... They accept or reject men and material, and inflict sanctions all according to their own interests. (de Grazia, 1978, p. 188)

In a section of one of his file studies (National Institutes of Health [NIH], and Department of Health and Human Services [HHS], September 1, 1993), Lang reported that, as part of an investigation into allegations of improper conduct relating to AIDS research in the NIH laboratory of Robert Gallo, the Appeals Board of the U.S. Department of Heath and Human Services (HHS) discussed a definition of scientific misconduct: "This definition cannot reasonably be read as encompassing falsification or any other conduct which does not *seriously deviate* from commonly accepted practices within the scientific community" (p. 5).

Lang commented on this definition as follows (in the September 1, 1993, section of the file study):

> The Board has ruled that scientific misconduct does not include "falsification or any other conduct which does not seriously deviate from commonly accepted practices within the scientific community. ... "According the the Board's logic, if falsification becomes a universal practice among scientists, then it receives the legal approval of government agencies which are supposed to overview the maintenance of scientific standards for government grants and government laboratories. (p. 1)

De Marchi and Franchi (1996) also commented on this situation: They observed that the definition of misconduct was changed after Gallo and others had been found to have engaged in questionable practices. The new definition, according to De Marchi and Franchi, served the interests of the science and pharmaceutical power structure.

IS FALSIFICATION A COMMONLY ACCEPTED PRACTICE?

Prior to the advancement of the Appeals Board definition, many codes and guidelines of academic and professional ethics included "falsification" as an example of misconduct or fraud. For example, LaFollette (1992) noted that the National Science Foundation considers falsification to be a part of its definition of misconduct. Along a similar line, Windom (1988) observed that the Public Health Service's definition of misconduct includes "fabrication, falsification, plagiarism, and deception" (p. 1). In fact, the association of falsification with misconduct had become so strong that Chalmers (1990) wrote, "Scientific misconduct is commonly conceptualized as deliberate falsification of data" (p. 1405).

In the wake of the Felig–Soman scandal at Yale's Medical School, the president and fellows of Yale University approved a policy statement that included these ideas: "Academic fraud is more than error; it may take the form of falsification or fabrication of data, plagiarism. ... It is hardly possible to exaggerate the damage that can result from such a breach of the academic commitment to truth" (*Yale Weekly...*, 1982).

Similarly, at Harvard the discussion of the John Darsee case—which is by now mentioned often among case studies of academic fraud and misconduct—included references to falsification. In one instance, the case is discussed with the title "Medical School Dean Releases Report on Falsification of Research Data," and the text includes references to the "discovery and admission of data falsification by Dr. Darsee," and to "all investigations and deliberations dealing with falsification of results" (*Harvard University Gazette*, 1982, pp. 1, 12). If the definition of misconduct cannot encompass falsification, Darsee's falsifications might not have constituted misconduct. At the same time, it is obvious that many persons in the scientific community did not approve of how Darsee conducted his research.

At this point, it should be obvious that the term *falsification* is similar to *national security* in the sense that both are very elastic terms that can be defined and interpreted in different ways at different times by different persons and organizations. Invoking the term falsification can lead to rhetoric versus reality gaps, and to double standards relating to toleration of falsification on the part of scholars and organizations. The greater the toleration of falsification that exists, the greater the proclivity might be to attempt to silence scholars who detect, expose, and try to correct the falsifications.

In fact, in the Appeals Board definition, the reference to "commonly accepted practices" is something of a recognition of a double standard. If something is commonly accepted, it might be generally accepted but not necessarily universally accepted by all scholars and institutions all of the time. Commonly accepted can easily be associated with commonly tolerated.

Falsification can be deliberate, or it can occur in an unwitting and unintentional manner. A false paradigm in history, for instance, that is believed to be true, amounts to a falsification of history. The persons who were involved in the original formulation of such falsification of history might have known that it was not true. Later generations of scholars who come across the falsified version might believe it is true, however, and include it in textbooks and classroom lectures. To the extent that scholars perpetuate a false paradigm of history believed to be true, they are engaging in a falsification of history, but they are doing so unwittingly, in good faith, and within the context of honest error. This type of falsification would be a component of paradigm dependency in academia.

Sometimes falsification is associated with intent to deceive, and sometimes it is regarded as honest error. A problem in such cases is that sometimes only the persons engaged in the falsification know for sure whether or not it was done deliberately. In such cases, a sense of democratic due process or fair play might result in giving someone the benefit of the doubt, based on the concept of being innocent until proven guilty. Until it is proven that falsification was deliberate, it might be considered, believed, or assumed that it was the result of honest error. Proof might be in the form of an outright admission, but short of such an admission, some doubt might linger. This sense of due process and fair play can therefore be a factor in the toleration of falsification, a factor viewed in a positive sense. In its broader definition, falsification can include fabrication of data, misrepresentation, plagiarism, obfuscation, prevarication, cover up, and so on. In one sense, any activity that actively obstructs knowledge of the truth might be considered part of a falsification process. Thus, secrecy and cover up can be components of falsification.

On the other hand, a relativist position that denies the existence of absolute truth might regard falsification as a relative, or even a fictitious, notion. If there is no truth, there cannot really be a falsification of the truth. A somewhat similar situation occurred in discussion of rules for the Olympic Games. For a long time, competition and participation were reserved for nonprofessional athletes. Then there was discussion of what really constituted a professional athlete and what really constituted violations in this regard. Finally, professional athletes were allowed to compete in some sports. At one point, someone commented to the effect that if there are no rules there can be no violations.

FALSIFICATION TREATED AS A SUBJECTIVE MATTER

Along a similar line, toleration of falsification can take place by regarding falsification as a subjective matter. Such a position is similar to a relativist one. What is considered to be a falsification by one person or institution might not be regarded as falsification by others. This was essentially the response of the president and the

Board of the College Art Association (CAA) in a letter written by CAA President Paul Arnold to Gordon Moran (personal communication, December 11, 1987; also known as The Arnold Letter). As the Guido Riccio controversy was unfolding and developing, certain practices were detected that seemed to be examples of misrepresentation, destruction of evidence, falsification, peer-review conflict of interest, and censorship. As a result, the CAA was asked to include these practices in its published ethics code as examples of unethical practices in art history. The Arnold Letter stated that the CAA "cannot" include such practices in the ethics code as examples of unethical conduct because the CAA was being asked to include "subjective matters," such as "fairness," and "respect."

In effect, the specific use of the terms *fairness* and *respect* in this case is itself an example of falsification, as in the specific requests to the CAA that led to the writing of The Arnold Letter, the CAA was not asked to include fairness and respect. Why these terms were brought up in this context remains something of a mystery.

In reply to The Arnold Letter, the CAA was asked to reconsider its position relating to unethical practices (falsification, etc.), and it was pointed out that the CAA had not been asked to include fairness and respect, and that inclusion of those terms in the letter written by Arnold amounted to a falsification. At a meeting of the CAA Board of Directors of April 16, 1988, the "board voted unanimously to reaffirm the position taken in Professor Arnold's letter" (G. Edelson, personal communication, May 8, 1988). After further correspondence and discussion on the specific subject, on August 9, 1988, it was stated that "the Board considers the matter closed and sees no reason to depart from its reaffirmance of the positions stated in the Arnold letter" (B. Hoffman, personal communication, August 9, 1988).

Because the CAA is a member of the ACLS, the President of ACLS, Stanley Katz, was asked (personal communication, February 26, 1988):

> Do you agree with the CAA Board that our requests for practices to be included in the CAA ethical code involved "subjective matters"? In other words, do you believe, in your role as a scholar, and in your role as President of ACLS, that, in terms of academic ethics, practices such as false statements, falsification, misrepresentation, censorship, conflicts of interest ... represent examples of "subjective matters"?

Several years have passed, and still no answers to these specific inquiries have been received from Katz, or, for that matter, from any other officer of the ACLS.

By contrast, Lang, who had been following the case, wrote, with specific reference to the CAA response in The Arnold Letter, "I do wish the CAA and similar organizations took cognizance of the facts of obstructions, evasiveness, falsifications, misrepresentation, which occur on a much more widespread basis than is usually recognized" (Moran & Mallory, 1991a, p. 63).

The legalistic position regarding falsification taken by the HHS Appeals Board, and the subjective position taken by the CAA (with the apparent consent, based on silence in the face of inquiry, of the ACLS president), contrast with the academic and professional policies, codes and guidelines in which falsification is considered an example of unethical behavior (even to the extent of being considered misconduct or fraud). Such strongly contrasting attitudes can lead to ambiguity. This ambiguity, in turn, can lead to arbitrary double standards, based on power, special interests, and vested interests, relating to whether falsification will be tolerated or punished.

A CASE AT HARVARD: DELIBERATE FALSIFICATION OR HONEST ERROR?

In *Le Bugie della Scienza* (the title of which in English would be *The Lies of Science*), Di Trocchio (1993) described a situation in scientific research in which falsification was both tolerated and punished during the development of the case. A summary of Di Trocchio's account is as follows. In March 1986, researchers led by Ellis Reinherz at Dana Farber Cancer Institute at Harvard University announced the discovery of Interleukin 4-A. Articles in *Science* and the *Journal of Experimental Medicine* gave details of the discovery. It turned out that the articles were erroneous, and a retraction was published in *Science*. Di Trocchio asked why the retraction took place so quickly, when in the Breuning and Baltimore cases it took a long time to ascertain that errors were serious enough to warrant a retraction.

Di Trocchio (1993) explained that the experiments that were crucial to the "discovery" were conducted by Claudio Milanese, a young Italian scholar sent to do research in the United States. In fact, Milanese was coauthor with Neil Richardson and Ellis Reinherz for one of the two articles, whereas the second article listed six coauthors. Before the retraction, two other articles on the subject were in the works for publication in *Science* and the *Proceedings of the National Academy of Sciences*.

At one point, according to Di Trocchio (1993), Reinherz held a press conference (to which Milanese was not invited). He also applied for a patent for the discovery and was negotiating a deal with a pharmaceutical company. Milanese was left out of the picture, and he returned to Italy.

However, then it turned out that further experiments were not working as expected, and Milanese was called back to the United States. Di Trocchio (1993) related that Milanese reminded Reinherz that even before the publication of the article in *Science* he had explained that the experiments were yielding some negative results. The experiments were repeated again, with negative results. Milanese returned to Italy once more. That left Reinherz with the problem of how to get out of the situation (i.e., how to make an about face and still save face).

According to Di Trocchio(1993), it was decided that because Milanese carried out the experiments, he must assume the blame for the failed (i.e., negative) results. Milanese was asked to sign what amounted to a confession. Milanese claimed he did not really know the cause of the errors involved. The head of Dana Farber appointed a committee to investigate the case. The committee concluded that Milanese was solely responsible. Letters were sent and phone calls were made to Italy, and Milanese lost his university research job and abandoned a career in academia.

In Di Trocchio's (1993) account of what happened to Milanese, it seems clear that a scientist was silenced on two occasions. First, at the press conference and in negotiations with a pharmaceutical company, Milanese was left out, even though his role as the conductor of the experiments would qualify him as a protagonist in these events. It would seem, in light of how things ended in this case, that the honorary coauthorships, and the credit for the discovery that went to Reinherz and others, would amount to a falsification of the scholarly record in terms of whose discovery it really was.

If scholars did not do the experiments, how could they be the coauthors who were the discoverers? Taking credit for the results of the experiments they did not do is a type of falsification that has become commonly accepted and tolerated in the form of so-called honorary authorship. To the extent that a scholar is not given due credit (at a press conference or in dealings with a drug company), the scholar is silenced.

Then, once the falsification (in the form of false and negative results of experiments) of the research was detected, the same scholar who was denied a part of his credit for the discovery was silenced by means of punishment meted out on the basis of intolerance for falsification. In this case, silencing took place in the form of abandoning a career in academia. So, on the one hand, falsification was tolerated, but, on the other hand, falsification resulted in punishment (although what might be considered falsification by the investigative committee in this case might also be considered honest error by the researcher who did the experiments).

There are some rather subtle aspects to the question of toleration of falsification in this case. In Di Trocchio's (1993) account, Milanese was quoted as saying that he did not have regrets about assuming most of the blame, but that he did regret that he did not prevent Reinherz from publishing the results that he (Milanese) knew were doubtful. In this specific instance, by remaining silent, Milanese was tolerant of potential falsifications that ended up being published in leading scholarly journals. At the same time, he allegedly had clearly explained, before publication of the articles, that the most recent experiments were not working according to the results obtained in the article submitted for publication. Therefore, the results about to be published were falsifications, or potential falsifications, in that they did not agree with the latest unpublished results. By not clarifying and confirming the results before publication (after being advised by Milanese that the latest experiments were showing some negative results), Reinherz would be, in these circumstances, showing a tolerance for falsification. Otherwise, he would have confirmed the results before publishing them. If confirmation could not be obtained, at least he could have decided not to submit the articles, or if he had already submitted them, he could have withdrawn them from publication, or perhaps he could have included a cautionary note along with the publication of the results. A silent withdrawing of the articles could have saved the embarrassment of a subsequent retraction letter.

SOME QUESTIONS ABOUT FALSIFICATION IN THE
FELIG–SOMAN CASE

It seems that some some double standards or ambiguities relating to toleration of falsification took place in the scandal at Yale involving Philip Felig. This case was reported in a two-part article in *Science*, with the first part entitled "Imbroglio at Yale (I): Emergence of a Fraud" (Broad, 1980). A summary of events reported in the article is as follows. A junior researcher at NIH, Helena Wachslicht-Rodbard, submitted an article to the *New England Journal of Medicine* (*NEJOM*). Her supervisor, Jesse Roth, was a coauthor. An anonymous reviewer for *NEJOM*, Professor Philip Felig of Yale, recommended rejection. Before returning the paper with its negative recommendation to *NEJOM*, Felig had his associate, Vijay Soman, read and comment on it. Soman made a photocopy of the manuscript, which he used for an article of his own in the same area of research. Soman sent his manuscript to the *American Journal of Medicine*, where Soman's boss, Philip Felig, was an associate editor. Felig was also a coauthor of this article. The manuscript was sent out for peer review to Roth, who had his assistant, Rodbard, read it. She read it and spotted plagiarism, "complete with verbatim passages" (Broad, 1980, p. 39).

Rodbard sent a letter to *NEJOM* editor Arnold Relman, along with a photocopy of the Soman–Felig article. Relman was quoted as saying the plagiarism was "trivial," that it was "bad judgment" for Soman to have copied some of Rodbard's work, and that it was a "conflict of interest" for Soman and Felig to referee Rodbard's paper. (Broad, 1980, p. 39) Relman then called Felig, who said, according to Broad (1980), that peer-review judgment was based on the low quality of Rodbard's paper, and that the work on the Soman–Felig paper had been completed before Felig received the Rodbard manuscript. (Broad stated that this last statement by Felig was incorrect.)

Relman published the Rodbard paper, in revised form. Roth called Felig (a longtime friend from school days) and they met to discuss the two papers, for which they were either coauthors or reviewers. Broad (1980) stated that prior to the meeting "Felig had not compared the Soman manuscript to the Rodbard manuscript" (p. 39), even though Felig was coauthor of one article and referee for the other! When he returned to Yale, Felig questioned Soman, who admitted he used the Rodbard manuscript to write the Soman–Felig paper.

Broad (1980) reported that Rodbard and Roth began to express disagreement about the extent of plagiarism involved. Rodbard wrote to the Dean of Yale's School of Medicine, Robert Berliner, who did not believe all that she wrote. He was quoted as writing back to her, "I hope you will consider the matter closed" (p. 38). NIH apparently put off (by dragging their feet or by stonewalling) an investigation. A subsequent audit of the records revealed, according to Broad, "gross misrepresentation" (p. 41). Soman admitted that he falsified, but claimed it was not "significantly different from what went on elsewhere" (p. 41). After further investigations, at least 11 papers were retracted. Soman was asked to resign from Yale University, which he did. Felig became Chairman of Medicine at the Columbia College of Physicians and Surgeons.

From the standpoint of silencing of scholars as a result of toleration of falsification, the Rodbard article was given a referee rejection by Felig, who then became a coauthor of essentially the same article, published under different authorship. If Rodbard had not persisted in order to gain what she considered to be academic justice, at least part of her work would have been published under the name of other scholars, and her own article would not have been published (after the negative referee report). It seems that Rodbard left NIH. Soman left Yale, and some of his articles (some coauthored with Felig) were retracted.

A VARIETY OF CASES OF TOLERATION OF FALSIFICATION

Indications of toleration of falsification can be noticed in a variety of situations and settings within academia and on its fringes. Several years ago, Lang made a successful challenge to the nomination of Samuel Huntington for membership in the NAS. At a chance meeting in the small Italian hill town of Montepulciano (in the province of Siena), a mathematics professor from Princeton, Enrico Bombieri, was drawn into a conversation about Lang's successful challenge of Huntington. As part of his challenge, Lang cited what he and other scholars considered to be Huntington's improper use of mathematics, resulting in falsifications of history (Lang, 1988). Bombieri defended Huntington during the conversation, which also touched on other aspects of falsification in academia. Part of the conversation with Bombieri was reported to Lang (G. Moran, personal communication, October 2, 1990) as follows: "What struck me most about the conversation was Bombieri's apparent lack of concern about falsification in academia ... and his apparent contempt for persons who try to expose and correct (you, Dingell, etc.) falsification."

For someone studying the phenomenon of toleration of falsification, the compilation of the *35th Reunion Directory* (Class of 1960, Yale University) was a real eye-opener. The compiler and editor was William Boardman, assisted by Peter Parsons and Huntley Davenport. The directory informs the reader that "The University has provided technical services to assist ... in producing this directory" (p.ii). During the production, Boardman, a County Superior Court Assistant Judge in Vermont, sent a letter to his classmates, dated September 20, 1994, stating:

> We were serious—we still are serious—about our *WARNING* to those who submit nothing: "you risk seeing something we made up appearing under your name." The editorial staff is determined that something shall be said about everyone, regardless of truth, decency. ... Of course we will strive to avoid the libelous, but not necessarily the false, the misleading, the scurrilous, or the innuendo-laden.

As mentioned earlier, one of the high points in the Guido Riccio controversy was the 1985 conference held in Siena. This conference was reviewed by Gardner (1989) in *Burlington Magazine*. His review included a description that amounted to a clamorous falsification of the events that actually took place. Gardner wrote:

Few can have attended a conference where the presence of the police was so apparent, and the presence of television and press so intrusive. *Frondeurs* simultaneously staged a lively counter-conference. The reason for this unwonted excitement was, of course, the debate over the authenticity of the Guidoriccio da Fogliano. (p. 489)

A journalist in Siena wrote that Gardner reported mendaciously, and another Sienese, Giorgio Sacchi, asked, rather sarcastically, how many *Frondeurs* were involved, where was the counter-conference held, and where were all the police located (Mallory & Moran, 1989, p. 24)? The fact is that there was no counter-conference (much less a simultaneous and lively one), no *Frondeurs*, and no apparent presence of police.

After this false account was published, the editor of *Burlington Magazine*, Caroline Elam, was asked to make a published correction. In a rejection letter, she refused to do so (personal communication, October 20, 1989). In this case, the falsifications were tolerated and allowed to be perpetuated, and, at the same time, the true version of events was silenced.

Several scholars have commented, in one way or another, about the tendency toward toleration of falsification in academia. Here are some examples. Hillman (1995), in "Honest Research," stated, "there are a large number of improper practices which are tolerated and accepted by the academic community, but hardly ever spoken about, and are often regarded as behavior acceptable to the research community ... they are so widespread and sometimes secret and not admitted" (pp. 56-57). Martin (1992) made similar observations in "Scientific Fraud and the Power Structure of Science": "A host of things go on in scientific research that could be open to suspicion. Some of these are accepted as standard practice, others are tolerated. ... Some individuals have tried to raise concern about these practices, but for the most part they are tolerated" (p. 84). Martin then described several specific case studies in which plagiarism and other falsifications were tolerated at some Australian universities.

In the view of DeFelice (1991), the widespread practice of "unearned authorship" (sometimes referred to as honorary authorship) itself creates a situation in which "researchers routinely accept a certain level of dishonesty and therefore defend larger transgressions that involve the same vice" (p. 104). He then elaborated:

By accepting or insisting upon unearned authorship, much of the scientific community has forfeited the right to bear witness. Thus when investigations reveal unbecoming conduct that involves the same crime, scientists close their ranks, because many are guilty of far less spectacular but similar infractions. (p. 104)

Hillman (1997) classified honorary or unearned authorship as "parafraud" (p. 126).

DeFelice's use of the words *routinely accept* finds something of an echo, if not at least a partial confirmation, in the sworn congressional testimony of Margot O'Toole during the *Cell*-Baltimore case:

Dr. Huber called me and told me that there was no doubt I was right scientifically.

However, she and Dr. Wortis were convinced that there was no fraudulent intent. She said a correction would have a devastating effect on Dr. Imanishi-Kari's career. They had therefore decided that no correction would be submitted. I was shocked. I said the paper had to be corrected because others were relying on it. Dr. Huber replied that there were so many faulty papers in the literature, that one more did not matter. (Lang, 1993, p. 7)

COVER UP AND TOLERATION OF FALSIFICATION

Another aspect of toleration of falsification is known as *cover up*, generally understood to mean the hiding of evidence of scholarly error or wrongdoing of one form or another. If falsification were openly tolerated, there would be no need to cover up the fact that falsification had been perpetrated and detected. If falsification were not tolerated, it would be punished, instead of having evidence of its existence covered up. It would seem, therefore, that toleration of falsification tends to exist in covert form, rather than openly and publicly. It might be widely tolerated, but it is usually not admitted publicly that it is widely tolerated.

Articles in *The Scientist* several years ago give firsthand accounts, told by Sprague (1987), Hollis (1987), and Jacobstein (1987), of cover-up activity at University of Pittsburgh, Case Western Reserve University, and Cornell University. In each case, these scholars tried to expose and correct serious errors. All three cases reveal similar patterns of institutional resistance to exposing and correcting the errors, and institutional retaliation against the scholars who tried to have the errors corrected.

In such cases, retaliation becomes a component of the phenomenon of toleration of falsification. A newspaper article describing the University of Pittsburgh case is entitled "Study Finds Reluctance to Expose Scientific Fraud." This article (Raeburn, 1987) discusses the same themes of resistance to correction of error, and of retaliation against scholars who try to correct error: "There is a generalized reluctance to take prompt corrective action in response to faulty, misleading, or fraudulent data ... 'Researchers may fear that if they raise such questions, they themselves will suffer.' They might be viewed by colleagues as troublemakers" (p. A-7).

There is a somewhat ambiguous or double-edged relation between cover up and toleration of falsification. The exposure of a false paradigm is embarrassing and uncomfortable to experts and specialists in a field of study, because as Schneider (1989) pointed out, "If the knowledge expounded by recognized scholars to their students should prove to be of dubious reliability, then their authority is open to question" (p. 137). As discussed earlier, much rhetoric states that a primary mission of the university is the pursuit of truth. The exposure of the perpetuation of clamorous falsifications (as in the case of false paradigms), or of massive falsifications of data in scientific experiments, would indicate failures in the pursuit of truth or commitment to truth, and might place the university's commitment to truth in question, just as unreliable knowledge propounded by an expert places the expert's authority in question. Cover up is prompted, at least in part, by an attempt to hide the fact that serious falsifications have been taking place. On the one hand, by covering up—rather than punishing or correcting—the falsifications, it would seem that falsification is being tolerated. On the other hand, cover up is sometimes—if not often—resorted to in an attempt to give the impression that falsification is not tolerated and has not taken place. However, by hiding and silencing evidence of deliberate falsification, the institution involved ends up perpetuating the falsifications for some time, and, thus, tolerates them (at least for the duration of the time they are perpetuated as a result of the cover up).

It seems that cover up is, therefore, part of a cycle involving toleration of falsification. The rhetoric states that truth is pursued and deliberate falsification is not tolerated. However, unearned authorship, and allowing faulty papers to abound in the literature of a discipline without correction are examples of some types of falsification that are tolerated. But such toleration is usually not openly acknowledged beyond the circles of the persons who are falsifying or tolerating the falsification.

Thus, toleration of falsification is not officially approved, but the approval exists unofficially. Then, scholars such as Sprague, Hollis, Jacobstein, Stewart, Feder, O'Toole, and Lang try to expose and correct the falsifications they have detected (without necessarily knowing at the time if the falsifications came about unwittingly or deliberately). At this point, the authorities involved have basically two choices: (a) investigate, and if falsifications have taken place, admit it and make corrections, and (b) cover up. Sometimes, when evidence of falsification is too strong to hide or deny, or if it has already become too widely known to be covered up effectively, authorities might try to justify falsification, either on the basis that it is a subjective matter or that it is a commonly accepted practice. Such justifications are usually not widely promulgated, however. In fact, after Lang's negative criticisms of The Arnold Letter appeared in a scholarly journal (Moran & Mallory, 1991a) the CAA revised its published ethics code (CAA News, 1996). Instead of considering misrepresentation to be a subjective matter that the CAA could not include in its ethics code as an example of an unethical practice (which is, in effect, the position the CAA leadership took in the Arnold Letter), the new ethics code states that "Art historians ... must guard against misrepresenting evidence" (College Art Association, 1995, p. 1). At this point, misrepresentation is not officially tolerated. In one sense, a cycle has been completed. (It is not known if there is a direct connection between the appearance of Lang's remarks in a publication and the CAA's revision of its ethics code. The revisions might have been formulated before Lang's remarks appeared in print.)

Swan (1994) illustrated another situation in which the CAA showed tolerance for falsification (in the form of tolerance, by means of silence, for a specific case of blatant plagiarism of an art historian's work). Swan wrote, "there is such a thing as unmistakable verbal theft ... this clear-cut case of plagiarism resulted in no official action or public notice, despite the efforts of the victim of the larceny. ... The borrowing is unacknowledged, and it is verbatim and blatant" (p. 45–46). Swan then related that "a letter of complaint" was written "to the College Art Association," and that "no action was taken" (p. 46). He mentioned further that "the CAA was arguably one relevant body to receive the complaint ... the rest was silence" (pp. 45–46).

A subtle form of toleration for falsification can occur when a professional society or association publishes ethics codes or guidelines, and then claims that it cannot enforce the codes, which serve as guidelines rather than laws. In fact, it seems that some organizations that issue ethical codes and guidelines do not publish, or do not have in place, mechanisms to deal with alleged violations that are brought to their attention.

When attempts to justify falsification are made, these attempts might indicate that academic discussion has escalated beyond the confines of the type of discussions held by the Fellows of Pierson College (as described in the Introduction), and of collegial and academic debate elsewhere in academia. At a certain point, debate becomes controversy and can escalate further to various levels of scandal. It is at the levels of controversy and scandal that attempts might be made to justify falsifications of one type or another. It is during the developments of controversies and scandals that some of the most strenuous efforts to silence scholars might take place.

7

Transition From Academic Discussion and Debate to Controversy and Scandal

Academic discussion, unless it is a monologue, implies that a group of two or more scholars, rather than one scholar only, are talking about a scholarly subject. The scholars might generally be in agreement, and discussion would involve elaboration of the main points that are agreed on. If during academic discussion there is major disagreement among scholars, the discussion might be called a debate. Both sides—or more than two sides—air their opinions and present their evidence, and everyone involved tries to evaluate and analyze the evidence.

Discussions and debate can be carried out in the classroom, during informal gatherings, in scholarly publications, or at meetings and conferences devoted to specific subjects. A real debate cannot take place unless opposing sides are involved. The concept of "debating the empty chair" does not involve a debate as much as it does an observation that the chair is empty.

SILENCE AND SILENCING

Discussions and debates can lead to controversies and scandals. As far as the silencing of scholars is concerned, it might be assumed that such silencing would take place more during controversies and scandals than during discussions and debates. Yet, scholars become silent on a subject when a discussion ends before the discussion becomes a debate. Similarly, scholars become silent on a subject when the debate on the subject ends. Even though there may be strong and unpleasant attempts to silence and censor scholars during controversies and scandals, the scholars who persist and who dare to try to overcome such attempts to silence them may end up—in totality, in the long run—writing and publishing more on the subject than they would have done if no one had attempted to silence them in the first place.

It may seem ironic and paradoxical, but, in some cases, authoritative scholars who decided to try to silence other scholars would have done better to let these other scholars have their say. In fact, sometimes the very attempts to silence scholars can be included among the reasons discussions and debates escalate into controversies and scandals.

DIFFERENT TYPES OF CONTROVERSIES

A comparison of various controversies indicates that some ideas are very likely to become controversial very quickly, whereas others may take a long time—even more than several decades—before they spark a controversy in academia. At the same time, some ideas might become highly controversial almost immediately, and quickly silenced, only to resurface at a later time and become the subject of avid interest that remains within the confines of polite academic discussion and debate, without any repetition of the harsh attempts to silence the idea that took place when the idea was first presented by a scholar.

ADOLFO VENTURI AND GUIDO RICCIO: NO DEBATE, NO CONTROVERSY

In 1907, a famous Italian art historian, Adolfo Venturi, wrote (in a monumental multivolume study of the history of Italian art) that the famous portrait of Guido Riccio on horseback was not painted by Simone Martini. He suggested the figure on horseback was an illustrative part of the large map painted below on the same wall. This map was believed to have been painted in 1345, a year after the death of Simone Martini. Venturi (1907) also doubted that similar large representations of a horse and rider would have been painted in the midst of other castles that comprised the 14th-century cycle of painted castles in the Palazzo Publico in Siena.

Venturi's comments were startling, if not revolutionary, in the face of what had become a paradigm in the literature. His observations seemed quite logical. As far as can be determined, his doubts about the attribution of the Guido Riccio portrait did not provoke a negative reaction (perhaps, in part, because these doubts were written in a footnote). But neither were they accepted. In fact, it does not seem that these ideas of Venturi were taken up or even cited, in the subsequent literature on Simone Martini in general and discussion of the Guido Riccio painting in particular. Venturi's comments, as startling as they were, were apparently the beginning and the end of the discussion. His comments in this case neither provoked discussion nor led to any debate or controversy. Instead, the result was silence on that particular aspect of the subject of Guido Riccio, and on that aspect of the painted map (Mappamondo) on the same wall in the Palazzo Publico in Siena. There does not seem to have been any specific attempt to silence Venturi by preventing him from publishing his revolutionary idea, but his idea was, in effect, silenced because other scholars ignored it.

A question remains whether his idea was ignored on purpose because of its revolutionary nature, or because scholars who were his contemporaries and immediate followers did not think, at that time, that his idea was very important. Another question that remains is whether or not his idea was silenced simply because scholars did not read his multivolume work attentively, with the result that the idea remained lost and buried in the footnote.

SEVERAL DECADES LATER: A LONG, BITTER CONTROVERSY ENSUES

In 1977, the following appeared in a brief article in an art history journal:

> Iconographical, documentary, and historical evidence, and the lack of spatial harmony between the equestrian figure and the landscape, all suggest, however, that the portrait of Guidoriccio was not painted at the same time as the scenes representing Montemassi and Sassoforte ... a date of 1352 or later would help explain several facts. ... The document of May 1330, which contains a payment for painting Montemassi and Sassoforte, makes no mention of the central figure. ... There is no known evidence that any of these other castles had a Sienese Capitano General painted in the foreground. ... This hypothesis for two separate programs for the fresco ... (Moran, 1977, pp. 82, 84–85)

Both the 1907 and 1977 items propose very much the same thing, namely, that the portion of the painting that represents the horse and rider was painted a couple of decades or so later than the rest of the painting. The 1907 hypothesis considers the horse and rider not as originally part of the scene painted in 1330 with the castle of Montemassi, but instead, as a symbolic figure painted over a large map depicted on the same wall (believed to have been painted in 1345). The 1977 hypothesis considers the horse and rider not as originally part of the scene painted in 1330 with the castle of Montemassi, but instead, as a memorial portrait painted in 1352 (or slightly later). Because it had been ignored by scholars and left out of the pertinent subsequent mainstream literature, the 1907 passage was unknown to the author of the 1977 article until several years after that article had been published.

Even before it was published in a scholarly journal, the hypothesis of the 1977 article touched off a strong negative reaction in the city of Siena and in the art history community. It eventually escalated into a controversy described as the "case of the century," "the hottest issue in art history today," "one of the great art historical questions of the century," "one of the most intense and acrimonious battles in the annals of art history," (Moran, 1991, pp. 164–5) and so on. If the 1977 article had been ignored the way the 1907 item had been, or if the 1977 article had been noted without an academic fuss made over it, perhaps things might have ended there, with the hypothesis returning to silence after 1977, the way the similar hypothesis was treated with silence after it appeared in 1907.

The Simone Martini attribution for the Guido Riccio fresco was a paradigm in both 1907 and 1977. There must be some reason, or more than one, to account for the greatly different reactions. One possible explanation is that in 1907 art history was not a fully established academic discipline in many universities, whereas it is at the present time. By 1977, however many professors had taught, to countless students in classrooms in the United States and Europe, that Simone Martini painted Guido Riccio. In fact, scholars waxed eloquently about it, in classroom lectures and scholarly publications, as an example of Simone's genius and originality. (In reality, such originality was so exceptional for a painting of the 14th century that it should have raised doubts about the attribution, rather than serving as a reason for giving Simone Martini credit for having more originality than he actually possessed.) Meanwhile, generations of Sienese school children had been brought into their city's Palazzo Publico (the city hall, which is also a famous museum and tourist attraction) and told by their grade school or junior high school teachers, in front of the painting, that Simone Martini painted the portrait of Guido Riccio for the glory of the Sienese republic of the 14th century. Besides, in 1907 tourism in Siena was a very small activity compared to the booming industry that it has become since the end of the World War II. After the war, the famous image of Guido Riccio on horseback began to appear often, in Siena and elsewhere, on tourist agency posters, brochures, postcards, covers of guidebooks, plates, ashtrays, cookie box covers, wine bottle labels, calenders, lampshades, bathroom tile, T-shirts, compartments of passenger trains throughout Italy, and so on.

The 1907 hypothesis fell into silence perhaps because of a lack of subsequent adherents to it, combined with a general lack of specific interest about it. What is certain is that it did not cause a fuss or a controversy in Siena or in the art history community. By contrast, when a very similar hypothesis was proposed several decades later, the keen interest and curiosity—if not stupor and shock—that it aroused made it more difficult to be passed off with silence. It was not merely a fine point of attribution and dating to be discussed by a handful of specialists in Sienese 14th-century painting with their colleagues and students, but it was a matter of great curiosity and concern among the citizens of Siena and the press. Under these circumstances, attempts to silence views that contested the paradigm-dependent views of the establishment scholars merely added to the curiosity and interest among segments of the public and the press.

ANOTHER CONTROVERSY, BUT WITH A DIFFERENT
SCENARIO

By comparison, another situation in the history of Sienese painting might seem very surprising, based on the different types of reactions that occurred. As early as the 17th century, a variety of secondary sources led scholars to believe that an artist named Barna painted a cycle of frescoes in the main church (Collegiata) of the hill town of San Gimignano in the province of Siena. There is even a legend that Barna slipped and fell from the scaffolding while painting in the church, and that this accident led to his death. (There is a plaque in the church, near the paintings, recounting this legend.) Like Siena, San Gimignano has become a thriving center for tourism, and in San Gimignano the large cycle of paintings attributed to Barna is one of the main drawing cards for tourists.

In 1927, the archivist and scholar Peleo Bacci made the startling proposal that the artist Barna never existed, and that the fresco cycle (representing scenes from the New Testament) was painted, instead, by Lippo Memmi, Simone Martini's brother-in-law and collaborator as a painter (Bacci, 1927). A swift, severe, and bitter rebuttal by a powerful art historian, Cesare Brandi (1928), was quick to appear, and the subsequent literature in art history followed the traditional view, by now an entrenched paradigm, that Barna painted the famous New Testament scenes. In effect, Bacci and his ideas on the subject were effectively silenced as a result of the stinging rebuttal. There was no debate and no controversy. In fact, it was certainly more revolutionary and startling to suggest that an artist, to whom a corpus of important works was attributed, did not ever exist, than to suggest that a part of a work (Guido Riccio fresco) was not painted by the same artist who was believed to have painted the rest of the work. In this sense, it was not a surprise that Brandi tried to silence Bacci in such a severe manner, or that other scholars did not attempt to rebut Brandi and support Bacci on this subject.

The hypothesis was thus nipped in the bud, and no debate evolved. In a sense, Bacci's idea was silenced, to the extent that no scholar gave it any backing or support in a scholarly publication. In this regard, it resembled Venturi's hypothesis about Guido Riccio. Both Venturi's idea, however, and Bacci's hypothesis still remained as part of the scholarly record.

Then, almost 50 years later, in 1976, two scholars from two different countries in two different articles independently revived the hypothesis that the famous paintings in San Gimignano were not painted by an artist named Barna. One article (Moran, 1976) stated:

> If this hypothesis is correct, it serves two major purposes. Most importantly, it vindicates Peleo Bacci, who was severely, unfairly, and unjustly attacked in print for suggesting that an artist named "Barna" might *not* have painted the Collegiata New Testament Scenes. Secondly, it clears the way for new, fresh investigations to determine just who did paint these frescoes. (p. 79)

Both of the 1976 articles closely followed Bacci (1927) in his belief that the frescoes were painted by Lippo Memmi. One article (Caleca, 1976) repeated the Lippo Memmi attribution, whereas the other suggested that Lippo's brother, Federico Memmi, might be the artist, in collaboration with Lippo.

This time around, Brandi did not respond negatively the way he did in 1928. Perhaps he was no longer keenly interested in this aspect of art history, and it seems he no longer had the clout and power he once had. But neither, for the most part, did other scholars respond in a harsh, negative manner that attempted to silence the idea. To the contrary, lively discussion took place in the scholarly literature (and presumably in classrooms as well), all within the parameters of polite academic debate. Some scholars have tried to hold onto the traditional Barna attribution, but a rather large segment of the specialists in the field, in Italy and elsewhere, have supported the view that members of the Memmi family were the artists who painted the work (Freuler, 1986).

In a sense, this situation was the opposite of the Guido Riccio case. For Guido Riccio, the paradigm-busting hypothesis was at first neither contested nor considered and it fell into silence and oblivion for several decades. When a similar hypothesis was presented decades later, it touched off a storm of strong negative reactions and developed into a controversy described as the case of the century. For the Barna case, a paradigm-busting hypothesis met quick, harsh criticism, so harsh that the hypothesis was in effect silenced in deference to the traditional view. When a nearly identical paradigm-busting hypothesis was proposed ("revived" might also be an accurate term) decades later, it provoked polite and lively academic discussion and debate, with much support for the paradigm-busting hypothesis. The bitter controversy that might have been expected to break out did not take place.

Why was there no attempt to silence the non-Barna hypothesis the second time around, the way the non-Simone Martini hypothesis for Guido Riccio was? Why, in this case, did the situation remain in the realm of polite debate instead of developing into bitter controversy? It certainly was not because the specialists in the Barna debate are a kinder, gentler, and more courteous group than the scholars involved in the Guido Riccio controversy, because they are, to a large degree, the very same scholars.

Perhaps there is a plausible reason, based on the specific evolution of the published studies relating to Barna and to Lippo Memmi. The large New Testament fresco cycle in San Gimignano was practically the only stylistic basis for attributing other works (wall paintings and wood panel paintings) to an artist named Barna. As scholarship on Barna and Lippo Memmi intensified between 1928 and 1976, scholars noticed the strong stylistic affinity between the known works of Lippo Memmi and the frescoes in San Gimignano attributed to Barna. This stylistic affinity was so strong, in fact, that other paintings attributed to Barna by some scholars were attributed to Lippo Memmi by other scholars.

The result was an overlapping of attributions published in the scholarly literature that seemed to be leading to an impasse, if not to a hopeless morass. By the mid-1970s, the time was ripe for Bacci's (1927) silenced hypothesis to get a new hearing, as a logical explanation for the impasse, and also as a means for breaking the attribution logjam, so to speak. In contrast to the Guido Riccio fresco, which since 1907 was becoming more and more entrenched as a Simone Martini paradigm as a result of rhetoric and hype from scholars and tourist agencies and tourist guides, the Collegiata New Testament fresco cycle was experiencing, in the scholarly literature since the late 1920s, something of a merger between the styles of Lippo Memmi and an artistic personality known by the name of Barna. If Bacci had written his ideas on the subject for the first time during the 1970s instead of the 1920s, he most likely would not have received any reaction similar to the negative one written by Brandi (1928).

As a result of this comparison of these two cases, Guido Riccio and Barna, a case can be made that there is a certain evolution of the scholarly record that can help determine whether a paradigm-busting idea or hypothesis will provoke discussion and debate or whether it will create a bitter controversy that might even develop into scandal. From 1907 to 1977, the Simone Martini attribution for Guido Riccio became solidified and entrenched by extensive repetition, eloquence, and even hype in the classroom and in the scholarly literature. The attribution was also reinforced by means of the painting becoming one of the major tourist attractions of Siena. Meanwhile, between 1928 and the mid-1970s, the traditional Barna paradigm was becoming undermined by increasing overlapping attributions to Barna and Lippo Memmi made by scholars who were working within the paradigm. The paradigm-busting hypothesis, abruptly silenced when it appeared in 1927, found a favorable "state of the research" situation when it was proposed again in 1976. In a sense, the timing was right, even though the hypothesis remained essentially the same. In 1927, the idea appeared to be a bold paradigm buster. By the 1970s, the same idea appeared as something of a logical adjustment to the paradigm.

LANG AND A SOCIOLOGICAL SURVEY

Sometimes a scholarly controversy originates by chance, and develops and escalates, at least in part, because of reactions to attempts to silence scholars and their ideas. A "second reminder notice" relating to a sociological survey did not trigger a controversy in 1969, but it did in 1977. In fact, the second notice of 1977 led to a controversy that involved the sociological establishment and, among other institutions, the AAAS, AAUP, American Council of Education (ACE), NAS, National Science Foundation (NSF), the *Chronicle of Higher Education*, Sloan Commission on Government and Higher Education, and the Carnegie Council on Policy Studies in Higher Education. The controversy lasted from about 1977 to 1980, dealt with defective studies in the field of sociology, and attempted to silence exposure and discussion of these defective studies. What started out as what might seem to be an innocent, bureaucratic, business-as-usual "second reminder notice" escalated into a controversy which is recorded in a book of 700 pages that documents "a major public controversy that involved a good part of the education network" (Lang, 1981, p. 1).

In 1969, Lang threw away a sociological survey sent to him. After the second reminder notice, he wrote to Clark Kerr, Director of the Carnegie Council on Policy Studies in Higher Education, to let Kerr know of the defects of the survey and of Lang's "contempt" for what Kerr "was doing." No reply from Kerr was received and that was the end of it. In this sense, Lang was silenced because Kerr preferred silence. It is not known if Kerr felt too busy to respond to Lang, if he thought Lang's criticism did not merit a reply, or if he actually agreed, to one degree or another with Lang, but decided not to discuss the issue further. In any case, discussion was nipped in the bud. No debate and no controversy emerged.

Then, in 1977, Lang received another survey. He threw that one away also, as well as the first reminder notice. At about the same time, Lang read an article about the work of Seymour Lipset, who directed the 1977 survey. A second reminder notice arrived, and Lang wrote a letter to "the surveyors," expressing his "exasperation." The letter was eventually reproduced, with Lang's permission, in the *Harvard Crimson*, which also reported that Lipset said "Lang sounds like a crackpot to me" (Lang, 1981, pp. 6–7). The controversy was off and running. Perhaps without a second reminder notice there would not have been any real controversy, much less one that lasted 3 years and filled a 700-page book.

In this case, a consistent attempt to silence Lang was a major cause of the escalation. According to Lang (1981), the controversy could have ended in January 1978, soon after it started. In a reference to Edith Uunila, Assistant Editor of the *Chronicle of Higher Education*, he wrote:

> I said she should ask the editors when they talk about me and the file (and they do) just to imagine what would have happened in January 1978 if instead of writing a tendentious article which caused Provost Garfinkel to link me with McCarthyism, *The Chronicle* had printed my 15 pages of comments. It is staggering in retrospect to think how differently things would have turned out: no *New York Review* article; no problem with AAUP; NO FILE!! (p. 588)

It also seems possible that the controversy could have ended even sooner if Lipset had not decided to insult Lang in print in a Harvard publication. Perhaps a more prudent reaction to Lang's disapproval of, and negative reaction to, the survey (e.g., stating something along the line that he would take Lang's observations into consideration in the compilation of future surveys) would have saved Lipset a lot of time and embarrassment.

THE *CELL*–BALTIMORE CONTROVERSY: DID IT HAVE TO HAPPEN?

Something similar seems to have happened in the *Cell*–Baltimore case, which turned into one of the most bitter controversies involving modern biomedical research. (Because, in this case, the situation escalated into more than one government investigation, and because disciplinary actions were taken, a case can be made that the controversy actually became a scandal.) In "Rockefeller U. Faculty Cool to President Baltimore," the following observations were made:

> The melee at the prestigious "Rock" thus further lengthens a grotesquely unpleasant affair that could have been nipped in the bud three years ago if Baltimore and his colleagues hadn't brushed off a young postdoctoral fellow who expressed solid reservations about portions of a paper they co-authored. ... Dingell would not have held hearings on the case. (Greenberg, 1987, pp. 5–6)

This passage sounds very similar to Lang's comments about how the controversy about the 1977 survey could have ended much sooner than it did.

Various observations that describe what took place arrive at similar conclusions:

> At the outset, the substance of the dispute was not unlike others that occur regularly in biology labs. It was simply a disagreement over scientific matters between two scientists. ... *Nature* was preventing the scientific community from learning of certain issues. ... Hence *Nature* has a substantial (but of course not exclusive) responsibility for the escalation of the whole case. (Lang, 1993, pp. 11, 31)

Just as the second reminder notice touched off events that led to publication of a 700-page book about defective sociological research, the refusal to publish a mere correction letter regarding specific biological research results touched off events that led to publication of *Science on Trial:The Whistle-blower, the Accused, and the Nobel Laureate*. In this book, the author, Sarasohn (1993), observed that the disagreement could have ended before it escalated into a controversy: "Baltimore ... truly could have stopped the dispute at many different points. ... The damage to his reputation would have been nil" (p. 266).

A letter of correction published in *Cell* in 1986, or soon thereafter, might well have been noticed by specialists, who could have taken note of the correction in their future research. Few, if any, other scientists might have given a second thought to the correction after they had read it. Instead, there was an adamant refusal to publish a correction, or to allow a correction to be published by other scholars. Events escalated to the extent that Baltimore resigned as President of Rockefeller University (Sarasohn, 1993).

From the very outset of the *Cell*–Baltimore controversy, there were attempts to silence scholars who tried to correct what they perceived to be serious error. In one sense, the attempts at silencing succeeded, as Margot O'Toole lost her job in academia, and Stewart and Feder have been punished by means of transfers within NIH. On the other hand, all three of these scholars were heard from extensively during the controversy, despite the attempts to silence them. If a correction letter had been published, Stewart and Feder probably would not have been heard from at all in this case, and it seems unlikely that any more than a few persons would ever have been aware that O'Toole was involved in the correction of the specific errors involved.

VELIKOVSKY: A FAR-RANGING, INTERDISCIPLINARY
CONTROVERSY

Not all controversies can be nipped in the bud. In some cases, the nature of the subject matter is so crucial, or so vast and far-reaching, or the alleged mistakes on one
side are of such great magnitude that even suppression of the issue for a long time will
not put an end to the controversy in all its aspects. The controversies that Velikovsky
touched off took place within several different academic disciplines. It is reported that
at one point, in 1950, an issue of *Science News Letter* "printed denunciations of
Velikovsky's ideas by five authorities in as many fields" (de Grazia, 1978, p. 29).
Velikovsky's most famous work, *Worlds in Collision*, became a best-seller despite (or
perhaps also because of) the fact that "Commentators ranging from the British
Astronomer Royal to the American science writer Martin Gardiner denounced the
book" (Cude, 1987a, p. 62). There seems little doubt that the massive attempts at
silencing Velikovsky and his ideas were aimed at nipping scholarly discussion in the
bud by preventing academic debate, thus hoping to prevent escalation to controversy.
Nevertheless, "In spite of the clamour against the heretic, his books have found an
enthusiastic following. ... A German edition went through five printings" (de Grazia,
1978, pp. 51–52). The September 1963 issue of *American Behavioral Scientist*
"chronicles more than a decade of controversy" (de Grazia, 1978, p. 54).

Velikovsky (1978) himself made some interesting observations relating to the
nature of academic controversies:

> And many of those who look to acknowledged authorities for guidance will express their
> disbelief that a truth could have remained undiscovered for so long. ... Never in the his-
> tory of science has a spurious book aroused a storm of anger among members of scien-
> tific bodies. But there has been a storm every time a leaf in the book of knowledge has
> been turned over. (p. 7)

Along a similar line, he quoted the philosopher Butterfield:

> But the supreme paradox of the scientific revolution is in the fact that things which we
> find it easy to instill into the boys at school ... things which would strike us as the ordi-
> nary natural way of looking at the universe ... defeated the greatest intellects for cen-
> turies. (Velikovsky, 1980, p. 9)

It seems that the current "ordinary natural way of looking at the universe" consists of a series of confirmations of Velikovsky's hypotheses and predictions concerning the planet Venus. The Mariner probes of Venus have apparently confirmed
his startling (i.e., startling to the establishment, but logical and natural to
Velikovsky) predictions that the surface of Venus was very hot, that its atmosphere
was filled with hydrocarbons, and that it rotated slowly and retrogradedly. These
were all crucial aspects that were foundations for his more comprehensive theories.
"What was unbelievable and heretical in 1950 is making great inroads into the sci-

ence that claimed dogmatic completeness and infallibility as recently as then" (Velikovsky, 1980, pp. 8–9).

Velikovsky's critics in the science establishment were not particularly quick to give him credit for these confirmations of his specific predictions, but it appears possible that in some areas other discoveries and observations will dovetail with his ideas, creating a situation somewhat similar to that of the Barna studies in art history, in which a theory that was not tolerated in the past eventually became the logical conclusion of subsequent studies that evolved. Velikovsky's studies, wide in scope, encompass various academic disciplines. For this reason, his revolutionary ideas might not become incorporated into mainstream orthodox studies quite as quickly as the revolutionary Barna theory did, but the trend might be heading in that direction after the discoveries about Venus revealed by the Mariner probes.

The Velikovsky case, from the beginning, was quite different from the Guido Riccio case, the survey of 1977 case, and the *Cell*–Baltimore case. If scholars ignored Velikovsky, instead of trying so strenuously to silence him, they would have given Velikovsky free reign to expand on and attempt to buttress his revolutionary ideas with further evidence. A letter of correction could have nipped the *Cell*–Baltimore case in the bud, but no letter of rebuttal or correction could have prevented Velikovsky's ideas from stirring strong controversy. If Lipset had not insulted Lang in a Harvard publication, there would most likely not have been any controversy, but an absence of insults against Velikovsky could not have prevented a controversy. If the 1977 Guido Riccio article was ignored or shrugged off (e.g., as being interesting but not important) by scholars, there probably would not have been a controversy that is still intensifying two decades later, but such a tactic would not have worked in the Velikovsky case, which would have continued nevertheless.

LONG-TERM CONTROVERSY ABOUT ANIMAL EXPERIMENTATION IN MEDICAL RESEARCH

In contrast to controversies that suddenly burst open into the academic science, such as those provoked by Velikovsky's studies, other controversies may simmer beneath the surface (as far as scholarship is concerned) for long periods of time, and have great difficulty breaking through certain silence barriers within academia and the mass media. Similar to the Adolfo Venturi hypothesis that doubted the traditional Simone attribution for Guido Riccio, some controversial ideas remain ignored in the mainstream scholarly literature for a long time.

From at least as early as 1873 to the present time, many scholars (more than 1,000) have been claiming and warning that animal experimentation in medical research (particularly drug research) can lead to serious error when the results are used as models for humans. In 1899, Wilson stated that such animal experiments are "inherently misleading in their application to man and therefore unreliable" (Ruesch, 1989, p. 230). Although there has been some recent rhetoric about refining, reducing, and replacing animal experiments in medical research, it is obviously a long way between the 19th century and the day that Bigelow envisioned, cited earlier, when "the world will look upon today's vivisection in the name of science the way we look today upon witch hunts in the name of religion" (Ruesch, 1978/1991, p.). Despite eye-opening titles that occasionally creep into the scholarly literature like *Fifty Years of Folly and Fraud 'in the Name of Science,'* by Bross (1994), and despite rather widespread international sales and distribution of books such as Ruesch's (1978/1991) *Slaughter of the Innocent*, animal experimentation for testing of drugs continues to be a methodological paradigm of the powerful academic–governmental–pharmaceutical–industrial complex.

One reason that a type of silence barrier has prevented the debate—long simmering beneath the surface—from breaking out into the open in academia and among the wider public the way the Velikovsky controversy did, is that the scientific problems involved have been deflected into discussions involving cruelty to animals. Various so-called animal protection organizations have been vociferous, but their efforts are geared more toward "humane" treatment of animals, rather than scientific discussions about tragic errors caused by misleading and unreliable results obtained from animal experimentation (e.g., thalidomide, DES, and SMON). Besides, Ruesch pointed out that infiltration into animal protection groups has been responsible for the fact that among these societies, issues of scientific methodology are not prominent. In fact, the Foreword of the published acts of a 1988 conference on animal experimentation begins, "Scientists are coming under increasing pressure from activist groups to stop animal experimentation branded as cruel and unnecessary for improving human health" (Garattini & van Bekkum, 1990, p. vii). The discussion is directed toward the public activists, not toward rebutting the many scholars who have questioned the scientific validity of using animals as models for humans in drug testing.

The 1988 conference was not a two-sided debate but a repetition of the orthodox view. The views of scholars like Ruesch and Croce were silenced. Croce (1991) wrote that animal experimentation is a "methodological error," and he elaborated:

> Which animal? There are millions of species of animal on the earth. So, which should we use? ... No experimentation carried out on one species can be extrapolated to any other, including man. To suppose that such extrapolation could be legitimate is the main reason for the failure and sometimes for the catastrophes which are inflicted on us ... especially in the area of drugs. Too little is spoken or written about certain facts. ... For example, in August 1978 only Japanese newspapers reported the appearance in Tokyo of 30,000 people paralyzed and blinded by Clioquinol. (pp. 13–14)

This situation might have reached proportions of a scandal in Japanese newspapers, but it did not provoke very much discussion, debate, or controversy in the scholarly literature.

Croce (1991) also related that, from 1972 to June 1983, the sale of more than 22,000 "medicinal preparations" had been prohibited because of harmful effects, and he noted that all those preparations "had passed with flying colors the animal experiments imposed by law" (p. 14). Croce then asked, "how many years must pass before it is realized that a medicine is dangerous and how many have fallen victim to it in the meantime?" (p. 14). As a partial answer to these questions, he cited a study discussed in Germany in 1976: "'6% of fatal illnesses and 25% of all illnesses are due to medicines'" (p. 14). More recently, a brief article in *USA Today* (1995), "Costly Treatment," cited a study that claims that "prescription drug-related medical problems ... cost the nation $76 billion annually. ... Drug-related problems can result from unforeseeable complications or side effects. ... Hospitalizations are the biggest part of the cost" (p. 9A). The term *unforeseeable* could refer to misleading conclusions derived from results of animal experiments. (The recall, or the prohibition of use, of drugs and medicines would be the medical equivalent of a retraction of a published scholarly article. It would be interesting to know if, when the thousands of medicines were recalled, the scholarly articles that announced their discovery and supported their use as treatments and cures were subsequently retracted. A study of this nature would involve service quality of academic libraries, a subject discussed later in chapter 13.)

Another disaster similar to those caused by thalidomide, DES, and Clioquinol might force the issue out into the open as part of a controversy that includes questioning the scientific reliability of the methodology of animal experimentation. Another possibility is that a trend toward refining, reducing, and replacing animal experimentation might eventually lead to its disappearance from medical research. In that case, a long-running debate might become resolved without ever becoming an acknowledged academic controversy. In such a case, a paradigm would not be overturned by a revolutionary idea, but would, somewhat similar to the Barna case in art history, evolve or transform, on a long-term basis, into another paradigm.

In the May 23, 1996 issue of *New York Review*, a book publisher was quoted as saying, "If Duesberg is right in what he says about AIDS, and we think he is, he documents one of the great science scandals of the century" (Horton, 1996, p. 14). This statement would indicate that a debate has evolved into a major controversy, and could escalate into a major scandal (if it is not already in the process of doing so). One of Duesberg's (1996a) main hypotheses is that HIV is not the cause of AIDS. Several months after the review article in *New York Review*, readers of an article in the *International Herald Tribune* might not have been aware that there had ever been a debate on the issue, much less a controversy, as they read Roberts' (1996) words: "HIV, the virus that causes AIDS" (p. 19). A fierce controversy might be raging among scientists involved in a crucial issue concerning public health without a large portion of the public becoming aware of it. Scholars might be able to overcome strenuous attempts to silence them among their colleagues, as the Horton review of Duesberg's publication testifies, but the scholars may still come up against strong silence barriers among the mass media, even though the pertinent material is of vital importance to the general public.

In his lengthy review of Duesberg's published AIDS research, Horton (editor of the *Lancet*) acknowledged that a controversy was in full swing: "The standoff between Duesberg and the AIDS establishment has become increasingly embittered and ugly. ... Parts of the lay press have also adopted a highly partisan position in the Duesberg controversy. ... An open debate with Duesberg could have grave commercial consequences" (Horton, 1996, p. 19).

This last observation is of utmost importance for the subject of silencing of scholars. De Marchi and Franchi (1996) stated that scholars who have attempted to debate the authorities on the subject of AIDS have come up against a wall of silence ("muro di silenzio"). Commercial interests are directly involved in much current scientific research. Duesberg (1996b) observed that the "commercialization of science" goes hand in hand with "consensus" of scholarly opinion:

> As the NIH budget has increased, so has the subsidized market for biotechnology products. The pharmaceutical industry, likewise, has profited from monopolies granted by the FDA. ... Naturally, some of these federally provided corporate profits find their way back to scientists in the form of patent royalties, consultantships, paid board positions, and stock ownership. These same scientists often sit in judgment of their fellow researchers as peer reviewers. ... Such commercial conflicts of interest have almost totally permeated biomedical scientific institutions today. ... It would be economic suicide for a scientist to advance research that would render his established commercial products obsolete. (pp. 454–455)

If peer reviewers are also holders of commercial interests, it would be not only economic suicide, but possibly also academic suicide for scholars, particularly non tenured scholars, to try to publish ideas and findings that are not in line with the consensus that shores up the commercial interests. In such situations, if scholars were in need of grants to enhance their careers, would they challenge the consensus, or would they tend to remain silent as far as a challenge is concerned? This question leads to the problem of scholars not saying and writing, for various reasons, what they really believe. In its totality, the reticence of scholars to say what they believe is perhaps the most insidious and the most widespread factor responsible for the silencing of scholars in academia. There is no way to determine just how many scholars have been silenced in this manner, nor is there any way to know the total impact such silence has had on the amount of error that remains uncorrected in the scholarly literature.

8

Saying What You Believe

I wasn't about to rock the boat by broadcasting my thoughts ... which could have threat-
ened my future in academic medicine. (Crenshaw, 1992, p. 17)

You realize I can't give you my *private* feelings on this matter. I'll just have to leave it
at that. (Hentoff, 1986b, p. 29)

The first of these quotes was from Charles Crenshaw, at that time a young untenured
academic in the field of medicine. The second was from Sidney Altman, who in 1986
was the Dean of Yale College and a member of the Executive Committee of Yale
College. These quotes show that the silencing of scholars that takes place because
scholars are afraid to say what they believe cuts a broad path through the academic
hierarchy from its lowest positions to the highest pedestals of academic power.
Problems associated with being afraid to say what you believe might involve, on the
one hand, personal discretion, prudence, or fear based on intimidation or academic
politics, and, on the other hand, institutional cover up and secrecy.

According to his own account, some of the "thoughts" Crenshaw did not broadcast for a long time related to his observations and conclusions about specific entry
and exit gunshot wounds. Based on his medical training and work, he had previously
had considerable experience distinguishing between entry and exit gunshot wounds.
Specifically, he served on emergency duty shifts at a city hospital in Texas where,par-
ticularly on Saturday nights, he treated many gunshot wounds.

Having remained silent, Crenshaw advanced in his academic career, becoming chairman of his department at his medical school. Who knows exactly how different his career might have been if he had spoken out and said what he believed at the beginning of his career? Who knows for sure how many other academics advanced their careers while remaining silent on certain subjects and issues? Likewise, the number of scholars whose academic careers were hampered or terminated because they decided to speak out in spite of attempts to silence them is unknown.

After being silenced for many years, and after much reflection, Crenshaw (1992) decided to tell what happened, in *JFK Conspiracy of Silence*. A few brief excerpts from the book give a good indication of why Crenshaw and his colleagues felt afraid to say what they believed:

> Dr. Crenshaw tells us he kept silent to protect his medical career. Dr. Charles Baxter ... had issued an edict of secrecy. ... No one ... would be permitted to talk about what he or she did or saw. ... Thus did Dr. Crenshaw and the other physicians ... enter into ... a "conspiracy of silence" to hide their knowledge. (Crenshaw, 1992, pp. xv–xvi)

The subject matter of Crenshaw's book concerns his doubts about the reliability of the Warren Report and its conclusions relating to the the death of President John F. Kennedy. It also concerns the pressures put on Crenshaw to refrain from saying what he believed:

> I believed the Warren Report to be a fable, a virtual insult to the intelligence of the American people ... a level of discretion we seldom discover, one that I have had to practice to protect my medical career. ... Southwestern Medical School ... and the U.S. Government have never been overly subtle about their desire for us doctors to keep quiet ... the doctors ... have always felt the necessity to continue what has evolved over the years as a conspiracy of silence. ... Just recently, a gag order was issued from Southwestern Medical School warning ... not to confer with Oliver Stone. (Crenshaw, 1992, pp. 3–5)

From the standpoint of silencing of scholars based on scholars not saying what they believe, it is difficult to imagine a more direct case than this one. There was no discussion, it seems, about openness and free exchange of ideas, or about academic freedom. Orders were given to remain silent, and the scholars did so in order to protect their academic careers. At the same time, historians and political scientists, among other scholars, have a keen interest in knowing the historical facts relating to the Kennedy assassination. Government secrecy on the subject and the long-term silence of scholars who feel intimidated to speak out deny scholars access to important material.

WORSE THAN A PACT WITH THE DEVIL

In an interview with Hentoff, Altman stated that he could not give his private feelings about whether or not a student at Yale should have been punished by the Executive

Committee (a disciplinary body at Yale University). Hentoff (1986b) seemed rather taken back by Altman's confession, and he commented on it:

> Later this year, I'll be spending several days with junior high and high school students. ... I shall tell them of my conversation with the Dean of Yale College, especially his final words. And I'll caution them that no job, no matter how important it appears to the outside world, is worth taking if you can't say what you think while holding that job. That's worse than a pact with the Devil because it's a deal you make with yourself to become less than yourself. (p. 29)

Despite Hentoff's caution about doing something worse than making a pact with the Devil, it seems that many scholars feel inclined to reject this caution in their pursuit of economic, academic, and career salvation. If some powerful professors can be silenced at Yale about the punishment given to an undergraduate, it can be imagined that there might be many other matters (administrative or intellectual) at Yale and throughout academia about which scholars feel they cannot afford to say what they believe.

The most obvious difference between the cases involving Crenshaw and Altman is that Crenshaw was a junior academic whereas Altman enjoyed a position of great power. It can readily be understood how Crenshaw could be intimidated under the circumstances, but the situation with Altman seems quite different. Crenshaw remained silent to protect his career, but Altman's career, by comparison, did not seem to be in similar danger. He had already attained some of the highest positions of power and prestige in academia (with his prestige to be enhanced further by an imminent Nobel prize). It would seem that his career would have survived intact if he had told Hentoff his private views about the punishment of a student at Yale.

If he was not protecting himself by refusing to say what he believed, who or what was being protected, and for what reasons? Perhaps only Altman knows for sure, and perhaps someday he, like Crenshaw, after much reflection, might reveal just what did take place at Yale and just why he felt he could not tell Hentoff his private views.

SILENCE AMONG GRADUATE STUDENTS

A case can be made that many scholars are already conditioned as early as graduate school to have a strong reticence, based on fear brought about by academic insecurity (or based on other reasons), to say what they believe. Diamond wrote, "I know of one case in which a dean warned a graduate student that he would lose all chance of academic employment if he did not 'cooperate fully' with the authorities, but I have no idea how widespread the practice may have been" (Lang, 1981, p. 61). Diamond's description by itself demonstrates the subordinate position of graduate students and their vulnerability in relation to saying things that might upset academic authorities.

In *The Ph.D. Trap*, Cude (1987a) commented that "the average doctoral candidate quickly learns to defer any controversial ideas" (p. 52). It would likely be academic suicide, as far as a career is concerned, for graduate students to insist that their dissertation advisors (and the members of the committee before whom they might have to defend their works) are very wrong about key aspects of their fields of study, no matter how much new evidence the graduate students accumulated during their studies.

Cude (1987a) described how student Lowell Holmes, who studied under Melville Herskovits (a colleague of Margaret Mead), discovered to his surprise that what he observed in Samoa was much different than that written in the famous work by Mead (1928), *Coming of Age in Samoa*. Herskovits had written in support of Mead's theories, and Cude wrote, "If Holmes had been foolhardy enough to press his own findings with logical rigor, in all probability he would never have won his degree, let alone a wider hearing in the professional literature. To say Mead had erred was simply out of the question" (p. 87). He received his degree after agreeing with Mead. The situation that Holmes faced is not very common, according to Cude, because to begin with, "topics requiring originality" are "avoided like the plague by doctoral candidates" (pp. 87–89).

Hillman (1996), who has been engaged in a long ongoing battle with the academic research establishment, commented on his experience:

> I learned several lessons from my time at the Institute of Psychiatry. Firstly, doctoral students have no redress against their supervisors, since their careers would be ruined if they made determined criticisms. ... As I traveled around, there was hardly a single place at which I lectured where several people did not come up to me when I had finished and say that they agreed with us. I always asked them their names. Would they be prepared to say in public ...? ... One lecturer ... said he would. All the others had reasons why they could not: they were writing theses, seeking lectureships, applying for grants. (pp. 101, 119).

At the same time, Hillman (1996) emphasized that in his classroom teaching he teaches his students "the accepted wisdom" because, as he explained, he "wanted them to pass their examinations" (p. 119).

Hillman's account can be regarded as a blend of cynicism, realism, and understanding in relation to his students as he continues to carry on his battle with the establishment. Regarding the situation within the establishment, he wrote:

> We must ask what has been discovered about the *genesis* of cancer, multiple sclerosis, Alzheimer's disease, or schizophrenia. The answer is remarkably little. ... If we leave aside my hypothesis that basic medical, biological, and pharmaceutical research has not been successful because it has not addressed the fundamental problems and assumptions inherent in most of the techniques, the current situation is dangerous because it suppresses free thought, without which the advance of knowledge can only be slow. (Hillman, 1996, p. 125)

Hillman's experiences, and his teaching, can suggest how thoroughly the fear to say what one believed permeates academia. According to his account, he felt it necessary to avoid telling his students what he believes on certain subjects so that the students could pass their exams. Then, in the course of his scholarly conferences in which he expresses controversial ideas, he comes across many scholars who say, in private, that they agree with him, but they are not willing to say so in public or the scholarly record.

LACK OF TENURE AND SILENCE, AND TENURE AND SILENCE

Once scholars get their graduate degrees, they become so-called junior scholars, and they are usually at the lower levels of the academic hierarchy. At this time, they may feel a sense of loyalty and admiration toward their graduate school advisors, or may even attain the roles of "disciples" of them. Moreover, junior scholars are often still beset by problems of economic and career insecurity that they faced as graduate students. These problems can continue to act as restrictions and restraints on their willingness to say what they believe. In fact, at this stage the lack of tenure and quest for tenure might add to the sense of insecurity if more scholars seek tenure in a department, or in a discipline, than there are tenured positions available. The intense competition for a limited number of tenured positions increases pressures along the lines of academic and departmental politics, which might place further inhibitions on scholars saying what they believe.

Tenure is usually associated with security in an academic career. Once scholars attain tenure, so the rhetoric goes, they should feel free to say what they believe in regard to the subject matter of their specialized field of study. Hillman (1995), in fact, recognized the pressure on junior scholars to remain silent on certain topics, but urged them to speak out once they get tenure:

> It is of crucial importance that the honorable research workers, who have to be quiet about intellectual doubts when in junior positions, should reassert their independence and honesty as soon as they are in a position to do so. This applies with particular force to thinkers and academics under former totalitarian regimes who are struggling to restore freedom of thought. (p. 58)

On the other hand, Altman was in a position to assert his independence, as far as tenure and power were concerned, but he still felt he could not say what he believed. For whatever reason, despite his tenure and power, Altman did not want to assert his independence in regard to the inquiries that Hentoff made.

Thus, even for scholars with tenure, their "position to do so" (as far as asserting their independence, and saying what they believe, are concerned) can still be far off. Once tenure is attained, there are still strong pressures that tend to promote orthodox thinking and to inhibit and silence dissenting ideas. By the time they have attained tenure, scholars have been teaching within the parameters of paradigms and tend to experience the paradigm dependency that this situation produces. Their expertise and intellectual authority for the subject matter they are teaching become identified with these paradigms.

Besides, if after gaining tenure scholars wish to publish, gain further promotions, win honors and prizes, and obtain research grants and editorial positions, they still have to pass peer review. If at any stage of their career they become known as whistle-blowers or trouble makers, scholars might face a halt or a slowdown to further career enhancement. Just ask Duesberg.

There is also the factor of so-called collegiality, which can inhibit scholars from saying what they believe. Scholars who say what they believe by adhering to new paradigm-busting ideas may be perceived as having betrayed their colleagues by placing their expertise and intellectual authority in doubt. It is also possible that such colleagues will let a colleague whistleblower know that they feel betrayed. In a sense, all these scholars are in the same boat (The Good Ship Collegiality, sailing along on the Paradigm Sea). In fact, it might be that one of the reasons that Altman told Hentoff he could not give his private views is that he felt he would be betraying his colleagues in the Yale administration and on the Executive Committee who agreed with the punishment of a student (even though the punishment was in direct contradiction of the contents of the Woodward Report, whose approval of freedom of expression on campus became part of university regulations). Although collegiality is often viewed in a positive sense in terms of courtesy and respect, it can also have a chilling effect that inhibits scholars from saying what they believe. Sometimes collegiality can take the form of closing ranks behind a scholar or group of scholars who have been accused of wrongdoing (plagiarism, unethical research practices, etc.) or who are under investigation. Such a form of collegiality might also have an inhibiting effect on the conduct of an investigation.

With a large portion of academic research being subsidized by government or industry (or a combination of both for the same research projects), pressure to conform is reinforced by the specific vested interests (political or commercial) toward which the research is directed. In addition, much research is also conducted by large academic research teams under a research director, or a small group of directors. It would seem that in order to become, and to remain, a participant on a research team, a large degree of conformity is required. This conformity might be viewed by the sponsors of the research and by the directors of the research in terms of loyalty. If researchers detect errors or other unwanted information during the research, feelings about seeming disloyal might prevent them from speaking out about the errors.

SOME CASE STUDIES

The documentation for particular cases of scholars being afraid or otherwise unwilling to say what they believe is enormous. Some selective examples can serve to show that such cases have existed for a long time in academia, and they occur in various academic disciplines. In addition to specific case studies, there has also been some general discussion of scholars being silenced from saying what they believe.

Martin (1986a) wrote:

> Samuel Epstein has documented the role of industry in promoting production practices in the face of evidence of their role in causing or promoting cancer. Scientists who have defended asbestos, certain pesticides, and other cancerous substances have received grants, consultancies, directorships and jobs. ... Those who have exposed the dangers have often been suppressed. (pp. 173–174)

In these cases, it does not seem that feelings about being disloyal are as great a factor as fear of being retaliated against, or suppressed, as far as remaining silent or speaking out is concerned.

In another publication, Martin (1992) continued on this theme:

> The flip side of bias built into the structure of science is suppression of dissent. The few scientists who speak out against dominant interests—such as pesticides, nuclear power or automotive design—often come under severe attack. They may have their reputations smeared, be demoted, be transferred, have their publications blocked, be dismissed, or blacklisted. (p. 88)

He added that intellectual silence can extend to political matters or alleged matters of national security: "The response of US universities to the First World War. A great many scholars who held dissenting views remained silent throughout the war" (Martin, 1986a, p. 175).

The John Coulter case in Australia has been described as one in which

> Dr. Coulter has been willing to speak out when others with the same knowledge have kept quiet. ... Coulter publicly pointed out that ethylene dichloride is highly toxic and a potential cause of cancer. Health Commission staff were aware of this hazard, but no one said anything publicly. ... It is now accepted by the US National Cancer Institute that ethylene dichloride does cause cancer ... in March 1980, Dr. Coulter was informed that ... he would be transferred and demoted ... instead ... Dr. Coulter was sacked outright. (Martin, 1986c, pp. 123–125)

It can be imagined that those "with the same knowledge" as Coulter had, and who remained silent, did not suffer the same fate that Coulter did.

THE DEAD SEA SCROLLS AND DEAD SILENCE

One of the great controversies in the field of religious history in recent times involves access to, and interpretation of, the so-called Dead Sea Scrolls. In their discussion of the controversy surrounding the scrolls, Baigent and Leigh (1993) alluded to the problem of scholars not saying what they believe:

Many scholars were intimidated against saying what they actually believed. Academic reputations are fragile things, and only the most audacious or secure individuals could afford to incur the risk involved—the risk of being discredited, of being isolated by a concerted critical barrage from adherents of the consensus. ... No one dared risk the wrath of the ... solidly entrenched consensus. ... Roth and Driver had been driven to silence on the subject. ... Everyone else who might pose a threat had been intimidated into compliance. (pp. 80–81, 119)

The phenomenon of being "isolated by a concerted critical barrage from adherents of the consensus" has perhaps played a major role in silencing scholars during the controversies in which Velikovsky was involved and in which Duesberg is currently involved. In *The Velikovsky Affair* (de Grazia, 1978), it was reported that "Several scientists and intellectuals who attempted his defense were silenced or sanctioned severely" (p. 173) and it is mentioned that in the field of sociology scholars "knew well that, by dealing with the attitude of some scientists toward Velikovsky's hypotheses, they were risking the wrath of well-entrenched academic power" (p. 156). It was also written that "as happens in most power situations the network of influence extends outward through former students, new appointments, and professional awards. ... The rank and file are likely to follow their leaders more than the dissidents" (pp. 190, 210). The leaders, in such cases, are able to help lead the rank and file to career enhancement. By contrast, a decision on the part of the rank and file to follow the dissidents would most likely lead to setbacks in terms of career enhancement.

AIDS research, for one reason or another, has become a source of case studies of scholars being afraid to say what they believe. In his aforementioned review article of Duesberg's works, Horton (1996) specifically made reference to the problem of scholars not saying what they think: "He recounts how scientists who have flirted with dissident views ... have been dissuaded from pursuing their alternative theories. ... Apparently under pressure from the company, two co-authors of the study withdrew their support from the clear implications of the trial that AZT was ineffective" (pp. 14, 19). Because AIDS is a topic that achieves headlines in the news media on an international basis, there may well be some scholars who have been silenced, but who, following Crenshaw's example, may say what they believe at some time in the future, when they feel it is the right moment. De Marchi and Franchi (1996) suggested that, for the time being, however, many specialists have resorted to a "terrible silence" ("terribile silenzio") as a result of the harsh treatment given to Duesberg. Regarding such treatment, it is reported that a powerful Italian specialist, Fernando Aiuti, actually went so far as to claim that Duesberg has behaved like a criminal and should be banned from the scientific community.

Duesberg (1996b) himself made several pertinent references, based on his personal experiences and observations:

Few scientists are any longer willing to question, even privately, the consensus views in any field whatsoever. ... Two health care workers ... told Duesberg under the condition of anonymity that they were directed not to report HIV-free AIDS cases as AIDS. ... The chilling effects of silencing tactics extend even onto the campus itself. ... Graduate students are discouraged from entering Duesberg's lab during their decision-making first year, advice that can be psychologically intimidating to such inexperienced students. Under the condition of anonymity, several students have confessed to such pressures more than once. (pp. 66, 274, 404–405)

Manwell and Baker (1986b) discussed the problem of scholars not speaking out in terms of *paralysis of conscience*. They asked, "Why do scientists, academics or other professionals fail to protect intellectual freedom and fail to protest injustice?" (p. 130). They also referred to "the need to encourage and to protect the tiny minority of scientists who are willing to speak out" (p. 130). The concept of paralysis of conscience can extend from fear of consequences to ambiguity or ambivalence about the specific definitions or interpretations of ethical problems, and further, to the practice known as cover up. A form of paralysis of conscience might be seen in the confession to Hentoff by the Dean of Yale College that he could not tell him what he really believed.

Fox and Braxton (1994) believed that "ambivalence over values" might cause scientists "to be reluctant to speak out about misconduct" (p. 380). This ambivalence is compounded by the fact that what may seem to be an obvious case of academic fraud in the opinion of a scholar might not be the same as the definition of fraud in a court of law. An accusation of fraud might end up with a lawsuit. The threat of a lawsuit, and the bigger threat of losing it because of differences in definitions of fraud, can be a very powerful silencing factor.

When paralysis of conscience moves into the realm of academic cover up, the scholars who are involved in not saying what they believe are found, for the most part, in the upper ranks of the academic hierarchy, rather than the lower ranks (where reasons for not speaking out are more likely to involve fear rather than an actual desire to hide the truth). Fox and Braxton (1994) observed that even though "scientists holding high rank, seniority, and administrative appointments as chairpersons enjoy a security that permits them to report or take action," they too might remain silent and be "pulled toward inaction" as the result of "institutional pressures for professional solidarity within their units" (p. 377). Horrobin (1990) described a case in which a "senior scientist's ... willingness to be ruthlessly unfair in the pursuit of his own ends is known to many members of the scientific community, yet no one has had the courage to try to put a stop to it" (p. 1440). Such a lack of courage might amount to cover up itself, or it might create the atmosphere or circumstances that might lead to cover up at some later time.

Some examples of scholars refusing to say what they believe took place in the *Cell*–Baltimore case. Sarasohn (1993) related that investigators discovered "serious problems" regarding the authenticity of data in one of Thereza Imanishi-Kari's notebooks. In this regard, Lang (1993) cited the Dingell investigations, which reported that a number of "prominent scientists, under a promise of confidentiality, examined the suspect notebook and agreed that it was obviously bogus. But the same scientists were unwilling to advance their professional opinions in public for fear of the disapproval of their colleagues" (p. 30). (These scientists must have been regarded as experts and authorities in their specialized fields, otherwise they would not have been asked to examine the notebooks. Nevertheless, for whatever reason, they too decided not to say what they believed in public.) Lang also concluded that panels of scholars "have actually contributed to intimidation or to covering up" (p. 44), and based on the developments in the case, Lang included panels at Tufts and MIT in this group.

Sometimes scholars refuse to say what they believe because they do not want to get deeply involved (even if their opinions might have considerable significance in a specific situation). They may not necessarily have any real fears of retaliation against them, and they may not be involved in a cover-up operation. Rather, they simply prefer to stay on the sidelines during a controversy in their field and let other scholars battle it out. This attitude might be motivated by prudence if scholars feel they do not have sufficient command of the facts of the case to commit themselves to one side or another. Or, perhaps their silence is based on a form of protective collegiality, in which they believe that some of their colleagues might be wrong but they prefer not to let their beliefs be known.

SILENCE AS A MEANS OF STAYING "OUT OF THE FIGHT"

A specific case of evasive silence took place in the Guido Riccio controversy. In 1986, Lang (personal communication, June 26, 1986) wrote, "I did give the documents on Guido Riccio to a person named Weil at the Humboldt dinner last Monday. ... She said she was 'trying to stay out of the fight', and was curious why I was involved." It would not be surprising if similar responses or attitudes were common in controversial issues in many other academic disciplines outside art history. Scholars may well have definite beliefs, ideas, and hypotheses on a subject, but they do not want them to become part of the scholarly record.

In his dealings with sociological surveys and the education establishment, which led to the creation of his book *The File*, Lang (1981) came to the conclusion that "there is a very large group which gives collegiality priority over the issues of validity ... an overriding concern of this group is not to get involved" (p. 693). Sometimes a decision to not get involved might be made because scholars do not feel they have enough time to devote to the subject. Sometimes, however, such decisions might be based on a fear that powerful academics might become upset by hearing scholars saying what they believe about certain issues. Sometimes there might not be actual fear, but a sense of prudence would be sufficient to cause silence.

STUDIED SILENCE IN THE FACE OF CHALLENGES

In contrast to the scholars who do not want to get involved, there are scholars who are directly and deeply involved in scholarly controversies who use silence as a tactic.

One such tactical use is what Rosand (1979) called *studied silence*, a refusal to reply in the face of specific challenges from other scholars. This might also be called hit-and-run scholarship (Moran & Mallory, 1991a, p. 59).

It seems that the National Cancer Institute (NCI) and Robert Gallo were involved in a type of studied silence situation recently, according to a published interview (Zimmerman, 1995). Gallo was asked, "What are the issues that NCI officials, and others, higher up, told you to remain silent on?" Gallo replied, "Basically, not to ever talk about ... Dingell ... or the patent for the HIV blood test. Basically, in the last few years ... not to talk to the press, period" (p. 1).

Studied silence on the part of scholars often takes the form of refusing to reply to letters of inquiry that seek information, opinions, or clarifications. Scholars might refuse to acknowledge receipt of letters, or they might acknowledge receipt but remain silent about the inquiries. Lang (1981) described examples throughout *The File*. Another example was cited in Chapter 6, in which the head of the ACLS, Stanley Katz, retreated into silence when asked if he approved of the decision of the CAA that falsification, destruction of evidence, misrepresentation, and so on, were "subjective" matters that the CAA "cannot" include in its ethics code as unethical practices.

More recently, Edmund Pellegrino and Michael Merson were asked, concerning AIDS research, what they thought of Lang's article on the subject published in *Yale Scientific*. Pellegrino is Director of the Center for the Advanced Studies of Ethics (Georgetown University), and a member of the editorial board of *Accountability in Research* and *Journal of the American Medical Association*. Merson is Dean for Public Health and Chair of the Department of Epidemiology and Public Health at the School of Medicine of Yale University. Previously, he was Executive Director of the World Health Organization's (WHO) Global Program on AIDS. Neither replied. It does not seem possible, given his activity with the WHO, and given his position in the field of public health, that Merson does not want to get involved, or wants to stay out of the fight. It would appear that there must be some other reason for his silence in this case.

Ruesch (1992) commented further about scholars not speaking out in the medical field:

The many honest and courageous doctors who have tried to voice their opinions in contrast with the "accepted" doctrines imparted by the Faculties ... have all been quickly discouraged from continuing or silenced. ... And it is because of such systematic censorship, running parallel with a constant flow of bombastic medical propaganda, that occasional outbursts of candor ... have quickly fallen into the trough of oblivion, never again to be resurrected by their chastened authors. (p. 11)

A recent newspaper article (Hanchette & Brewer, 1996) seems to illustrate a situation similar to what Ruesch (1992) described. So-called Gulf War syndrome is a topic that has become a mystery for doctors and medical researchers, and also something of an embarrassment for the military and the government. According to the article, as many as 80,000 persons might be affected. Now, according to the article, some doctors and researchers are being fired after "describing research results to colleagues" (p. 3A), or after coming up with theories such as those that "Iraqi nerve gas may have combined with oil fire residues and chemicals to suppress immune systems and trigger genetic alteration" (p. 3A). The article states that government officials claim the firings are part of general budget and bureaucratic cutbacks. On the other hand, it seems strange that a series of cutbacks would be directed against medical researchers involved in research that appears to be so crucial. Could it be that these researchers are being considered to be whistleblowers? In this case, it is interesting to observe that a hypothesis is made that various chemicals have suppressed the immune system. The hypothesis that HIV is the cause of AIDS would be based on the idea that HIV suppresses the immune system. In this case, findings and hypotheses that various chemicals also suppress the immune system might cause some doubts about the official HIV–AIDS hypothesis.

The various issues involved in scholars not saying what they believe, for whatever reasons, lead to discussion of what academic leaders can be expected to do in cases of controversial issues, vested interests, and conflicts of interest. Such discussion involves the various meanings of trust, the relation of trust to skepticism, and the role of whistleblowers in the scholarly pursuit of truth.

9

Trust, Skepticism, and Whistleblowing

Among the most treasured and essential ideals of science are collegial relations based on common pursuits and mutual trust. ... Interfering with collegiality is perilous for science. ..." It is uncomfortable to live with error but important to remember that correcting a specific error at the expense of collegial trust will not and cannot restore that comfort. (P. Woolf, personal communication, July 23, 1987)

This quotation is from an informal peer review of a proposed rebuttal article that purported to correct alleged errors found in a published article in the field of biomedical research. The peer-review judgment advised against publication of the rebuttal article, and the concept of "collegial trust" was invoked in support of a recommendation not to publish. On the other hand, Woolf (1986) is also on record as stating that scholars should accept criticism:

Scholars ought to be able to tolerate a good deal of mutual criticism. ... Although such professional criticism is uncomfortable, even painful for all the parties concerned, scholars cannot afford to be too thin-skinned if they are to maintain scholarly standards and professional autonomy. (p. 8)

Woolf's apparently contradictory statements indicate that trust, skepticism, and whistleblowing are important factors in discussions of silencing of scholars. These factors often intertwine and overlap. Whenever trust, skepticism, and whistleblowing are discussed in this context, however, they should also be analyzed within the parameters of rhetoric versus reality, double standards, and paradigm dependency. The word *mutual*, as used by Woolf in "mutual trust" and "mutual criticism" implies a common and universal application rather than one based on favoritism and special privilege. *Collegiality* is an academic term for politeness and courtesy, which might also include benefit of the doubt relating to questions about honesty and good faith.

The word *trust* abounds in the literature about science. As an example, Nigg and Radulescu (1994) wrote that scholarly publishing in science takes place "in an environment ... fundamentally based on trust" (p. 168). When it is stated that a person can be trusted, it often means that the person is honest and acts with integrity. Sometimes it is felt that a person or groups of persons can be trusted based on past behavior. At the same time, trust might be tied in with a sense of dependency, as in situations in which persons have no other choice than to place their trust in experts or leaders. In such cases, trust might become more a matter of hope than of belief or conviction. In any case, in terms of scholarship and scholarly communication, the word *trust* is usually associated with an assumption of honesty and integrity on the part of scholars, and this assumption is mutual (at least according to the rhetoric).

On the other hand, trust is also associated with plausible possibility and logical expectation, based on specific and particular circumstances. There is often a negative connotation involved, such as the feeling that persons or institutions cannot really be trusted to make certain types of decisions in cases involving conflicts of interest, special interests, vested interests, and paradigm challenges. In the midst of all the rhetoric about mutual trust, just what can academics be expected to do (i.e., trusted to do) within the reality of conflict of interest situations and vested interest situations?

Skepticism is another word commonly used in the literature and rhetoric of academia and science. It is associated with intellectual curiosity, critical inquiry, critical analysis, and basic scientific methodology itself. In this respect, it is an essential element in scholarly research and scholarly communication. Schmaus (1987) stated that "The growth of scientific knowledge, then, does not depend so much on the honesty as on the skepticism of scientists" (p. 4). However, because skepticism might also conjure up negative impressions along the lines of suspicion, doubt, and cynicism, it is sometimes given a clarifying, positive, and uplifting adjective, such as "healthy" skepticism ("enlightened" skepticism might be another example). Skepticism is not an adversary that places doubt on trust and honesty. On the contrary, it is an ally and colleague of trust and honesty, all involved together in the advancement of knowledge.

At this point, along come some whistleblowers. If they are traffic police, they might blow the whistle to halt traffic to allow schoolchildren to cross the street safely. Or, they might blow the whistle to stop a car that committed some traffic violation that endangered pedestrians or other drivers in traffic. Such whistleblowers are usually looked on favorably as protectors of society.

How are academic whistleblowers looked on? Do such whistleblowers enjoy the "collegial relations based on common pursuits and mutual trust" that Woolf claimed are among "the most treasured and essential ideals of science?" Do academic whistle-blowers do good or do harm in academia, in terms of "growth of scientific knowledge" (or growth of knowledge in fields other than science)?

In a sense, academic whistleblowers are scholars who have been successful in the exercise of their skepticism, to the extent that such skepticism has resulted in the discovery of error (ranging from so-called minor error to the more spectacular error consisting of a false paradigm that became entrenched in the scholarly literature). But when is such a whistleblower regarded as a successful skeptic and a discoverer?

Harvey is now regarded as the scientist who in the 17th century discovered the circulation of blood. This discovery is now acknowledged as important enough to be cited in textbooks and encyclopedias. According to words attributed to him, Harvey himself did not believe that he would be hailed (collegially or otherwise) as a great discoverer by his colleagues:

> But what remains to be said about the quantity and source of the blood which thus passes, is of so novel and unheard-of character that I not only fear injury to myself from the envy of the few, but I tremble lest I have mankind at large for my enemies, so much doth wont and custom ... and doctrine .., and respect for antiquity, influence all men. (Nissani, 1995, p. 168)

WOOLF, THE U.S. CONGRESS TASK FORCE ON SCIENCE POLICY, AND BALTIMORE

In effect, Woolf's quotes at the beginning of this chapter can perhaps be understood best in terms of rhetoric versus reality situations. Her idea that "scholars ought to be able to tolerate a good deal of mutual criticism" serves as effective rhetoric of a generalized nature for members of Congress who heard her testimony. It seems obvious that powerful academics might not appreciate her words as much as the Congressmen serving on the Task Force on Science Policy might, if these words were spoken in specific relation to alleged errors in the works of academic authorities.

In fact, the informal peer-review remarks, "It is uncomfortable to live with error but important to remember that correcting a specific error at the expense of collegial trust will not and cannot restore that comfort," were related to whether or not Stewart and Feder should publish a rebuttal article in the journal *Cell*. (The rebuttal article discussed errors in the *Cell* article for which Baltimore was a coauthor.) The key phrase seems to be "correcting a specific error at the expense of collegial trust." This is a long way—in a brief period of time from when it was written—from the belief that "scholars ought to be able to tolerate a good deal of mutual criticism." It is also a long way from the concept of considering collegial trust in terms of honesty and integrity versus fraud and misconduct. (In their rebuttal article, Stewart and Feder discussed some alleged errors, but they did not speculate about any possible misconduct or fraud.)

By associating specific error with collegial trust, as Woolf did, it is no longer a matter of a scholar's honesty that is being trusted or distrusted, but the scholar's infallibility as an expert. No matter how Woolf's words are interpreted, the impression remains that she is saying that the rebuttal article, with the exposure and discussion of errors in the *Cell* article, should not be published because the article indicates that the authors of the rebuttal article do not trust the authors of the *Cell* article. (Otherwise, the question of trust would not have been raised by Woolf.)

However, Sarasohn's (1993) book and Lang's (1993) article in *Ethics and Behavior*, which deal with the *Cell*–Baltimore case in detail, both emphasize that the rebuttal article, as well as O'Toole's original activity in this matter, were concerned with the correction of error. O'Toole, Stewart, and Feder were not showing any lack of collegial trust for anyone's honesty or integrity. They merely wanted to see the errors corrected. It was the data that were not trusted in this case.

By contrast, how did mutual trust or collegial trust fare, in terms of the way some coauthors of the *Cell* article (and the leaders of the science establishment who rallied around them) treated Stewart, Feder, and O'Toole? Sarasohn (1993) reported that "the talk around Cambridge and Boston was that O'Toole's documents might not be genuine data. ... Baltimore attacked O'Toole's motives" (pp. 36–37). Sarasohn then cited a memo from NIH official Joseph E. Rall to Stewart and Feder that affirmed that "it could equally well be that the seventeen pages you have are falsified" (p. 40). Moreover, Sarasohn wrote, "During one phone call, Stewart claimed, Baltimore said that O'Toole had stolen the documents and called Stewart a vicious person" (p. 41).

At this point, it seems clear that, on the one hand, an appeal was made to collegial trust as a reason to silence scholars (and the ideas they are expressing in a rebuttal article), whereas on the other hand, as part of an effort to silence the same scholars, collegial trust and mutual trust were abandoned, as evidenced by use of words such as "attacked O'Toole's motives," or "stolen" and "falsified." Thus, in this case, mutual trust comes into the picture as part of the rhetoric of science, but in reality the concept of trust was invoked in a one-way-only manner that resulted in a strenuous attempt to silence scientists.

In the famous peer-review experiment by Peters and Ceci (1982), articles published by famous scholars from prestigious institutions were resubmitted to the same journals, with the names of the authors and institutions changed to ones that were less prestigious or fictitious. Several of the articles that were previously published were rejected the second time around because of defects in methodology or for other reasons. It seems that some prestigious names were trusted more than less prestigious names. The trust was not mutual in this case.

TRUST, SKEPTICISM, AND VESTED INTERESTS

It would seem that a similar experiment (hypothetical or real) could be envisioned to test the concepts of collegial trust, mutual trust, and skepticism, in terms of what scholars might be expected to do (i.e., trusted to do) in vested interest situations and conflict of interest situations. Such an experiment could also test how what they might be expected to do compares to the rhetoric about trust, skepticism, and the advancement of knowledge.

Suppose that two lengthy, detailed studies were drawn up, with one study concluding that there is no definite proof that tobacco causes lung cancer or any other serious illness, and with the other study concluding that not only has nicotine in tobacco been proven to be addictive, but also that damage to human health caused by tobacco is, in fact, much greater than has previously been reported or suggested. Both studies are sent to the same two scholars for their peer-review recommendations.

Now suppose, in this hypothetical case, that one of these scholars is a long-term senior research consultant for a major tobacco company and owns shares of that company's common stock (and also has the opportunity to exercise options to acquire many more shares). Furthermore, the scholar is a well-paid consultant to tobacco industry associations, and is a professor of agriculture whose chair is endowed by a tobacco growers' association.

The other peer-review referee in this hypothetical situation is an environmentalist activist on campus, and a leader of a lobbyist group that is trying to get the government to place tobacco on a list of addictive drugs that includes heroin and cocaine and is trying to have cigarettes, cigars, snuff, chewing tobacco, and pipe tobacco banned. Would any sociologist, or other scholar writing about higher education or about the sociology of science or peer review, expect both peer-review referees to exercise the same amount of trust and skepticism in reviewing both articles for scientific rigor, error, methodology, and accuracy?

WHISTLEBLOWING

The fact is that there are vested interests and conflict of interest situations, ranging from paradigm dependency to specific individual and institutional financial and commercial interests, that exist in academia. The potential magnitude of such financial and commercial interests is enormous. For example, Levin (1996) reported that the School of Medicine at Yale University has become "a major enterprise of biomedical research and clinical practice that generates more than 40 percent of the University's revenues and expenses" (p. 24). If whistleblowers were afforded collegial trust and given appreciation for the correction of errors that their skepticism produces, they might have excellent opportunities in many academic disciplines.

A major problem, however, that whistleblowers face is the fact that scholars, like other persons, do not appreciate being proven wrong. There might also be a connection or correlation between a scholar's power, prestige, and reputation and the scholar's lack of toleration for correction of the scholar's errors.

Minor errors are usually allowed to be corrected, but they do not necessarily involve whistleblowers and whistleblowing. If Baltimore and the authorities at MIT and Tufts University had allowed some errors to be corrected in the infamous *Cell* article, the corrections might have been considered part of the so-called self-correction of science, with specialists adjusting their future research accordingly. O'Toole would not necessarily have been known as a whistleblower in this case, but instead, as another one of many scientists who exercised healthy skepticism. She became known as a whistleblower only after she and Stewart and Ned Feder tried to have corrections made after: (a) some authors and authorities refused to admit that serious errors were made, and (b) obstacles prevented the correction of error.

The *Cell*–Baltimore case, in this sense, illustrates some aspects of academic whistleblowing. Major breakthroughs in medical research by establishment scientists are not usually regarded as whistleblowing, but the major breakthrough arrived at independently by Semmelweis relating to the cause of childbirth fever is regarded as a classic case of whistleblowing. The perfection of miracle drugs and miracle cures has become part of the research paradigm that might involve specific vested interests and conflicts of interest. If a scholar discovers, however, that a miracle drug does not really work, after all, or is causing tragedy and death and suffering (e.g., DES, thalidomide, and SMON), scholars who discover the defects of the medicines become known as whistleblowers.

In theory, academic whistleblowers are scholars who believe they have detected serious error, and they try to correct it. In reality, however, the term *whistleblower* is usually reserved for scholars whose detection of errors and their attempts to correct them have hit a raw nerve in terms of paradigms, vested interests, or conflicts of interest.

Along this line, in the case of the Guido Riccio controversy, in 1907, Venturi detected what he thought was an error in attribution for part of a Sienese painting, and he published it (in passing, in a footnote) in an authoritative and monumental history of Italian art. Although, by 1907, the attribution to Simone Martini for the Guido Riccio fresco had become a paradigm, the discipline of art history was not yet developed enough, and the vested interests built up around the painting were not yet strong enough, to bring Venturi's comments to the level of whistleblowing. Instead, his insight did not lead to correction or even to discussion. It was ignored by scholars for a long time. In this sense, Venturi's opinion, as revolutionary as it was, did not draw the attention necessary to qualify it as an act of whistleblowing.

Although Venturi's publication about Guido Riccio did not differ much in content from that that was written about the same painting in 1977, it was the different reaction of the establishment from 1977 onward that turned the situation into one of academic whistleblowing.

When, in the 17th century, Harvey tried to convince the medical profession about the circulation of blood, he became a whistleblower. At the present time, medical researchers who routinely agree with and follow Harvey's findings in their development of miracle drugs are not known as whistleblowers or followers of a whistleblower, yet they are working within the paradigm that a whistleblower introduced.

SILENCING OF WHISTLEBLOWERS

Obviously, there are attempts to silence scholars who are whistleblowers, and these attempts have been taking place in academia for centuries. In fact, to the extent that progress in science and in medicine, and the advancement of knowledge in other disciplines as well, have taken giant steps forward as a result of paradigm changes brought about by discoveries made by scholars (or groups of scholars), the history of science and of medicine and intellectual history are histories of whistleblowing. As discussed earlier, establishment scholars have a vested interest in paradigms in their disciplines based on their own sense of reputation, prestige, expertise, and authority, all of which might be placed in doubt and question if the paradigm were suddenly proven wrong.

With the rise of the industrial–governmental–academic complex, vested interests have expanded greatly into financial as well as intellectual areas, leading, in turn, to some conflicts of interest. Under these circumstances, the areas in which academic whistleblowers operate become more complex and more expansive in dimension. In any case, similar knee-jerk reactions to whistleblowers seem to prevail at present as they did in the past. The overriding reaction seems to be that the ideas of the whistleblower must be silenced.

In order to silence the whistleblowers' ideas, there are often attempts to discredit the whistleblowers. Among the first casualties of the discrediting process is the sense of trust, mutual trust, or collegial trust that the scholar who is being discredited might have enjoyed previously. Strohman (1995) described the "before and after" whistleblowing situation experienced by Duesberg:

> In 1987 Peter Duesberg was at the top of his career and the future was promising. ... He was the recipient of a seven-year Outstanding Investigator Award Grant from the National Institutes of Health that provided him with hundreds of thousands of dollars to conduct his research. ... His brilliance as an experimental virologist was acknowledged around the world and his prizes for leadership are many. Now, in 1995, he has no grants from the National Institutes of Health. (p. viii)

Furthermore, Strohman (1995) stated that the editor of *Nature* asked Duesberg to "quit his role as critic," and that the editor has "used his power as editor to enforce Duesberg's silence in the journal" (p. xi). Likewise, Horton (1996) wrote that Duesberg is

> a brilliant virologist, and the former recipient of an award for outstanding investigative research from the National Institutes of Health. ... Yet, he is now perhaps the most vilified scientist alive. His work inspires excoriating attacks. ... What extraordinary course of events has led him to be dismissed by his peers and ridiculed by his colleagues? (p. 14)

In this case, and in many other cases, it seems that the "extraordinary course of events" is all part of a common phenomenon in the history of academia in which a scholar becomes known as a whistleblower. In the *Cell*–Baltimore case, when O'Toole attempted to correct errors in the published article in question, the coauthors of the dubious article neither received excoriating attacks, or were they dismissed nor ridiculed by their peers. Nor, for that matter, was there an attempt to silence the authors. To the contrary, they were merely asked to publish a correction. However, according to Woolf, such an attempt to publish such a correction of another scholar's published work was itself an example of withholding, or denying, "collegial trust."

SILENCING BY MEANS OF ISOLATION

In contrast to mere suggestions to publish corrections of error, it would seem that excoriating attacks and ridicule by colleagues are certainly more evident manifestations of loss of collegial trust in academia. Whistleblowers are not only denied mutual trust, for the most part, but attempts to silence them are also linked with attempts to isolate them. This isolation process might take place even if the attempt at isolation has to be propped up by falsifications and misrepresentations. In such cases, factors of double standards, rhetoric versus reality gaps, and toleration for falsification can all come into play.

A glaring case of falsification and misrepresentation in an attempt at isolation of a whistleblower took place in the Guido Riccio controversy. Giovanni Previtali was quoted (in a Sienese newspaper) as claiming that doubts about the establishment view about Guido Riccio were "only the invention of a non-expert who has not found anyone who agrees with him" (Mallory & Moran, 1996, p. 142). Previtali continued, "This American was mistaken from the beginning ... and he is spending all his life trying to demonstrate that the fresco is not by Simone. Poor man, by now he has taken on the form of a monomaniac" (p. 142). Some scholars, including Previtali himself, knew that his ideas contained falsifications in this case. Aside from the fact that Venturi expressed similar doubts about the painting in 1907, by 1984 other scholars in the United States and Italy, and also in England, had already cast some doubts of their own on the traditional establishment viewpoint (Falcone, 1991).

Complete isolation means that a scholar is alone, a single voice in the wilderness. No other scholar shares the same ideas. Previtali was trying to convey such an impression at a time when other art historians were actually joining in to voice what was becoming at least a small chorus of doubts. In addition to claiming, falsely—as Previtali did—that a scholar and whistleblower is actually isolated, attempts might be made to misrepresent what a scholar said or wrote.

Along with misrepresentations, attempts might also be made at intimidating other scholars so that they will not support the whistleblower's ideas, or even associate with the whistleblower. Once again, a very clamorous example of such a misrepresentation occurred during the Guido Riccio controversy. When the destroyed part of the lower border of the Guido Riccio fresco became a focal point of discussion that was becoming embarrassing for the authorities, Roberto Barzanti (1988), former mayor of Siena, Vice President of the government of Europe, and head of the Department of Culture of the government of Europe stepped in. He described as a sensationalistic shot ("sparate sensazionalistiche") the observation that a part of the fresco had been destroyed in 1980–1981, and he implied that the observation was merely pure fantasy. Yet, if Barzanti had taken a good look at the fresco either before or after he published his statement, he would have clearly seen that the observation that part of the painting had been destroyed was an accurate description rather than fantasy. For the purposes of discussion of whistleblowers and their treatment by authorities, Barzanti's words can serve as an illustration of how mutual trust can become practically nonexistent.

Rose (1978) described a variation on the theme of isolating and silencing whistleblowers. According to her account, at one point in the Velikovsky controversy, there was going to be a debate sponsored by the AAAS:

> Originally, Dr. Velikovsky was promised that the panel would consist of three opponents of his views and three (including himself) defenders of his views. This promise was flagrantly broken, and the panel was rigged in such a way that only Velikovsky was allowed to speak in his defense ... there were four-to-one odds. ... When the Cornell volume was published David Morrison and Isaac Asimov were added to the negative side, and Goldsmith wrote a long "Introduction." Velikovsky's lecture was dropped. (The four-to-one odds became seven-to-zero odds). (p. 68)

In this case, the specific silencing of scientists and their ideas from the published scholarly literature might be described as a fabricated isolation.

LAFOLLETTE AND THE WHISTLEBLOWER AS NEMESIS

In her description of whistleblowers, LaFollette (1992) wrote:

> As their efforts continue, they attract vigorous criticism, especially if their targets are senior scientists. They may even be accused themselves of hidden motives, of secretly harboring revenge. If their allegations later prove to be correct, society will probably applaud their courage and persistence—but it will be a bittersweet victory. (p. 137)

LaFollette (1992) compared whistleblowers to the concept of *nemesis*, in a negative setting, rather than to scholars who try to correct alleged error in spite of all the obstacles placed in their way. Although LaFollette made her own distinction between whistleblowers and "nemesis figures," she described Stewart and Feder as nemesis figures although they are, in fact, better known in scientific and academic circles as whistleblowers. She also indulged in a sort of pop psychology, in explaining that "the nemesis cannot stay quiet" (p. 147) and "the nemesis may also feel more vindictiveness toward the transgressor and all he represents than empathy for the party wronged" (p. 147). She also asked why "scientists ... so often criticize the truth-seeking nemesis?" (p. 147).

One explanation she cited is that the "nemesis disrupts the tidy order of science and must be removed either temporarily or permanently from the scientific mainstream" (p. 148). Needless to say, in such cases "removed" in effect means silenced.

SILENCE AND UNRESPONSIVE INSTITUTIONS AND INDIVIDUALS

Relations among trust, skepticism, and whistleblowing can be discerned in LaFollette's (1992) further comments about nemesis figures and whistleblowers:

> We may simply have to tolerate their presence until universities and research organizations find ways to treat well-intentioned questions about research conduct fairly and seriously. Concerned scientists have stepped into the nemesis role to force ethical responsiveness in seemingly unresponsive institutions. (p. 154)

In this passage, "unresponsive" can be associated with stonewalling, silence, or cover up. From the standpoint of silencing of scholars, the situation proceeds as follows: Whistleblowers raise questions and try to correct errors. The whistleblowers and their ideas are suppressed, and the silence that ensues is continued on the part of the institutions in the forms of stonewalling and cover up.

In this context, the word *unresponsive* in relation to the correction of error can refer to individuals as well as to institutions, and LaFollette and her book provided an interesting and paradoxical example relating to the term. LaFollette devoted much of the discussion under the subchapter "Protecting Individual Rights" to the case of David Abraham, a scholar of German Weimar history whose work was allegedly found to be marked by the falsification, if not fabrication, of some documentary evidence. According to LaFollette (1992), the American Historical Association (AHA) refused to "initiate a formal investigation" (p. 172). She then stated that Abraham "could only write his own letters for publication in subsequent issues of the same journals his opponents had already exploited. By the time Abraham replied in a later issue to one accusing letter, another letter with new allegations was published elsewhere" (p. 172). She also referred to the "nebulous nature of the charges" (p. 173) and stated that "gossip and innuendo ruled the process" (p. 173) and that Abraham was driven out of the history profession of academia.

Even a cursory reading of LaFollette's (1992) account by someone who was not familiar with the details of the case might conclude that Abraham was mistreated and was silenced unfairly. However, to anyone who had been following the case closely, LaFollette's narration might have caused the red flag that warns of falsification to start waving furiously. Instead of being forced to write "letters for publication in subsequent issues of the same journals his opponents had already exploited" (p. 172), in some cases Abraham was allowed much more space in the same issue of a journal than his opponents used, and in other cases his opponents were shut out of journals that took Abraham's side. For instance, the AHA's Executive Director, Samuel

Gammon (personal communication, December 19,1983), pointed out that the AHA had published an "exchange" between Abraham and his critics. Gammon added that "The Professional Division and the Executive Committee of the Council reluctantly agreed to publish the Turner letter, provided Abraham had a right of response," and also that the AHA leadership "believed that essentially scholarly debate belonged in the pages of scholarly journals of record." Furthermore, in the June–September 1984 issue of *Central European History*, Abraham (1984a, 1984b) had about 88 pages to present his case, whereas his critic, Feldman (1984a, 1984b), expressed his views in less than half (about 40 pages) that number. Abraham (1985)was also allowed to publish a rebuttal article of more than 20 pages in *Vierteljahrschrift fur Sozial-und Wirtschaftsgeschichte.* Instead of comprising gossip and innuendo, these exchanges among specialists in history journals seemed to be an actual working out of the self-correcting process that is often referred to in the academic rhetoric. In effect, in this specific case, that which Rennie and Flanagin (1995) described as part of the only real peer review is described by LaFollette (1992) as essentially gossip and innuendo.

It seemed obvious that LaFollette's (1992) description amounted to a blatant falsification of what actually took place. She was asked (G. Moran, personal communication, September 19, 1993) how she could have made such clamorous error in a book devoted to the discussion of falsification and the correction of error. She was also asked if she had trusted someone unwisely, instead of actually checking the record first. In any case, she was asked how she made the error, and a request was made of her to correct the error. More than 3 years have passed, and no reply has been received from her. The answer remains a secret, and this secrecy is a result of LaFollette's silence based on unresponsiveness.

BLIND TRUST AND EXCESSIVE TRUST

It might be that LaFollette's (1992) falsifications resulted from her placing what amounts to blind trust, untempered by skepticism, in sources that turned out to be unclear, misleading, or unreliable. Baltimore's reflections on the controversy in which he was a leading character include comments about his "trust in the efficacy of the peer review process," and observations that he might have been "blinded to the full implications of the mounting evidence by an excess of trust" (Lang, 1993, p. 69). His reference to "excess of trust" would seem to imply that trust itself should be viewed with a certain amount of skepticism, as a sort of brake or harness on excessive trust. An excess of an excess of trust might amount to blind trust.

In some cases in which persons (nonspecialists, journalists, and the general public) do not understand the technical terminology and in which persons are dependent on the actions of experts, blind trust is all that people can have, if they have any trust at all. On the other hand, conflict of interest situations might arouse skepticism to such a degree that trust, if not negated, is placed in doubt. It might well have been specific conflict of interest situations in medical research that led Pradal to ask, "Whence comes this blind trust, when intelligence should in fact lead us rather toward mis-trust?" (Ruesch, 1989, p. 89).

A more generalized skepticism about trust and error is found in Brian Martin's (1996) analysis. He observed that experts have often been mistaken in the past, and, as a result, he asked, "Why should the public trust them now?" (p. 3). Trust in this sense refers to infallibility, of trusting experts not to make serious mistakes. If the term *cover up* were substituted for *mistakes* in this instance, skepticism about trust would refer to honesty and integrity of the investigators and the investigation process. Martin's ideas find an echo in Wade's (1995) observation that "scientific establishments have been wrong in the past," and that "in cases of scientific fraud, universities have proved as zealous as the Pentagon in discouraging whistle-blowers" (Wade, 1995, p. 14).

In these contexts, trust can also refer to reliance on. Lang, who recently wrote a letter (personal communication, January 11, 1996) to the Council of the NAS relating to AIDS research, stated, "As I have written before, it is left for individual scientists to propagate correct information, since scientists cannot rely on the official media such as the *New York Times* and *Science.*"

TRUST AND FEAR

Fear, and particularly fear of the unknown or a fear of catastrophes, can elicit or pro-voke trust in political leaders and scientific leaders. It can be warranted and justified in some cases, but it can also represent a source of exploitation, or simply colossal blunders. The so-called swine flu scare is such an example, according to Duesberg (1996b), who recalled that "the naive legislators easily could be manipulated by the CDC's alarmist rhetoric" (p. 142). Duesberg expanded on this theme:

> The CDC has nevertheless continued to exploit public trust by transforming seasonal flus and other minor epidemics into monstrous crises and by manufacturing contagious plagues out of noninfectious medical conditions. The fear of infectious disease had now been revived on a mass level for the first time in decades, and the lay public had no choice but to trust their appointed experts for answers. (pp. 137, 158)

If fear provokes dependence and blind trust, or inevitable trust, in experts, the opposite might be said for secrecy. Although appeals to secrecy might work, in rela-tion to trust, in the name of national security (but not all the time, as Relyea [1994] showed), secrecy in peer review and scholarly communication breeds skepticism and suspicion. In Sharp's (1990) analysis of "publication bias," no less than nine pro-posals are listed to improve fairness in peer review. He observed that "implicit in many of them is a lack of trust in the ability and integrity of the reviewer" (p. 1391). One of the nine proposals is to abolish secrecy. Secrecy in peer review (in its broad-er definition) is one of the most effective weapons for silencing scholars in a demo-cratic society.

10

Peer-Review Secrecy

There is not a crime, there is not a dodge, there is not a trick, there is not a swindle, there is not a vice which does not live by secrecy. Get these things out into the open. (Ruesch, 1995, p. 3)

If peer review, in its broader definition, consists of the total assessment that a work receives, referees' reports and editorial decisions are a small but crucial part of the entire peer-review process (which, in theory, is a continuous, open-ended process that proceeds as long as the work is discussed by peers). Within the total process, secrecy can assume various forms in relation to various audiences. The most common forms of secrecy are described as anonymous refereeing and double-blind review.

At the same time, the very concepts of suppression, censorship, and cover up all imply secrecy, in the sense that there are attempts to keep certain persons or groups from having knowledge of specific facts and ideas. In terms of silencing of scholars, secrecy and peer review would go hand in hand.

As discussed earlier, important knowledge remains secret (i.e., hidden) when false paradigms act as impediments to discovery. In this sense, secrecy has something of a passive nature, in contrast to intentional suppression and censorship. The common phrase "unlocking the secrets of nature" implies that the secrecy was not caused by peer-review suppression, but rather that peer-review approval of original research allowed, or helped, the secrecy to be overcome.

In some cases, secrecy imposed by peer-review suppression might have a specific impact and might appear significant to a small number of specialists in a given academic discipline (and might also be of interest to sociologists studying academic behavior), but might not be of any special concern to other scholars. In other cases, such as studies of infectious diseases or highly toxic poisons in consumer goods (or in the air or the water supply), secrecy might affect the public at large, and thus all scholars regardless of their disciplines.

It would seem that in the halls of academia, where the rhetoric praises and underlines the importance of mutual trust, free exchange of ideas, free flow of information, and open debate and discussion, secrecy would be most unwelcome. Yet, it is obvious that secrecy is entrenched in academia, with terms like *anonymity, blind review, double-blind review, and confidentiality* used, instead of the word *secrecy*, in a manner that deflects attention away from the direct contradiction between secrecy and mutual trust and open discussion.

WHY SECRECY?

Perhaps a hypothetical situation can help in understanding some aspects of the nature of secret peer review. Suppose that a scholar is asked by an academic publisher to be a peer-review referee for the manuscript of a book that the publisher is considering. The policy of secrecy is used, on the basis that secrecy will protect the referee from retaliation in the case of a negative judgment about the manuscript, thus allowing the referee to give "honest" opinions. Suppose that the referee gives a scathing negative review, and as a result the publisher informs the author that the manuscript is rejected. The author goes to another academic publisher, and the book is eventually published.

Now suppose that the referee who gave the secret scathing negative judgment of the manuscript is asked to write a book review now that the manuscript is published. What does the reviewer do in this case? There would seem to be several possibilities: (a) write another scathing review, perhaps even more negative, in order to keep sales, distribution, and access to the author's ideas as low and as limited as possible; (b) insist that the published book review is anonymous, or published under a false name; (c) write a less negative review this time, or a balanced review, or even a favorable one, in order to avert retaliation; or (d) decline the invitation to write the review, out of fear that negative comments will result in retaliation.

The last of these possibilities would seem to be the most logical. The result would be that another scholar would be sought to review the book, and the scholar who declined to review the book would end up with one less entry on his or her curriculum vitae. The third possibility, if enacted, would indicate that published peer review (e.g., book reviews) is not as forthright and "honest" as secret peer review. The second possibility (i.e., anonymous book review) might conflict with the editorial policy of the journal or newspaper, and therefore amount to a result that is the same as a decision to decline to write the review.

The most interesting possibility is the first one; that is, writing of a signed negative review after writing a secret negative review of the same work. It would demonstrate that there really was no need for secrecy in the first place. In this case, anonymity would not have affected the contents of the review, which would have been very negative whether it was signed or whether it was secret. The overriding factor was the negative nature of the review, not whether it was written openly or in secret.

The fact is that scholarly journals do publish signed reviews (book reviews) that are strongly negative. This fact might lead to at least two questions. First, was the favorable secret peer review that recommended publication erroneous (in the sense that the work should never have been published if it was as bad as the negative review claimed it is)? Second, if the editors of these journals can find competent reviewers who are willing to write negative reviews openly (in the form of book reviews), why cannot the editors find reviewers for unpublished manuscripts without resorting to secrecy? In other words, why is there really any need, at all, for secrecy? If these editors believe in mutual trust and open communication, why do they not abolish secrecy in their own editorial process? Certainly fear of retaliation would not really be a reason after all, as demonstrated by the published negative reviews that are signed.

HIDDEN RESPONSIBILITY

Other factors, however, might benefit from secrecy. One of the most obvious of these is conflict of interest of a personal, institutional, collegial, financial, or other type of nature, particularly if members of the editorial leadership are themselves directly involved. Conflicts of interest can also overlap with responsibility for publication or rejection. Who was responsible, for example, for approval of all the articles of Darsee, Breuning, Felig, and so on (and their many coauthors) that were published and then subsequently retracted because of the clamorous errors in them? Editors might be able to claim, with justification, that the material was highly specialized and that it was necessary to rely on (i.e., trust) the judgment of specialists. The editors can thus avoid personal responsibility for having published clamorous errors. Responsibility would then be shifted to hand-picked peer reviewers. The hands of these referees may well also be clean, without washing, if they made honest miscalculation of judgment. However, if their hands have been dirtied as a result of some conflict of interest that prompted a favorable recommendation, there is no need to wash the hands, because the dirty hands remain a secret.

Editors who can find scholars who do not hesitate to write signed negative reviews, and editors who, at the same time, allow scholars to write secret reviews, are at best really paving the way for the exploitation of conflicts of interest, and paving the way for referees to avoid personal responsibility. At worst, such editors are enabling scholars to hide potential or actual conflict of interest situations.

In contrast to the responsibility for secret peer-review approval of articles that end up being retracted, there is also a question of responsibility for the secret peer-review rejection recommendations for works that later became so-called citation classics, or rejection of works that lead directly to high honors such as Nobel prizes. In "Have Referees Rejected Some of the Most-Cited Papers of All Times?" Campanario (1996b) discussed some rejected papers that were eventually published and led to Nobel prizes, and he also discussed other rejected works that eventually became among the most highly-cited articles in their fields. He stated that the present peer review system "often allows excellent manuscripts to be criticized by referees with vested interests" (pp. 302), and he added, "We could even speculate on the fact that some good papers that would have received many citations were never published because of the delays due to reviewing and initial rejection" (p. 308). Once again, editors can claim lack of expertise and necessity to rely on the judgments of referees who are specialists. The referees might have been involved in what amounts to variations of the paradigm-dependency phenomenon. They just could not fathom the importance of the new material because of their conditioned ways of thinking within the paradigm. In this case, their rejections would remain within the realm of honest error.

On the other hand, reasons for rejection in the cases discussed by Campanario (1996b) might have been motivated by, and based on, conflict of interest situations or vested interests. Whatever the reasons for such rejections—conflicts of interest, paradigm dependency, or honest errors of judgment or miscalculation—it is important to keep in mind Dalton's (1995) observation that "secrecy permits referees to get away with slipshod work" (p. 235).

DISTRUST AND THE ORIGINS OF SECRECY

It seems obvious that, in effect, peer-review secrecy originates with the editor's distrust of the author, or perhaps of the referee. If an author asks the editor for the name(s) of the referee(s), and the editor refuses to give the answer, the author might ask why. If, in this situation, editors reply that they are simply carrying out editorial policy, the author might ask what the basis is for such a policy. If editors reply that they can expect more honest opinions from referees if their names remain secret, the author might ask the editors why they do not choose referees they can trust to give honest opinions for which the referees will take personal responsibility. The author at this point might also make a specific request to have such referees review the manuscript in question.

At this point, if editors trusted the author, they would either agree to use such referees (e.g., referees whose names are known to the author and who will assume personal intellectual responsibility for their peer-review judgments), or else admit that they cannot find any such referees. If they claim the latter, it would mean that referees would not review manuscripts unless their identities remain secret. In such a case, editors could claim that the referees, not the editors, are responsible for peer-review secrecy.

If, on the other hand, editors admit that they use secrecy in their peer review in order to protect their referees from retaliation from the authors, then it is obvious that the secrecy is based on the fact that the referees do not trust the author. In such a case, it would be the alleged untrustworthy nature of the author that is responsible for peer-review secrecy.

Another alternative is for editors to say that they trust both authors and referees, but despite this trust they prefer to conduct their peer review in secret. In this case, however, they would then be admitting that they themselves are responsible for conducting secret scholarly communication operations that directly contradict their own professional rhetoric about open discussion and free exchange of ideas.

In any case, editors, referees, and authors are scholars and colleagues in their disciplines. Editors most likely have been, and continue to be, authors. The same is true for referees. Thus, when secrecy exists within the peer-review process of the literature of a scholarly discipline, no matter how the responsibility for secrecy is analyzed, it shows that scholars in that discipline tend to show a distrust, instead of mutual trust, toward each other, despite all the rhetoric to the contrary.

SECRECY AND VESTED INTERESTS

Once secrecy is established by means of editorial policy, this secrecy confers power to editors and referees to promote their own vested interests and special interests that remain hidden from other scholars and from the public. If they feel they have to falsify in order to promote these interests, secrecy allows them to avoid responsibility for falsifications.

In an academic climate in which editors and their institutions, friends, and colleagues and referees and their institutions, friends, and colleagues, are in keen competition with other scholars for grants, promotions, prizes, consultantships, and financial gains from research results (e.g., patents and contracts), the question arises whether anyone should be trusted with the peer-review secrecy that can conceal vested interests. Other questions might also arise. For example, if editors do not trust referees to give honest opinions if their names are revealed, why should editors trust them to reveal their conflicts of interest if these conflicts can be hidden by the secrecy of the referees' identities?

No matter whether editors trust neither referees nor authors, or whether they trust both groups, or trust one group but not the other, the questions just asked lead back to the question of why editors really want to operate within the realm of secrecy in the first place. It would seem that the best way to dispel any distrust on the part of any of the parties involved (authors, editors, and referees) would be to have all of their peer review actions and decisions out in the open so that they could be judged by their peers.

It may well be that the two-part article "Imbroglio at Yale: Emergence of a Fraud" would never have been written if peer review had been open instead of secret. As mentioned earlier, Broad (1980) related that Arnold Relman, editor of the *New England Journal of Medicine*, sent Helene Wachslicht-Rodbard's manuscript to Philip Felig for review. Felig showed the paper to his colleague Vijay Soman, and Felig then wrote Relman that the paper should be rejected. Soon after the rejection, Felig and Soman were coauthors of a very similar paper, containing some material from the rejected paper, that was sent to *American Journal of Medicine*, where Felig had an editorial leadership position.

If Felig and Soman had known beforehand that Felig's rejection advice and Felig's name as the author of the rejection advice were both to be communicated to Rodbard, maybe it would have seemed too risky for Felig and Soman to send their specific article, as it was written, to any journal. On the other hand, if the rejection advice could not be traced back to Felig, then Felig and Soman could have claimed they arrived at the same conclusions first. In this case, the conflict of interest would have remained secret if Relman had not been led to reveal to Rodbard (in the wake of her suspicions of plagiarism) that it was, indeed, Felig who recommended to him that Rodbard's paper be rejected (Broad, 1980)

As long as the names of referees remain secret, it is impossible to know how many other cases of similar referee activity have taken place. It is also impossible to tell precisely how many attempts at plagiarism by means of peer-review secrecy have been successful. It is obvious, however, that open peer review in the place of secret peer review would allow easier detection, with the result that fewer attempts at plagiarism of this type would take place.

Secrecy can cause doubts and problems at various other levels in addition to those involving referee reports. In the *Cell*–Baltimore case, it was reported that the NIH "decided to protect its five-member investigating panel from outside scrutiny, going so far as to keep their names secret" (Mervis, 1989, p. 1). It was also stated that Paul Friedman, who had previously handled important investigations in academia similar to the one involving Baltimore, "scoffs at the need to keep secret the members of the investigative panel ... anonymity is hardly the answer. It just isn't right to hide their names from everyone else who's involved in the investigation" (Mervis, 1989, pp. 1, 4). In such a case, it would not be possible to know if the secrecy was actually protecting the investigative panel members from the persons being investigated (and from their friendly colleagues), or if it was hiding evidence of a possible conflict of interest, based on collegial cover up, with the intention of absolving the persons under investigation. In any case, the decision to have scholars serving on a secret investigating panel was made at about the same time as an editorial appeared in *Science*, stating that "today's scientists need to realize that errors must be handled ... in full view of an anxious public" (Koshland, 1988, p. 637). Rhetoric and reality emerge again.

Problems of peer-review secrecy have been discussed in relation to doubts about the effectiveness or safety of the Salk polio vaccine:

> In answer to these charges there has been a curious silence. ... The charges of secrecy and restriction of pertinent data to a small handful of selected physicians is not a new one. It has been made twice by Dr. Wendell M. Stanley, Nobel Prize winner ... Dr. E. M. Krumbiegel ... Prof. Dr. Redeker ... Dr. Sven Gard ... have also made the same charge. (Ratner, 1988, p. 329)

Situations like this one might lead to the inference that as the commitment and stakes get higher, the perceived need for strategic secrecy and silence becomes greater.

COVER UP

One form of secrecy involved in high-stakes situations in which financial rewards and reputations are on the line is cover up. Problems associated with cover up came up during various phases of the *Cell*–Baltimore case. In this regard, Lang (1993) stated that "in some cases panels have actually contributed to intimidation or to covering up" (p. 44). Lang also pointed out that Imanishi-Kari herself was quoted as saying, "If OSI reaches the conclusion that there was misconduct on my part, then you have to conclude that MIT covered up and Tufts covered up" (p. 44). Lang then observed that "The OSI has now reached that conclusion" (p. 44).

Di Trocchio (1993) discussed the Stephen E. Bruening case at length, with considerable attention to the activities at the University of Pittsburgh and the NIH that resulted in long delays in investigations concerning misconduct. Sprague (1987) mentioned that the investigations dragged on for a long time, with the final report appearing "three years and five months after the investigation started" (p. 12)! Secrecy in peer review goes hand in hand with cover up of conflict of interest situations.

Secrecy in peer review (in its broad definition) also occurs when review of data is not allowed because of confidentiality, or when source material of one form or another is kept hidden from researchers. Hammerschmidt and Gross (1995), in their recent study of biomedical fraud, made some pertinent remarks on the subject:

> The author ... declined to produce the primary data for independent review. ... Even after fraud is suspected, the confidentiality that rules in peer review favours the perpetrator by inhibiting the investigation. ... We suggest that potential authors routinely give biomedical journals the right to scrutinize research records on demand. (pp. 3, 6, 10)

In his review of *Confronting the Experts*, Gratzer (1996) described similar problems involving secrecy: "So the evidence that sewage would not always sink and disperse ... was suppressed. Beder gained access to forbidden documents and fought her way through a morass of evasion and obfuscation by politicians and others" (p. 35). In *Intellectual Suppression*, Pugh (1986) stated that, in some cases involving university investigations, "elected representatives of academic staff" become "caught up in a conflict of interest situation" and, as a result, they might "prefer silence and secrecy" (p. 238).

Peer-review secrecy might often be involved in situations dealing with toxic, poisonous, and harmful substances. In "Hidden Hazards," Kasperson and Kasperson (1991) asked, "How is it, then, that certain hazards pass unnoticed ... growing in size until they have taken a serious toll? How is it that asbestos pervaded the American workplace and schools when its respiratory dangers had been known for decades?"

(p. 9). A partial answer might be found in a closed circle comprised of vested interests, conflicts of interest, and peer-review secrecy.

It would seem that if peer review were open rather than secret, conflicts of interest could be detected more easily, and the healthy skepticism that would be stimulated by such detection might result, in turn, in a greater possibility for the detection of error, or even for the accurate prediction of error. If peer review were based on trust and free of conflict of interest, there should be nothing to fear in terms of retaliation, and nothing to hide, and there would not seem to be any reason to prevent openness from replacing secrecy.

According to Walker (1994), there were gag clauses in experiments for testing AZT in treatment of AIDS patients. Scholars and doctors participating in the so-called Concorde Trials had to agree to have approval from Wellcome before publishing material based on the trials. The gag rule, it seems, extended to requiring doctors not to complain or object if they were not granted permission to publish their material. It would seem obvious that such gag rules impose a type of peer-review secrecy on certain findings and ideas.

In the case of AZT, negative criticism seems to have been muted at an early and crucial stage. When more vociferous negative criticisms were made, such as in Lauritsen's (1993) *Poison by Prescription: The AZT Story,* in Duesberg's (1996b) *Inventing the AIDS Virus,* Martin Walker's (1994) *Dirty Medicine,* and in *AIDS: La Grande Truffa,* by De Marchi and Franchi (1996), it appears that AZT had become an entrenched paradigm as a medicine for AIDS, if not the medicine. These later doubts seemed to have been brushed aside as AZT continued to be used widely. Some of Duesberg's criticisms of AZT have been taken up by the Italian press. An article in a leading national newspaper, the English title of which would be "Why We are Losing the War against AIDS," repeated Duesberg's claim that AZT is not only ineffective, but also dangerous. This article is, in effect, a discussion of Horton's (1996) review, which was translated into Italian in *La Rivista dei Libri* (Prattico, 1996). It is obvious, however, that a challenge to an entrenched paradigm is more difficult than a challenge, presented during open debate among scholars, that reveals evidence before the medicine attains paradigm status that the medicine is useless and dangerous.

SECRECY IMPEDES THE STUDY OF PEER REVIEW

Wenneras and Wold (1997) emphasized that an "in-depth analysis" of peer review "can be achieved only if the policy of secrecy is abandoned" (p. 343). Along this line, it is stated that the "policy of secrecy in evaluation must be abandoned" (p. 341). It would seem logical that one of the best forums for discussion of secrecy in peer review would be a conference or congress specifically organized to discuss peer review. A recent attempt, however, to engage in such a discussion at the International Congress on Biomedical Peer Review and Global Communications in Prague was rejected. The identities of the referees in this case remained secret, and the Congress

Director, Drummond Rennie, and the Congress Coordinator, Annette Flanagin, did not give the slightest hint to the author about what the referees said in their secret reports. The closest thing to a specific reason given (D. Rennie and A. Flanagin, personal communication, March 7, 1997) for the rejection of the paper, "The Peer Review Process and Questions of Trust, Openness, and Correction of Error," was that "priority" was given to "new and original research" and to abstracts that are "most relevant to and critical of the processes of peer review and scientific publication."

In their studies of peer-review practices at the Swedish Medical Research Council (MRC), Wenneras and Wold (1997) were able, by means of the Freedom of the Press Act, to gain access to much material that would otherwise have remained secret. Based on this material, Wenneras and Wold concluded that peer review at the MRC was characterized by sexism and nepotism. In terms of nepotism, they observed that "applicants who were affiliated with a committee member" received more favorable treatment than applicants "who lacked such ties" (pp. 342–343).

Regarding the influence of, and affiliation with, "committee" members, it would be interesting to know what Wenneras and Wold, or other scholars, would find if they could gain access to the secret peer-review material relating to the 1997 Prague peer-review congress. The program of this congress reveals that 3 days of this congress are devoted to peer review, with a fourth day devoted to the effects of electronic publishing on peer review. The program for the 3-day program on peer review includes 47 papers. No fewer than 11 members of the committee (i.e., advisory board) that organized (and that controls) this congress, including Rennie and Flanagin, had their papers receive peer review acceptance. In fact, four of Rennie's papers were accepted, as were four of another advisory board member, Richard Smith. (In addition to Rennie and Smith, three other advisory board members had more than one paper accepted.) In fact, 22 of the 47 papers that were accepted are authored by members of the advisory board or by their coauthors (or coauthors of their coauthors). These facts indicate that nepotism in peer review is not limited to the practices of the MRC (Campanario, 1996a). Under these circumstances, it is easy to understand that a paper dealing with questions of "openness" in peer review was rejected.

It is obvious that the secrecy of peer review makes it difficult, if not impossible, to study the secrecy of peer review, or to make a comprehensive study of peer review itself. A rather strange and somewhat inexplicable episode illustrates this point. In 1990, *Library Journal* sent out a request to a scholar to write a review of Noble's (1990) book *Bookbanning in America*. The review was written, as requested, and sent to the book review editor of *Library Journal*. Some time later (a few years or so), the author of the review wrote to the publisher, inquiring about where reviews of the book had been published, because it was not possible to trace or track down any published reviews. The publisher replied with a list of several publications, including *Library Journal* and *Wilson Library Bulletin*.

By the middle of 1996, it was possible to trace, through *Library Literature's* review sections from 1989 through 1994, notices of reviews of Noble's book published in *Choice* (January 1991), *ALA Booklist* (October 1990), and the *Newsletter on*

Intellectual Freedom (March 1991), but not the other journals that the publisher mentioned. This represented a very strange and confusing situation and another letter of inquiry was sent to the publisher (G. Moran, personal communication, May 9, 1996), which containing the following:

> I am very interested in the situation at *Library Journal* and *Wilson Library Bulletin*. Do you know if these two journals actually published reviews of *Bookbanning in America*? If so, could you please kindly send me copies of the reviews, or at least let me know which issues contain the reviews? If these two journals did not publish reviews, despite your listing them as reviewers of the book, do you have any idea why they did not?

Meanwhile, more than one letter had been written to the book review editor of *Library Journal*, asking about the publication of the review of *Bookbanning in America*. No replies have been received from *Library Journal*, nor has a reply been received from the publisher in response to the last letter of inquiry. It seems possible that reviews of the book were suppressed after they had been requested, written, and sent in. In any case, it does not seem that the book review department officials at *Library Journal* or the head of the publishing company are willing to discuss what took place. Secrecy seems to reign, and authors of the unpublished reviews are silenced in this case.

All this secrecy about suppression of reviews that the head of the publishing house thought would be published is baffling. Somebody, or a group of persons, might have been upset or uncomfortable about some aspect of the book, or about the specific reviews that were written but remain unpublished. Perhaps the following passages from the book have some bearing on the situation:

> Usually, challenges to books galvanized from the Right. ... the bookbanner had seemed to materialize from the conservative side. ... Now all of a sudden the bookbanner came from a different direction. ... Here is where bookbanners on the left have joined bookbanners on the right in lockstep. ... The consequence has to follow: no one is safe from assuming that what didn't offend in one generation might continue to not offend in another generation. (Noble, 1990, pp. 270, 273–274)

It might be that, somewhere along the line, these passages (and others related to them) hit a raw nerve relating to political correctness that led to some peer-review secrecy and silencing of scholars as far as the unpublished reviews are concerned. At any rate, political correctness itself has become one of the most acute problems of all concerning the silencing of scholars.

11

Politically Correct

As the religion professor delivers a lecture ... at the Chicago Theological Seminary, a school official sits nearby with a tape recorder, a kind of word cop, in case the professor says anything sexually offensive. ... Professor Snyder recited a story from the Talmud, the writings that make up Jewish civil and religious law. ... A woman in the class was offended ... because she believed the story justified brutality toward women. She filed a complaint ... Mr. Snyder, an ordained minister ... has used the Talmudic lesson in the classroom for more than 30 years. The university issued a formal reprimand and notified every student and teacher at the school. (Johnson, 1994, p. 1)

This situation at Chicago Theological Seminary shows that silencing of scholars by means of application of so-called political correctness pressures is a complicated subject, filled with ambiguity, contradictions, trendiness, and changing academic attitudes based on the political fashion of the time. In this case, a passage from a sacred scripture that had been used for decades by a professor, Graydon Snyder, to illustrate questions of ethics and morality to his students was suddenly declared politically incorrect. Furthermore, the professor was punished for using the passage as part of classroom discussions.

It would seem that the term *politically correct*, as it has been applied on campuses, is itself inherently self-contradictory in a democracy, where it is not politically correct, by nature of democracy itself, to impose a specific politically correct stance that curtails freedom of expression and academic freedom. As discussed in Chapter 1, dictatorships impose political correctness within their territorial jurisdiction.

INTELLECTUAL FREEDOM AND THE DELETION OF
POLITICALLY INCORRECT LANGUAGE

A recent publication of the Office for Intellectual Freedom (OIF) of the ALA reveals some problems involving intellectual freedom and the ambiguous, complicated, and contradictory nature of political correctness. It would seem that officials of OIF would be allies of Snyder and other scholars whose writings or teaching materials have clashed with political correctness on campus at a given time. In fact, the January 1991 *Memorandum* (with its *Attachments*) by Krug and Levinson, sent to "Chapter Intellectual Freedom Committees," included the following ideas:

> Everyone has the right to freedom of opinion and expression. ... We know that censorship, ignorance, and limitations on the free flow of information are the tools of tyranny and oppression. ... Any effort to restrict free expression and the free flow of information aids the oppressor. ... We believe that ... pressures towards conformity present the danger of limiting the range and variety of inquiry and expression on which our democracy and our culture depend. ... It is wrong that what one can read should be confined to what another thinks proper. ... Freedom is no freedom if it is accorded only to the accepted and the inoffensive. ... We realize that the application of these propositions may mean the dissemination of ideas and manners of expression that are repugnant to many persons. (Krug & Levinson, 1991, Attachment I, pp. 1–2; Attachment VII, pp. 1–2, 4–6)

These are strong words. There would seem to be little doubt that the ALA OIF leadership affirmed, with this issue of *Memorandum*, that a truly politically correct stance allows freedom of expression and freedom to read. Professor Snyder, after reading these words and ideas, might feel he was justified, after all, to cite and discuss passages from sacred scripture (e.g., the Talmud) that some persons considered to be sexist and, therefore, politically incorrect.

In this same issue of *Memorandum*, however, one also read, "The Intellectual Freedom Committee, and the Freedom to Read Committee of the Association of American Publishers ... recently completed a review of the document. ... Editorial changes have been made to delete sexist language" (Krug & Levinson, 1991, p. 3). After reading about this combined action of these two committees, authorities at Chicago Theological Seminary might feel justified in deleting sexist language from classroom discussions, including sexist language and ideas in sacred texts that constitute religious law. After all, if the OIF itself felt that expressions that are sexist should not be allowed in their own literature, why should academic authorities allow similar expression (i.e., sexist) in their classrooms or elsewhere on campus?

A CASE STUDY OF POLITICAL CORRECTNESS
AT ITHACA COLLEGE

Officials at Ithaca College in Ithaca, New York instituted a "remedial action" program for a tenured professor who was found to have used "sexual innuendo" and "sexual allusion" during teaching. Such innuendo and illusion were considered unacceptable, based on principles of political correctness that held sway at the time. A Memo by the Provost, dated November 13, 1992, indicated that unacceptable "examples of language" included "a climaxing moment," and the professor's suggestion to cello students to create "a tone that is transparent like a negligee." The remedial actions included the instructions to "stop immediately the use of sexual innuendo in any and all ... teaching settings," and also "to purge all sexual allusions from ... presentations." Classes of the professor were monitored by an Ithaca College authority to observe compliance. The "transparent like a negligee" phrase had apparently been used for years by the professor as a teaching device, similar to the use of the passage from the Talmud by the scholar at Chicago Theological Seminary.

Monitors (or other persons) at Ithaca College discovered that subsequently there was "continued use" of sexual allusions and innuendo in the classroom, including phrases such as "tuning is an intimate experience," "we only leave the womb once," and "follow through with an olympic stroke." The President of Ithaca College then wrote, in a communication to the professor, dated August 17, 1993, "your behavior cannot and will not be tolerated by Ithaca College. Accordingly, you are hereby dismissed from your employment with Ithaca College, effective immediately." As far as can be determined, the Board of Trustees and the leadership of alumni groups of Ithaca College approved of this firing of a tenured professor, or at least gave their consent by silence in the face of letters of inquiry about whether they approved of the action. This case at Ithaca College leads to the question of whether or not it is possible to eliminate and "purge" all sexual allusions and innuendo from all "teaching settings" without removing books from the college library that contain such allusions and innuendo. Students in all disciplines might go to the library, in the wake of a class lecture or discussion, to look for material that discusses the subject matter in more detail, or to look for background material on the subject. Such consultation of material could easily be described and defined as being within teaching settings.

Suppose that the Ithaca College professor had refrained, once remedial actions had been put into effect, from making any more sexual allusions and innuendo in the classroom (and in the studio or concert rooms where the students practiced and rehearsed their music). Suppose also that students, after attending classes that were free of sexual allusions and innuendo, went to the library in search of background material relating to their courses. Such background material is filled with what college authorities might regard as sexual allusion and innuendo. For example, students might come across the following passages (among many similar ones) in material relating to their courses: "frankly sensuous passion ... purely sensuous effect" (Grant, 1965, pp. 414–415). Students doing research on the music of Richard Strauss might read a reference to "a physique suitably voluptuous for shedding the seven veils" (Kupferberg, 1975, p. 99), and other music students might find this passage in a book by the famous musician Yehudi Menuhin (1981): "Like love which requires two to become one, so violin playing becomes alive with the complete integration and coordination of both hands" (p. 126).

Now suppose that a student checked out from the library one or more books with such allusions and innuendos, brought the books into class (while the political correctness monitors were present), and started to discuss the contents of the books with classmates and with the professor. Would the monitor (perhaps a dean, in this case) and authorities punish the student as well as the professor? Would the monitor confiscate the books?

Cornog and Perper (1992) wrote an article "For Sex, See Librarian," in which they invoked the ethical "framework" of the "Freedom to Read ideal" (p. 12). They explained that the Freedom to Read ideal was formulated by the ALA, with its "watchword" of "All points of view on all questions" being "surely known to all librarians" (p. 9). They stated further that "the Freedom to Read ethic" has become "the official ... stance of professional librarianship" (p. 9). According to this ideal, in the view of Cornog and Perper, the librarian "accepts the *totality* of outpourings of the human mind and soul concerning sexuality and all its moral issues" (p. 12). The Freedom to Read ideal, it would seem, also allows access to readers of this totality, and not only to librarians (unless the ALA, in formulating the ideal, and Cornog and Perper, in invoking it, were speaking for themselves only, rather than for the public at large, which would include professors and their students).

The Cornog and Perper (1992) article appeared at about the time of the political correctness episode at Ithaca College. Inquiries were made (G. Moran, personal communication, October 28, 1993) of Cornog and Perper in relation to their article, to the Freedom to Read ideal, and to the Ithaca College situation, based on the following: A hypothetical situation is described in which a powerful right-wing political leader, known for his outspoken views against pornography, after leaving his job with the government, became the president of a university or college, and, once in office, sent a written message to all faculty members. The message, in this hypothetical case, instructed faculty members to purge all sexual allusions and innuendo from all teaching and classroom settings. Further, the message would state that monitors would be sent into classrooms where there were reported violations. Professors who continued to use sexual allusions, or what the monitors interpreted as sexual innuendo, would be fired.

Cornog and Perper were asked: "If a powerful group of academics said such things, is it somehow different" than if a powerful political leader, now turned academic administrator, said the same things? They were also asked if "the same words would have an ethical justification *if* or *because* powerful academics wrote them?" Another pertinent question was asked: "And from the standpoint of the 'Freedom to Read ideal,' do you think it is really possible to 'purge all sexual allusions' from 'instructional presentations' and ... teaching settings without 'creating' an ethical basis to purge such material from the academic libraries also?" No reply has been received, and silence reigns.

It is not known how many scholars have actually been silenced, to one degree or another (ranging from deletion and suppression of specific teaching material, to being fired), as a result of political correctness censorship. Limbaugh (1993) described a case at the University of Alaska where a professor described a situation in which, in Limbaugh's words, "the faculty was under pressure to graduate some native students who had not yet mastered the required skills" (p. 235). It was reported that the professor was declared a racist, was not allowed to teach courses in the education department, and was investigated by the university authorities and also by the U.S. Office of Civil Rights. The professor apparently was not intimidated, and she defended herself from the charges. Limbaugh wrote, "She fought back and she won. We don't hear much about the thousands of political correctness victims who roll over and lose. But their numbers must be legion" (p. 235). In one era and in one place there was Kristallnacht, and in other times and other places political correctness knocked.

In some states such as Michigan and Wisconsin, codes restricting speech that have been drawn up by university authorities have been overturned by the courts or by specific laws (Johnson, 1994) However, formal codes are not needed for powerful academic authorities to equate unwanted speech with intolerable behavior. There is no reference, for example, in the August 17, 1993 communication (in which the Ithaca College President fired a professor) to the violation of a specific speech code, but rather to "behavior" that "cannot and will not be tolerated."

Ambiguity regarding expression and behavior can work in favor of the censors and suppressors. Burning something might be an evil act or a protected means of expression. Burning a flag might be considered a means of expression, whereas waving a flag or merely displaying one might be considered an intolerable act amid the ambiguity that pervades the political correctness scene.

It would seem that the concept of labeling as a form of censorship is also fraught with ambiguity. In *Memorandum*, Krug and Levinson (1991) included an attachment, *THE FREEDOM TO READ* (Attachment VII), which speaks out against the "prejudgment of a label," on the basis that "labeling presupposes the existence of individuals or groups with wisdom to determine by authority what is good or bad for the citizen" (pp. 4–5). In this case, reference is made to the labels "subversive" and "dangerous" (p. 4). (Other potential labels might include "immoral," "pornographic," "sexist," "racist," and so on.) It is not specified in the attachment whether labels are written or verbal, nor is it specified whether the concept of labeling applies only to books already in a library collection, or also extends to books that are being considered for library acquisitions. In any case, in the midst of these negative comments about labeling, it seems that Krug and Levinson (1991) and their colleagues decided to label (verbally) parts of one of their own attachments (e.g., Attachment VII) as "sexist" and, as a result, decided to make deletions in the text: "Minor editorial changes have been made to delete sexist language" (p. 3).

CAMPUS PUBLICATIONS AND POLITICAL CORRECTNESS

In fact, much of recent political correctness censorship has been directed against expression that has been given the label of "sexist" or "racist." Campus publications have been among the targets for such censorship. For example, an editorial in *USA Today* with the title, "Keep Our Speech Free" (*USA Today,* 1993) affirmed that "At 29 campuses in 14 months, PC thieves swiped thousands ... of newspapers they deemed offensive. ... University of Maryland's *Diamondback* lost 10,000 copies to snatchers who labeled it 'racist'" (p. 8A). And at Pennsylvania State University "women ... stole 4,000 copies of the *Lionhearted*" (p. 8A).

The suppression of publications on campus has been a long-term aspect of political correctness. What is being censored, suppressed, and silenced at the time depends on what the specific political trends or fashions are that determine the specific politically correct stance of the day. Schrecker (1986) related that in 1947, "the dean of students refused to let the organization put out its magazine, *The New Student,* as an official Harvard publication. Claiming that the format was too polished to be the work of undergraduates, the dean ... called in *The New Student's* editors and grilled them about their politics" (p. 87). The student magazine soon was forced to cease publication. The editors and their magazine were leftist. McQueen (1988) reported that, a few decades later, Dartmouth officials punished student editors of *Dartmouth Review*: "Dartmouth spokesman ... says ... *Review* editors were suspended after they provoked a verbal battle ... and Dartmouth English professor ... Jeffrey Hart ... testified that university officials abhorred the *Review's* call for greater emphasis on traditional college humanities courses" (p. 3). The student editors and their publication in this case were conservative.

THE CHANGING WINDS AND TIDES OF POLITICAL CORRECTNESS

What is consistent in these cases is the effort of powerful academic authorities to silence campus publications that the authorities feel are not politically correct. What changes is the notion, on the part of academic authorities, of what is politically correct or incorrect. At one point, Harvard authorities silenced leftist publications, and at another point Dartmouth authorities acted to silence conservative publications. At certain times, academic freedom, intellectual freedom, and freedom of expression might be considered the most politically correct values, whereas at other times academic authorities might consider academic freedom to be less politically correct than other forms of political correctness that are in vogue at the moment.

This last statement can be illustrated by whether or not scholars will be invited to speak, or whether they will be banned (silenced) from speaking on campus. It can be further illustrated by whether or not scholars, once they are invited to speak, will actually be allowed to speak or will be drowned out (silenced) by one heckling tactic or another. It can be illustrated even further by whether or not they will be allowed to speak and at the same time be protected from criticism by means of drowning out (silencing) the criticism.

Many Communist or Marxist scholars were banned (silenced) from speaking on U.S. campuses from 1939 to 1941, and later during the Cold War and McCarthy era. Schrecker (1986) observed:

> As the Cold War intensified, academic authorities became increasingly reluctant to let Communist, and later merely controversial, speakers address their students. Speaker bans were hardly new. In the previous red scare of 1939–1941, Harvard, Dartmouth, Brooklyn, Cornell, Vassar, New York University, Princeton, Oberlin, Swarthmore, and Smith all barred Party leader Earl Browder from speaking. During the late forties and early fifties, college restrictions against outside speakers intensified. Faculties were often as repressive as administrations. The Faculty Lecture Committee of the University of Michigan routinely refused to let left-wing student or faculty groups bring speakers onto the campus. (pp. 89–90)

It was not considered politically correct to allow them to speak.

As the Cold War cooled down, it came to be considered politically correct to allow controversial speakers to speak on campus, in the name of academic freedom. In effect, political correctness on campus became associated, to one degree or another, with academic freedom. However, this does not mean that in specific cases various means were not employed to favor one ideology over another. Sometimes, conflicting notions of what is politically correct exist at the same time, and attempts are made to enforce them. For instance, the following appeared in an editorial entitled "Yale's Beastly Behavior" (Wall Street Journal, 1986): "Free speech and academic freedom have not got much respect from liberals these last few years. Reagan officials have to avoid certain campuses." Meanwhile, Relyea (1994) and Pell (1984) gave detailed accounts of how President Ronald Reagan and leaders in his administration tried to enforce their own ideas about what was politically correct.

Schrecker (1986) documented many cases of leftist scholars who were not allowed to speak on campus because their ideas were not considered politically correct at the time. By contrast, Lang showed how, in the mid-1980s, it was deemed politically incorrect to point out and discuss defective scholarship of the Marxist scholar Jon Wiener, who had been invited by the American Studies Department to speak at Yale. Lang related that he had become aware of defective scholarship and "defamatory journalism" practiced by Wiener, and, as a result, he asked the "Chairman of American Studies for the opportunity to speak." This request was denied. Lang stated that he "had trouble" delivering a critical statement about Jon Wiener's scholarship during the public discussion of this forum organized by the American Studies Department, because of restrictions imposed by Jean-Christophe Agnew (who was then Director of Undergraduate Studies of the department), and because, as Lang described it, "there were catcalls and shouts of 'throw him out'." In addition, Lang related that he had "asked American Studies for a copy of Mr. Wiener's remarks so that he could analyze what was said, but that no text has been provided." (Lang's documentation for this event, and for events stemming from it, are found in his "file" study "The Teaching and Learning File," a copy of which was given to the main library at Yale University.)

A case can be made that in this episode it seems that Agnew and others present at the meeting felt that academic freedom was not as politically correct as the perceived need to protect a Marxist scholar from adverse criticism relating to defective scholarship. A scholar's point of view was silenced at the meeting to protect another scholar. Thus, from a historical and chronological standpoint, factors relating to political correctness at one point silenced Communist–Marxist scholars, at another point tolerated them, and at still another point protected them from criticism of defective scholarship. Now that the Soviet empire has collapsed, the Cold War has been put in the deep freeze (or has already melted away), and Marxism has been discredited, perhaps sometime in the future notions of political correctness will not enter into suppression, promotion, or protection of Marxist studies or discussions. Instead, criticism of Marxists and of specific Marxist scholarship might be regarded as a normal aspect of specialized political science research. Promotion of Marxism might someday be revived on a large scale, or attempts to revive Marxism might be viewed as the equivalent of trying to bring a dead horse back to life.

It should be emphasized that historical trends regarding political correctness in relation to anti-Communism, pro-Marxism, or post-Marxism are not clear cut, but may be overlapping during a specific year or years. At about the same time that criticism of a Marxist scholar was being silenced at Yale, a Marxist scholar at McGill University, David Mandel, was apparently becoming a "victim of unprofessional" conduct on the part of university authorities. As Cude (1987b) described the case, Mandel's "publications were Marxist, he had cancelled classes to show solidarity with striking McGill maintenance workers and his sympathies were pro-Palestinian on the Mid-East situation. While his students admired him, some of his fellow professors detested him, and so they hired an American instead" (p. C7). That specific decision was seemingly "in defiance of Canadian immigration regulations" (p. C7), which state that non-Canadians can be hired only in the absence of Canadians who qualify.

The changing winds and fortunes of political correctness indicate that academic "politics" can be an important aspect of success or failure. Many leftist scholars lost out in the 1950s, and others struck it rich a few decades later on the same campuses where their predecessors lost out. Mandel lost out at McGill at a time that his fellow Marxist Wiener was being protected from criticism at Yale.

A VARIETY OF CASE STUDIES

The concept of political correctness can be extended far in more than one direction. Devastating charges of being subversive, racist, anti-American, anti-Semitic, sexist, and so on, can be exaggerated and falsified, but also made to stick (resulting in punishment). In hindsight, many such charges might be considered as serious violations of academic freedom, unfair and unjust, or tyrannical denials of due process.

Political correctness can also be related to intellectual paradigms in academia. There is an interesting case in which it seems that ideological and intellectual paradigms are intertwined. Greenhouse (1988) related that, about half a century ago, Bourgin wrote a dissertation at the University of Chicago, in which he challenged "a then-common notion that ... Roosevelt's social programs departed from the lassez-faire principles of the U.S. government in its early days" (p. 1). His dissertation was rejected and he did not get his degree. A few decades or so later, he showed his failed dissertation to Arthur Schlesinger, Jr., who "praised the work as pioneering, and who enthusiastically urged Chicago's political science department to take a fresh look" (p. 1). They did, and this time around the dissertation was deemed of sufficient quality (politically correct?) and the scholar was finally awarded his degree. Greenhouse mentioned that one member of the dissertation committee (the second time around) that accepted the work remarked, "The world is full of former graduate students who have failed to get their PhDs" (p. 1).

It might be that when Bourgin was writing his dissertation, Roosevelt's policies were about as politically correct to the University of Chicago political science department as Ronald Reagan's policies were at Yale in the 1980s. In any case, Bourgin and his ideas were silenced. Who knows how many of the many former graduate students who have failed to get their degrees might have been silenced for reasons of political correctness rather than for defective scholarship?

The silence imposed by political correctness can extend beyond the classroom or publications and dissertation committees. During a wedding reception in England around 1990, a Yale alumnus related that at a recent gathering where the famous Yale singing group, Whiffenpoofs, were performing, he requested one of the group's traditional and favorite old-time standby songs, "Daddy Is a Yale Man." He said that he was told that it had been banned and that they would not sing it (apparently because it was sexist).

My Fair Lady was a spectacular success as a Broadway musical in the 1950s, and became a multiple-Oscar winner as a movie. Who knows if the same play would have been boycotted, picketed, panned, or even banned from New Haven if it had opened there around 1990, instead of on Broadway in the 1950s. The lyrics and dialogue are at least on the same scale as "Daddy Is a Yale Man," as far as political correctness is concerned.

As has been shown, notions of political correctness change as political trends and fashions develop in varying directions. The pace and degree of these changes are not always predictable. This unpredictability itself can also lead to silencing of scholars who might become cautious and prudent to avoid getting into political correctness predicaments. Noble (1990) asserted that "once a restriction is placed upon free expression, it will be enforced in ways no one can truly predict ... one man's limitation will be another's unburdening, making it impossible to forecast what will develop" (p. 237). Such uncertainty is underscored in Kimball's (1990) remark that "it is a sobering irony that what began as an appeal by the Left for free speech at Berkeley in the sixties has ended with an equally fervent appeal by the Left for the imposition of censorship" (p. 69).

Ladd and Lipset compiled "The 1977 Survey of The American Professoriate" and sent it to many scholars. Not all of them filled it out. One professor wrote that "the contents of that questionnaire, if answered correctly by any but milk-toast, middle-of-the-roader academics, could jeopardize the employment status of people even slightly off-center in either political direction if the political climate were only slightly less tolerant than at present" (Lang, 1981, p. 213). That scholar's reaction can give a good idea of how sensitivity to political correctness might lead scholars into silence. At what point does prudence and caution become transformed into intimidation that results in silence in certain subjects?

In addition to notions of political correctness dealing with sexism, racism, multiculturalism, and ethnic diversity on a general level, there are narrower aspects of political correctness that apply to specific academic disciplines, departments, or research centers. Sometimes they might be referred to as academic politics, departmental politics, politics of science, or similar names. As mentioned, Gallo and his AIDS research was involved in the politics of science, and he was silenced about public discussion of "Dingell ... or the patent for the HIV blood test." (Zimmerman, 1995, p. 1)

Gallo's politics of science in this case was conditioned by controversy over specific governmental subsidized research that was under investigation. By contrast, the case of Scott Nearing shows that academic politics can be broad-based as well as specific, as his scholarly ideas were considered politically incorrect by a variety of sources that had differing political orientation. He "was dismissed from the Wharton School of Economics in 1915 due to his opposition to child labour in Pennsylvania" (Martin, 1986a, p. 181). He was also "charged with sedition over his anti-war book *The Great Madness*" and he could not enter Britain "because of his outspoken opposition to colonialism" (p. 181). But Nearing's political views did not please the Communist Party either, which expelled him in 1929 "for refusing to change his views in his book on imperialism" (p. 181).

In her studies of the effects of McCarthyism on academia, Schrecker (1986) stated that "medical schools ... seemed to care less about academic freedom than other types of educational institutions," and she pointed out that Jefferson Medical College "was particularly insensitive to such concerns" (p. 244). In light of her comments, it is interesting to note that some recent studies in the field of medical research actually use the term *politically correct* in discussion of suppression of research findings, theories, and ideas. In *Dirty Medicine*, Mumby (1992) said:

> I feel that everyone ought to be warned what is in the wind. What is being attempted here is a serious hijacking of a statutory body, the General Medical Council, for the express purpose of suppressing freedom within medicine and eliminating people who practice medicine which is not politically correct. (Mumby, cited in Walker, 1994, p. 557)

Duesberg (1995) discussed his battles with the AIDS establishment by making use of the same term:

> The AIDS virus also proved to be the politically correct cause of AIDS. No AIDS risk group could be blamed for being infected by a God-given egalitarian virus. ... Once accepted as the politically correct explanation of AIDS, the HIV hypothesis has become the central investment for a whole generation of AIDS scientists, AIDS companies, AIDS journalists, AIDS politicians and gay activists. ... Claiming this priority, the virus-AIDS orthodoxy justifies intolerance, even censorship, of all those who question infectious AIDS. ... (pp. 515–516)

He also wrote, "In this era of centralized, government-sponsored science, an article against politically correct science can be fatal for a journalist" (Duesberg, 1996b, p. 335).

In her discussion of women's studies and "feminist critique," Hannah (1986) observed that in Australia after World War II, universities expanded within "the English tertiary system with its classical traditions and conservative outlook. ... The almost total absence of women both as teachers and students ... was taken to be the natural order of things" (p. 201). This reference to the "natural order of things" perhaps could be the equivalent to the nature of political correctness at that time. More recently, some persons might consider it the natural order of things for a theology professor to be punished for discussing (as he had been doing for many years) a passage from the Talmud, or for a music professor to be punished for mentioning a "tone that is transparent like a negligee."

Barbash (1996) described an interesting case involving the concept of political correctness. Cambridge University Press asked a "panel of experts" to review a manuscript for a book that had been submitted by a scholar at the State University of New York at Stony Brook. The panel "enthusiastically endorsed" it. A Cambridge University Press official was also quoted as stating that "there was no doubt the manuscript was extremely high quality" (p. 9). Nevertheless, the publisher decided to cancel publication of Anastasia Karakasidou's book. It was not politically correct in some circles, so much so that the author, it seems, has even received death threats. In the wake of the decision not to publish the book, three peer reviewers and editorial board members of Cambridge University Press "have resigned or dissociated themselves from the publishing house" (p. 9). In this case, both the publisher and the publisher's peer reviewers agreed that the scholar's work was of high quality, but the scholar was silenced nevertheless as the publisher caved in to political forces that did not consider the work politically correct.

Why did the peer reviewers protest the cancellation of this book? One of them, Hertzfeld, claimed the publisher "was acting to protect commercial interests in Greece" (Barbash, 1996, p. 9). Yet, many publishers act, on an almost daily basis, to protect their commercial interests in one location or another. Was Hertzfeld concerned, instead, about the silencing of Karakasidou because such silencing is contrary to the academic rhetoric about open debate, free exchange of ideas, and academic freedom? Or, is it possible that Hertzfeld felt that the author of the book stated the politically correct point of view in the book and that it should not be opposed? If the author's political adversaries had submitted a manuscript to Cambridge University Press, would the same peer reviewers have approved it, and would they have protested in the same manner if the publisher had canceled the book, under political pressure, despite peer-review approval?

A recent newspaper article by Carvajal (1996), with the headline "U.S. Holocaust Debate Is Silenced," begins, "At the urging of a German publisher and its controversial American author, New York University abruptly canceled a long-planned symposium of Holocaust scholars" (p. 2). The symposium was organized by Deutsches Haus and participants were to include scholars from Harvard, Rutgers, Bryn Mawr, Columbia, and Tel Aviv University, and attendance of about 200 persons was expected.

It is considered a violation of political correctness to attempt to deny that the Holocaust took place (not to mention a violation of the ethical requirement of a scholar's commitment to truth), or to give it a lesser than historical dimension. At the same time, it also seems that in some circles it is considered politically incorrect to claim that a large section of the German population itself was responsible, to a degree, for the Holocaust. In any case, the official reason given for the cancellation of the New York University symposium was that Goldhagen's (1996) book, *Hitler's Willing Executioners: Ordinary Germans and the Holocaust*, was to be discussed at the symposium, and because Goldhagen would not be present "the organizers decided to cancel the symposium because they considered it unfair to discuss his book without his participation" (Carvajal, 1996, p. 2).

By contrast, it seems that discussions of a book by Velikovsky used a different standard for fairness:

> The ... settings provided for the discussion of Velikovsky's work were mostly arranged ... by hostile critics or intimidated moderators. He was excluded from discussion of his own work. ... The *Proceedings of the American Philosophical Society*, which in 1952 carried extensive attacks upon him, would not suffer his reply. (de Grazia, 1978, pp. 173–179)

Was it fairness, or questions of political correctness, that caused the New York University symposium to be silenced?

According to a recent article by Williams (1996), it has not been politically correct in Italy to discuss the use of poison gas by the Italians against the Ethiopians in 1935. In the article, "Italy Peers Reluctantly into 2 Faces of Its Wartime Past," Williams claimed that "60 tons of a poison ... were dropped on Ethiopian soldiers" (p. 6). An Italian historian, Angelo Del Bocca, was quoted as saying, "There has not been a government that has favored a serious discussion of what we did in Africa" (p. 6). Because Italian universities are, for the most part, under direct central government control, it is understandable how "serious discussions" of a subject not politically correct had been silenced.

It was politically correct, it seems, to protect "Europe's beef market," but not politically correct to warn about health dangers. At least that is one of the themes of an article by Buerkle (1996) that begins "The European Commission sought to silence a German scientist who warned about a risk to human health from 'mad cow' disease more than one year before Britain admitted a probable hazard" (p. 1). At present, it seems that scientific evidence for mad cow disease and a direct relation to human disease is scanty. If strong evidence were to come to light in the future, demonstrating that mad cow disease was becoming rampant and also that there was a direct link to human diseases, then it might become much more politically correct in this case to warn about health dangers than it would be to protect a region's beef industry.

A good idea of how political correctness tends to silence scholars might be conveyed by the following passage:

> Ideas and activities once tolerated came under attack. Professors and administrators responded by revising the normally vague definition of academic freedom to exclude in a surprisingly explicit way the types of behavior the rest of the community did not like. (Schrecker, 1986, p. 14)

The same could be true for the observation that "what had been tolerated before becomes intolerable now" (Schrecker, 1986, p. 20).

The professor who was suddenly punished in the 1990s for describing a story from the Talmud, as he had been doing for decades before then, might regard these passages as pertinent references to his own case. And the tenured professor who was fired from Ithaca College for saying things like "a tone that is transparent like a negligee" (as he had been doing for years), might believe that these passages could refer to his own situation. However, neither of the two passages was intended to be prophetic. The first one describes academic freedom cases from the end of the 19th century to the 1950s. The second is from the commencement address that the President of Columbia University delivered in 1917.

The cases discussed in this chapter are merely a small sampling of the documentation that demonstrates how academic freedom can take a back seat to whatever politically correct stance holds sway and is being enforced according to the political climate of the day on campus. Intimidation leads to a chilling effect, which in turn leads to a silencing effect. Part of this intimidation results in the form of not citing works that might otherwise have been cited and discussed. This can lead to an "out of cite, out of mind" phenomenon that silences scholars and their ideas.

12

Out of Cite, Out of Mind

The figure of Guidoriccio da Fogliano is therefore the illustrated figure of the topographical map of the Sienese republic. (Venturi, 1907, p. 614)

In reality we have in the so-called Guidoriccio a remaining external part of the map. (Zeri, 1988, p. 52)

The first of these passages is from about seven decades before the Guido Riccio controversy broke out. The second is from about a decade or so into the controversy, when it was at an intensive phase. Both represent very similar ideas, and have been overlooked, ignored, and not specifically cited by scholars who have attempted to shore up the traditional paradigm that Simone Martini painted the figure of Guido Riccio on horseback. More revealing, a recent extensive study by Kupfer (1996) of the map in question does not even cite, much less discuss, the items from 1907 and 1988, even though the authors of both items, Venturi and Zeri, specifically claimed that the figure of Guido Riccio was an actual integral part of the very map that was the precise subject matter of Kupfer's study. This situation illustrates that scholars' ideas can fall into the silence of oblivion as a result of the out of cite, out of mind treatment.

WHO DISCOVERED THE CAUSE OF CHILDBIRTH FEVER?

Silencing of scholars and their ideas by means of the out of cite, out of mind treatment can have tragic consequences. The suffering and deaths caused by childbirth fever serve as a grim reminder. Semmelweis is often associated with the discovery of the cause of childbirth fever. However, according to Ruesch (1978/1991), the original discovery did not belong to Semmelweis:

> Others before Semmelweis had suggested that puerperal fever might be a contagious disease, and that hygiene could prevent it; but they had been laughed at. ... In 1795 Scotsman Alexander Gordon gave ample proof that the disease was contagious, in a paper titled "Treatise of the Epidemic Puerperal Fever of Aberdeen," in which he stressed the need for disinfection. ... Although the evidence he offered was indisputable, it went under amid the general hilarity of the medical giants. ... In 1843 Oliver Wendell Holmes ... wrote "The Contagiousness of Puerperal Fever." It also met vigorous opposition from the leading obstetricians, and its facts began being acknowledged only after it had been enlarged and reprinted in 1855. ... English historian, Lord Moynihan, called it "one of the greatest essays ever written in the history of medicine." Semmelweis had not heard of the English works when he came to the same conclusions. ... Semmelweis returned to his native Budapest and published a book about his findings. But as his countrymen, too, derided him ... he died without witnessing the triumph of his ideas. ... Semmelweis and the few of a like mind obtained recognition a quarter of a century later. (pp. 166–168)

The out of cite, out of mind situation goes even further, in this case. de Grazia (1984) pointed out that Gordon, Holmes, and Semmelweis were all preceded by Charles White, who, in 1773, "had insisted upon absolute cleanliness in the lying-in hospital" (p. 28). As de Grazia observed, "It took about a century from White's obsessive insistence upon cleanliness in Manchester's lying-in wards to consensus about a matter that should have been simple enough to grasp" (p. 29). Who knows if other scholars did not precede White in relation to the cause and prevention of childbirth fever?

WARNINGS ABOUT POTENTIAL DANGERS AND DISASTERS

In 1895, Charles Bell Taylor wrote, "It is not true that we owe our knowledge of drugs to experiments upon animals. The effect of drugs upon animals is so entirely different from their effect on man that no safe conclusions can be drawn from such investigations" (Ruesch, 1989, p. 242). These themes, and variations of them, have been repeated often, as Ruesch (1989) related, by doctors and medical researchers through 1950. These were, in effect, decades-long warnings about potential medical disasters that might occur if animal experimentation was relied on for the safety and efficacy of pharmaceuticals. Ruesch (1978/1991) wrote that, between 1967 or so and the end of 1970, "a long line of medical authorities had testified that the generally accepted animal tests could never be conclusive for human beings" (p. 361). These testimonies were, in effect, authoritative and expert explanations about why the thalidomide tragedy happened. The thalidomide case was not the last of its kind. Other similar tragedies have occurred in its wake, after approval for marketing of drugs was given following animal experiments with the drugs (Ruesch, 1992).

These examples illustrate different types of out of cite, out of mind situations. The startling 1907 observation about the painted image of Guido Riccio was not assimilated into the art history literature and classroom teaching relating to either the Guido Riccio fresco or to the painting of the map (Mappamondo) on the same wall. In 1977, a similar hypothesis was made, and it caused a violent reaction. It might be that the 1907 reference, found in a footnote in a large volume dealing with a survey of 14th-century art, went unnoticed. A recent monograph study of the Guido Riccio case, *Simone o non Simone*, by Ragionieri (1985), deals at length with a description of the painting written in 1916, but does not deal at all with the 1907 item.

It might be, in this case, that every scholar who has studied Simone Martini, in general, and Guido Riccio, in particular, since 1907 has conducted research that was, to some degree, incomplete, inattentive, and sloppy. It might be that everyone overlooked Venturi's 1907 observation and therefore missed its significance. If that was the case, the item was not cited by scholars because it was not known to them.

In the childbirth fever situation, it seems that some scholars were aware of the 1773 work of White. They were also aware of the ideas of Gordon written in 1795, but, instead of giving them wide circulation, scholars derided them. The same seems to be true for the 1843 work of Holmes (father of the famous jurist). Diffusion of the ideas of these three scholars remained, it seems, within the circle of scholars opposed to these ideas.As a result, these ideas did not get carried forward in the mainstream body of literature so that Semmelweis could become aware of them before he arrived at the same conclusions (or very similar conclusions). It was not sloppy research as much as a short circuit, or breakdown, in the scholarly communication process that prevented Semmelweis from having knowledge that was crucial for his work.

In the case of the thalidomide tragedy, citations that were serious, insistent, and fervent warnings stretching over a long period of time were, in effect, ignored and not cited as animal experimentation continued as the prevailing paradigm. Then, in the wake of the tragedy, the ideas that had been ignored were, in a sense, transformed into alibis to explain what happened. Because animal experimentation is misleading and unreliable, the medical and academic authorities testified (echoing the chorus of many scholars who had previously said the same thing in hopes of avoiding medical disasters), and because such experimentation is required by law before drugs can be marketed, the company that did the animal experiments and marketed the drug based on the results of the animal experiments cannot be guilty of violating the law. (The logic, in any case, goes something to that effect.)

The thalidomide case involves selectivity in the use of citations. In his discussion of precursors of Velikovsky's ideas and theories, de Grazia (1984) equated citations to a form of intellectual snobbery: "The recounting of one's precursors has in it an element of snobbery, like the genealogical research that discovers barons but not brigands, big shots rather than bums" (p. 335). Citations and intellectual snobbery can also affect service quality and access to material in libraries. A case was published by de Grazia (1984) in which a local library in Kansas "has refused to accept or acquire" a copy of *A Struggle With Titans*. The reason for such refusal, as reported by de Grazia, was that "the standard reviewing media have ignored it" (p. 264).

CITATION AND IMPACT

If ideas, discoveries, or hypotheses are not cited (or applied) at all after they are initially presented by scholars, they cannot have any impact. In other cases, scholars' works might be cited often, and even discussed at length, but with the express purpose of preventing any impact and of preventing future citations of a favorable nature.

Other ideas may enjoy very wide circulation and citation, but they do not obtain any meaningful impact because they are kept out of official policy and establishment thinking. As a result of his persistence (and of the logic of his evidence and argumentation), Duesberg's ideas about AIDS and HIV have attained wide circulation in articles, books, interviews, reviews of his books, conferences, and lectures. At the same time, a very large majority of the mass media have continued to repeat over and over again the official establishment view, as if Duesberg had not written any dissenting views on the subject at all. The mass media thus help create the impression that the HIV–AIDS hypothesis is a proven fact of paradigm status, instead of letting the public know that it is a hypothesis adhered to by the establishment, but also one that is keenly debated and contested by scholars. For example, on the ABC News broadcast of May 7, 1996 (and on the repeat on Italian TV on the morning of May 8), HIV was referred to as the virus that causes AIDS without a hint that such a hypothesis is the subject of intense scholarly debate. (Similar statements to that of the ABC statement have been repeated often in the media since then).

By contrast, sometimes ideas can have a widespread diffusion and a long-lasting, far-reaching impact, but scholars who were key figures in the formulation of those ideas are not cited. The theory of evolution is often associated with Darwin. However, Manwell and Baker (1986a) observed:

> It is generally accepted that Alfred Russel Wallace independently discovered the theory of evolution by natural selection and published the outline in the same year as Darwin. Furthermore, it is known that there were important predecessors who had formulated the essential elements of the theory. (p. 284)

Perhaps there was some intellectual and social snobbery at play in this case, as Darwin came from a family that Manwell and Baker described as "wealthy and intellectually prominent" (p. 284). Darwin's publication on the subject is also more extensive and exhaustive, solidifying his position as originator of the theory.

Something similar apparently took place with the studies of the physicist Lise Meitner, who became a collaborator of Otto Hahn until she was forced to flee from Nazi Germany. She continued some collaboration from Sweden, and it seems a major breakthrough occurred in their research about this time. But according to Bartusiak (1996),

> Hahn published the chemical evidence for fission without listing Meitner as a co-author. ... In the history of modern physics there are names that perpetually resonate. ... The name of Lise Meitner has diminished to a footnote. ... Fortunately, attention is gradually being refocused on this remarkable woman. (p. 12)

Like the studies of Wallace, Meitner's studies had a great impact in academia, but the spotlights of citation attention have been shining on other scholars who get the lion's share of the credit for such impact.

PEER REVIEW AND ITS EFFECT ON CITATIONS

Problems related to the out of cite, out of mind factor are obviously tied up with peer review when there is deliberate attempt at peer-review suppression. Not only are unwanted ideas rejected from publication, but citations are deleted from manuscripts that are accepted. There can also be tendencies toward self-citation and mutual citation of colleagues, with exclusion, or near exclusion, of citations of works of scholarly adversaries.

Peer-review rejection, however, might also take place because editors and referees are not able to fathom the current or future significance of the work. In such cases, rejection is not so much the result of deliberate suppression as it is the result of lack of knowledge and lack of expertise. It is often difficult, even with the benefit of hindsight, to determine where deliberate suppression ends and honest peer-review error in judgment begins. The result is the same, however, if important ideas are suppressed and false (and possibly dangerous) ideas prevail in the mainstream literature. In "Have Referees Rejected Some of the Most-Cited Papers of All Times?," Campanario (1996b) quoted Glenn:

> Who Knows. ... how many papers which could have had an important impact on the discipline lie buried and neglected in obscure journals because of unfair rejections ... or how many incorrect conclusions published in major journals have found their way into textbooks to be taught to unwary undergraduates or have influenced personnel and policy decisions. (pp. 307–308)

Along a similar line, Gibbs (1995) referred to a "vicious circle of neglect" and "publishing barriers" that can "doom good science to oblivion" (p. 92). As the information explosion expands from a proliferation of journals published in the traditional manner to the apparently limitless boundaries of electronic publishing, the Internet, and so on, there is a corresponding increase in the potential for important scholarly ideas to fall into the silence of out of cite, out of mind oblivion. Language barriers add to the problem, particularly in the case of languages that are rarely found in the literature of a scholarly discipline.

HYPOTHESES TRANSFORMED INTO PARADIGMS

As an idea is cited by various scholars over a period of time, the nature of the idea may be transformed, even to the extent that what was originally presented as a hypothesis eventually is placed in the scholarly record as a fact. At that point, scholars might not even bother to look for dissenting views published in the past, with these uncited dissenting views reduced to silence as a result. Rose (1978) reported that Velikovsky came across this problem in his studies of ancient history:

> There are numerous examples of tentative proposals becoming canonical, simply because of the passage of time. Back in the nineteenth century, Boeckh *guessed* that the dates of Eudoxus might be 408–355. Eventually, all of the qualifications were dropped. Today, many dictionaries and encyclopedias and other reference books give those dates as if they were beyond question. In 1938 de Santillana discovered that it is far more likely that the dates were really 390–337. But the "traditional" dates ... have become so widely circulated and so well entrenched that Santillana's better dates ... have so far not even been much noticed, let alone accepted. (p. 40)

In AIDS research, the famous Gallo–HHS news conference spoke of a "probable" cause, but the word "probable" soon got the out of cite, out of mind treatment in the official policy and among the mass media.

NONCITATION, FOLLOWED BY SURPRISE AND ASTONISHMENT

There are some situations that are presented in the mass media as if they were surprising and startling events and episodes to journalists, and to establishment researchers and administrators. They appear to be surprising and startling not because they are new, but rather because earlier discussions by scholars had been given the out of cite, out of mind treatment. A recent article by James (1996b) indicated that the world's population is faced with a serious resurgence of tuberculosis, which might kill 30 million people in the next decade or so:

> Specialists say that developed countries that thought tuberculosis was vanquished are facing a resurgence of the disease, often in a deadly new and virtually incurable form. ... Sir John Crofton ... called the Milan hospital outbreak ... "terrifying" because it involved a strain of the disease deadlier even than the Ebola virus or the bubonic

plague ... Italy dismantled its network of tuberculosis sanatoriums and clinics in the 1970s believing the disease to be a thing of the past. ... The Milan outbreak involved a strain of the disease resistant to seven of the nine drugs known to be effective. (p. 5)

Altman (1995) also reported on the situation, stating that "a worldwide surge in drug-resistant strains" of tuberculosis is taking place, and that "there are more cases of tuberculosis today than ever worldwide" (p. 3). Ruesch (1978/1991) related that, as early as 1962 and 1963, it was pointed out by Dr. Raiga that "the number of staphylococcal strains resistant to penicillin has been steadily growing" (p. 282). Ruesch also observed that, in 1972, during testimony before the U.S. Senate Monopoly Subcommittee, it was revealed that typhoid bacilli had become resistant to antibiotics (p. 283). He also stated:

When at the end of the forties the price of penicillin suddenly dropped owing to over-production, the doctors began using it indiscriminately, even for minor flus or common colds, thus depriving the organism of the faculty to develop its own natural defenses. The doctors used the available antibiotics ... without realizing that they were not only weakening the human organisms, but at the same time strengthening the various strains of bacteria, to such an extent that some of them would eventually defy every type of antibiotics. So modern science had begun in the forties already producing stronger and stronger bacteria. (p. 280)

From these passages, it seems that the situation is complicated by the fact that either too light a dosage or too heavy a dosage of antibiotics can result in the survival of more resistant forms of bacteria. If that is true, perfecting the right dosage for specific treatments of specific patients might become something akin to a lottery or roulette, for who knows exactly what is precisely the right amount in each case? The lack of certainty, and the resulting risk, seem so great that a resurgence of diseases such as tuberculosis might well have been anticipated and expected, rather than appear as a sudden surprise. In any case, the out of cite, out of mind form of silencing of the works of scholars that took place in this situation could well have been a factor in the great surprise that was reported relating to the resurgence of tuberculosis.

Another similar example of out of cite, out of mind at work was illustrated by Ruesch (1993). He alluded to headlines in the *New York Times*, from 1993, that read "Many Say Lab-Animal Tests Fail to Measure Human Risk" and "Animal Tests as Risk Clues: The Best Data May Fall Short" (p. 1). If one did not already know that these headlines were from 1993, one could imagine that they were describing the defense of Chemie Grunenthal at the thalidomide trial in Germany a few decades earlier. Soon after these articles appeared in the newspaper, Ruesch observed:

All that the *New York Times* has reported with blue-eyed wonderment had been printed and disseminated 15 years ago by America's biggest publisher, when Bantam Books' Publicity Department sent out 3,500 review copies of *Slaughter of the Innocent* to the "science writers" on its list, and not one seemed to have glanced at it, or caught the message. The book disappeared under silence. (p. 1)

ON SITE AND IN SIGHT, BUT OUT OF CITE

A recent article in *Time* (Gray, 1996) stated that a statue was sighted each day by employees and visitors in a building in New York City, but no one paid very much attention to it until it was recently cited as a work by the famous artist Michelangelo. (On site, and in sight, but out of cite until there was more insight?) The same article pointed out that the poem, "A Funerall Elegie," is on the minds of Shakespeare scholars after it was recently cited as a work by Shakespeare. Gray (1996) observed, "What we could safely ignore or overlook before now commands our reverent attention" (p. 77).

By contrast, it can be risky and dangerous to ignore or overlook many ideas in some academic disciplines. It took centuries after the first observations that citrus fruits and other foods prevented or cured scurvy before it was accepted that scurvy was caused by a deficiency in diet rather than by other factors (Duesberg, 1996b) The earlier observations fell under a long out of cite, out of mind silence, rather than being continually discussed and tested.

Aronson (1986) related an out of cite, out of mind story about the Dutch scientist C. A. Pekelharing. He gave a talk in 1905, which was published in Dutch in 1907, but was apparently not included in an index of pertinent works:

> No active nutrition researcher had apparently ever heard of or cited Pekelharing's remarkable statement until 1926. ... In his Nobel speech Hopkins counted Pekelharing among his predecessors ... commenting that "it is indeed astonishing that the results of such significant work ... should not have been rapidly broadcast." (p. 643)

Aronson (1996) mentioned that Pekelharing's work did not appear in an index. If scholars do not locate important scholarly works in indexes, catalogs, or on library shelves, the scholars might not be able to cite certain works or ideas. Indexes and library shelves are only part of the picture, however. The reference of Hopkins to "rapidly broadcast" invokes a broader sense of scholarly communication, one that might include scholarly conferences and informal contacts among scholars. In fact, Hopkins might have been referring to a type of informal communication among scholars known as *invisible colleges*.

At any rate, out of cite, out of mind situations in academia lead to discussion of the role of academic librarians in scholarly communication, and in problems relating to the silencing of scholars.

13

Role and Responsibility of Academic Librarians

If anyone had told me that the kind of censorship you expose occurs in the Western World to the extent that you are now documenting, I would not have believed it. I thought the libraries, at least, would be above reproach. (S. Lang, personal communication June 26, 1986)

One of the primary themes of this book is that many important ideas and many scholars have been silenced, in one form or another, and for one reason or another, for long periods of time. Lang's words about libraries being "above reproach" reflect a common opinion among many scholars that academic librarians should not be willing participants in this silencing process. If the theme of silencing ran throughout the previous chapters, one of the main themes of this chapter would be access that helps break through various silence barriers.

Lang's "above reproach" remark can serve as a reminder that scholars have to depend on libraries, usually to a very large degree. A case can be made that delayed recognition of important ideas might have been delayed for much longer periods of time had it not been for the work of librarians who provided access to material that facilitated further research and discussion and, eventually, recognition. However, a more proactive approach in many cases might have led to quicker recognition.

DISTINGUISHING BETWEEN TRUE AND FALSE

Another major theme of this book is that the truth is often silenced along with scholars and their ideas. Librarians are expected to be above reproach in helping scholars
search for the truth, rather than leading them down false paths. In this respect, librarians are often dependent on specialist scholars. Or, a mutual dependence might exist
between scholars and librarians, as Swan (1992) discussed in "Scientists and
Librarians: An Ethical Bond Must Unite Them" (p. 11).

It is obvious that academic librarians are not expected to be able to distinguish
between truths and falsehoods among all the contents of the scholarly literature in
their library collections. The reality is that the literature is too extensive and often too
specialized and technical to allow librarians to make such distinctions. However,
should academic librarians care, and should they be concerned, if they discover that
specific material that purports to be true and authoritative might be blatantly false?

An unusual example of untrustworthy material in academic libraries is found in the
field of art history. As of December 1994, some of the leading art libraries and public
libraries in the United States owned the book *Due Pietre Ritrovate di AMEDEO
MODIGLIANI*, published a decade earlier (Durbè, 1984). Unless there is some
explanatory material attached to the book (or next to the book on the shelves), or written on the catalog entry, students and scholars might not be aware that the book (a catalog for a Modigliani centennial exhibition) was sequestered soon after it was
published. Television, magazine, and newspaper stories narrate that the two sculptures
in question are not masterpieces by Modigliani, as the experts all claimed in the catalog. One sculpture was created, according to these stories and to testimony, in 1984
by five university students as a prank, and the other was made by a local painter as an
artistic happening. What do the librarians say?

Another example involves art library slide collections. In 1980, a fresco of high
quality was discovered under the plaster of a wall in the Siena Palazzo Publico, and
the fresco was uncovered. Slides of the fresco were made in Italy by the specialist firm
Scala, and are distributed in America and Canada through Sandak, an imprint of
Macmillan Publishing. The fresco depicts a castle in the midst of some buildings, sur-
rounded by a protective wooden fence, with two figures standing to the left of the castle and buildings.

The label on the Scala slide carries the attribution for this fresco painting to
Duccio, the famous 14th-century painter who was a contemporary of Simone Martini,
and the subject listed on the Scala slide is "Surrender of Giuncarico." Librarians, professors, and students who use this slide for study or for classroom presentations might
not be aware that the Duccio attribution and the Giuncarico identification for the castle were made by scholars who first enthusiastically attributed this fresco to Simone
Martini, with the specific identification of the castle as Arcidosso (rather than
Giuncarico). Furthermore, other scholars have accepted and retained the Simone
Martini and Arcidosso hypotheses for the painting, and still other scholars have published opinions on the painting with attributions to Pietro Lorenzetti, Ambrogio

Lorenzetti, and Memmo di Filippuccio. In terms of publications, the Duccio attribution is a minority view that has not been accepted and followed by other scholars, particularly the Duccio specialists who have rejected the attribution.

Jannella (1989) described the lack of agreement in this case as an "incredible difference of opinions" (p. 63) and added:

> The observer may be surprised by this variety of attributions, especially since the artists mentioned are all so different. But for the public in general ... and also for those who take a professional interest, the main problem was how to form one's own opinion. How disorienting ... when learned art historians contradict one another so drastically? It is difficult to find one's way through this maze. (p. 63)

How do art librarians and slide librarians react?

These two situations show how librarians can be confronted with difficulties in attempting to help scholars gain access to the truth. Who knows how many such problems relating to other disciplines have turned up, or still exist, in academic libraries?

INACCESSIBLE AND IMPOSSIBLE TO OBTAIN

During the Guido Riccio controversy, Martindale (1986) wrote that "the accumulated bibliography is enormous, much of it in inaccessible journals" (p. 260) About a decade later, Kupfer (1996) stated, "Hayden Maginnis generously furnished me with copies of articles pertaining to the *Guidoriccio* debate from the *Notizie d'Arte*, which proved otherwise impossible to obtain, at least from research libraries in this hemisphere" (p. 286). (It should be pointed out that copies of the allegedly "inaccessible" journals that Martindale referred to were actually placed into his own hands, or else were located at his fingertips in the library of the Archivio di Stato di Siena, where he was doing research. In addition to journal articles, that library also has a collection of newspaper articles on the subject, among which there is material that had previously faced peer-review rejection by journals.) Meanwhile, practically all of the scholarly literature that supports the establishment view is quite easily accessible in research libraries in more than just "this hemisphere" to which Kupfer referred.

This episode relating to accessibility leads to discussion of how academic librarians see their roles in scholarly communication, particularly during scholarly controversies that include dissenting views (sometimes published in so-called minor publications) that challenge establishment views (ones that are usually already found among the mainstream literature of the libraries' holdings). Some might feel that with the information explosion and rapidly changing technology it is enough of a job to try to keep up with the administrative chores of acquiring and processing material, without getting involved in questions of accessibility of pertinent, but minor, material, or getting involved in disputes over the reliability of material among the libraries' holdings.

In the case of the Modigliani centennial book (exhibition catalog), librarians might say that because the book and exhibition enjoyed the patronage of the president of Italy and were organized by leading government officials and reputable scholars, if there is anything wrong with the book, it is up to scholars to find out what it is. The same attitude might be held for "retractions" in the scientific literature. If works have been retracted, scholars should be able to find the retraction notices. The librarian's responsibility would end when the journal (or other material) with the retraction notice is processed. If that specific journal is not included among the library's holdings, scholars will have to find out about the retraction elsewhere.

INQUIRIES AND RESPONSES

Inquiries relating to scholarly communication that involve problems of access, the handling of gifts to libraries, or other questions are not necessarily welcome for one reason or another. Sometimes librarians might be unsure of how to answer, so they might become hesitant or evasive or remain silent. In the Guido Riccio controversy, some problems of these types have come up. An editorial by Pacey (1992) in *Art Libraries Journal* gives some idea of what took place: "Some years ago a number of prominent art librarians received long letters from an art historian. ... Some of us were perplexed as to how to respond" (p. 3). The editorial then revealed that Swan (1991) published an article in *Library Trends* relating to this case, and that his article "explores the ethical implications of this case, including the 'lack of response of librarians'" (Pacey, 1992, p. 3). In his article, Swan (1991) concluded that "the difficult truth is that librarians must be both neutral champions of access to all points of view *and* advocates for the important views that are suppressed or unrepresented" (p. 273).

This editorial and the conclusion by Swan (1991) bring to mind some ideas from *Writings on Scholarly Communication* (Morton et al., 1988). The introduction read, in part, "At many points the scholar's world and the librarian's concerns overlap" (p. 22) Morton et al. (1988) also observed that "librarians and scholars are not in the habit of spending much time together or looking at what the other is reading" (p. 22).

Swan's (1991) remark about "advocates for the important views that are suppressed or unrepresented," and Morton et al.'s (1988) references to librarians and scholars spending time together indicate that, at the least, academic librarians and scholars should engage in discussion and, at the most, librarians and scholars are, in a real sense, partners, colleagues, and fellow travelers in the scholarly pursuit of truth. Not all persons view the situation in this same light, however.

In terms of fellow travelers, perhaps a parallel can be drawn between scholars and librarians, on the one hand, and travelers in a Tuscan tale, on the other. The tale illustrates alleged differences and rivalry between Sienese and Florentines. In this tale, a person is wandering in the Chianti countryside between Florence and Siena, looking for the way to Paradise. The person becomes lost, and asks a passerby, who happens to be Florentine, where the road to Paradise can be found. The Florentine replies, "You are egocentric to believe you deserve to get to Paradise. What makes you think I am obliged to tell you where that road is?"

After that insult, the person makes the same inquiry (about the road to Paradise) of the next person who is encountered, who turns out to be Sienese. The Sienese replies in the following manner: "What a delightful question! I am flattered that you think I might know the answer. In fact, I am searching for the same road myself, and would be pleased to have your company. If we search for it together, perhaps we will have a better chance of finding it." (It seems that this version of the tale was told by a Sienese. Florentines might relate the tale with a different slant.)

If the Florentine and the Sienese in the tale become academic librarians, and if the inquiry about the road becomes the inquiries in the "long letters" mentioned in the *Art Libraries Journal* editorial, and if Paradise is viewed in terms of access to scholarly information, then Swan's (1991) reference to advocates of suppressed views and Morton et al.'s (1988) remark about scholars and librarians spending time together can be seen as having the same purpose.

Librarians and scholars spend time together when librarians seek expert advice from peer-review authorities and specialists about which scholarly material their libraries should acquire. Such activity takes place within the concept of service. Librarianship is often viewed in terms of service. The concept of service might imply a sense of subordination, based on expertise, or lack of it, when academic librarians seek advice from peer-review authorities about which scholarly material to acquire. At the same time, any sense of subordination of this type should be nullified by the realization that scholars are dependent on librarians.

Certainly academic librarians can be more than efficient, valuable, and helpful providers of administrative service. As professionals, they can become, in effect, partners and colleagues of scholars, and, based on some recent library literature, there are some indications that this view is becoming recognized as a vital aspect of scholarly communication. On the other hand, as in any profession, hierarchies and bureaucracies are part of the library profession, with the result being that internal politics become involved. Politics of academic librarianship can intertwine with academic politics in a way that can tend to subordinate librarians to powerful academic leaders and peer-review authorities.

After one of the so-called "long letters" (mentioned in the editorial in *Art Libraries Journal*) was written to members of the Executive Committee of the International Federation of Library Associations (IFLA), the Secretary General of IFLA, Margreet Wijnstroom (personal communication, December 10, 1986) wrote, "I would suggest you let the matter rest, and in any case cease to bother the members of my Executive Board and my staff with matters beyond their control. ... You may regard this note as my final reaction to any further letters you may have in mind." (In this case, Wijnstroom's note was the first reaction, as well as her final written reaction to the inquiries in question.)

In reply to some inquiries, Beth Houghton, at the time Chair of Art Libraries

Society/ UK & Eire (ARLIS/UK & Eire), gave some helpful advice and comments. At the same time, however, she would not reveal the names of her fellow executive leaders at ARLIS/UK & Eire, stating that she spoke, in her role as Chair, for the organization. However, when the Guido Riccio controversy intensified (including discussion of art library practices), Houghton later said she did not want to be quoted, because she had been expressing her personal opinions on the subject. Among his responses to inquiries relating to the same subject matter, Anderson wrote:

> I cannot for the life of me understand ... how a library, which exists to give service to its users, could refuse to let those users know about the materials being catalogued and not being catalogued. I can think of no reason to justify this action, and I would state it to anyone anywhere at any time. I am completely dedicated to the concept of service and will go out of my way at any time for anyone to give superb service. My goal as a librarian is to make every effort to do whatever users would like, to try to react positively to their suggestions rather than negatively, to be on the alert at all times to find ways to improve service to them, to have them leave my presence better off than they were before we came into contact. ... That is how strongly I feel on the issues you raise. (Moran & Mallory, 1988, pp. 129–130)

Comparing reactions of librarians to the reactions of persons in the version of the Tuscan tale described earlier, it would seem that Wijnstroom's reply would resemble the reply of the Florentine passerby: It would appear that Houghton tried to be like the Sienese passerby, but pressures of one form or another (collegial, professional, or political) inhibited her from carrying through completely.

On the other hand, Anderson's remarks would epitomize the Sienese traveler's willingness to help. Furthermore, as he expressed it, Anderson's concept of library service is so expansive, encompassing, generous, and enthusiastic in nature that it would seem, in terms of academic librarianship, to go beyond the realm of subordinate service, to the extent of identifying, in a real sense, with the actual specific research goals of the scholar. On a practical level, Anderson may not have all the time available, or the necessary resources required, to actually carry out all the help he would like to give, but the level of volition to help scholars would tend to make him as much an intellectual colleague as a helpful librarian.

PEER-REVIEW APPROVAL AND LIBRARY ACQUISITION DECISIONS

In an article on scholarly communication, Osburn (1989) wrote to the effect that academic librarians should carry out the wishes of academic peer review authorities: "We have discovered our place in what is now called the scholarly communication system. ... The relative importance of a given output of scholarly communication is determined through its acceptance or rejection by the peer review authority in each field" (pp. 277, 281). He also observed that the system is already overloaded as a result of the information explosion, and he implied that material that peer review authorities do not approve is "noise" (p. 285). (Such a reference to noise brings to mind the title of the song "The Sound of Silence," because, in effect, Osburn was suggesting that if peer-review authorities decide to silence scholars, academic librarians should also participate in the process of silencing them.)

Osburn's (1989) views have merit to the extent that scholars using academic libraries would have access to the latest material related to paradigms taught in the classroom, and access to research results that have been subsidized by the leading organizations that award research grants. However, to the extent that this material is marked by protection of false paradigms, double standards in peer review, secret peer review, toleration of falsification, and intimidation of various types that lead scholars to not say what they believe, there is the possibility that Osburn, and academic librarians who follow his advice, will become an integral factor in the silencing of scholars. In effect, academic librarians might get caught up in carrying out a phase of the suppression decided on by peer-review authorities.

By contrast, Berman proposed a proactive stance for librarians when academic controversies arise. At one point he wrote specifically about the Guido Riccio controversy, but the thrust of the message would also apply to controversies in any academic discipline:

> Good library procedure would dictate—with respect to a major intellectual and academic dispute like that surrounding Guido Riccio—that extra measures be taken to IDENTIFY AND MAKE AVAILABLE THE ENTIRE SPECTRUM OF VIEWPOINTS AND DOCUMENTATION. ... Beyond that, given the unquestionable interest in this particular matter, a proactive, truly helpful and alert librarian would also prepare—and possibly duplicate for broad distribution—a special bibliography on the case. Such a resource list should be posted prominently in the library and updated frequently. (Moran & Mallory, 1991b, p. 347)

It is interesting to place Berman's words "IDENTIFY AND MAKE AVAILABLE THE ENTIRE SPECTRUM OF VIEWPOINTS," written in 1986 and published in 1991, next to the words of Kupfer cited earlier, published in 1996, which reveal that some of the published Guido Riccio material remains "impossible to obtain, at least from research libraries in this hemisphere."

In *Memorandum,* a monthly publication of the ALA's OIF, Krug and Levinson (1991) seemed to give support for Berman's views: "It is in the public interest for publishers and librarians to make available the widest diversity of views and expressions, including those which are unorthodox or unpopular with the majority" (p. 3 of Attachment VII).

In effect, scholars are silenced to the extent that their published views are not made available. Therefore, the ideas of Berman and the policies of the ALA (as found in the item from *Memorandum),* if put into practice, would help prevent scholars from being silenced. A problem relating to rhetoric versus reality can remain, however. For example, Kaplan (1986) wrote about problems of availability of viewpoints that she faced while doing research in various libraries:

> Intellectual suppression is an issue that concerns us especially. I was alerted again to this problem very forcefully when I visited Europe a few months ago in order to complete some research on the feminist debate. I visited many libraries—mainstream libraries in West Germany—and wherever I went, catalogues were silent on publications by feminists. ... Denial of access to a wide audience and reading public is a scandalous way of muting women. (p. 2)

Furthermore, Kaplan (1986) seemed to imply that librarians were active participants in a silencing of scholars process when she wrote that "it seems that every attempt is made to drown out as many ideas as possible as quickly as possible by isolating them in specialized bookshops and a few, not well known archives" (p. 2).

LOOKING "ELSEWHERE" FOR SCHOLARLY MATERIAL

The material that Kupfer (1996) was seeking, but proved "impossible to obtain," was not material approved by peer-review authorities of the art history establishment. Likewise, the publications "on the feminist debate" that Kaplan (1986) tried to find in libraries in West Germany were not in the mainstream of scholarly publications. These situations would indicate that, despite the views of Osburn (1989), peer-reviewed scholarly material is not necessarily sufficient as far as scholarly communication and scholarly debate are concerned. Instead, it would seem that in situations where publications relating to an academic debate or controversy remain "impossible to obtain, at least from research libraries in this hemisphere," or where "catalogues were silent on publications by feminists," or in other similar situations, academic librarians should heed Berman's suggestion to go beyond the peer-reviewed scholarly literature and look elsewhere in order to identify and make available all points of view.

During the *Cell*–Baltimore controversy, Lang (1993) came to similar conclusions about the need to look elsewhere: "One could not rely on the establishment press for systematic and correct information. One had to look elsewhere" (p. 34). He added, "full documentation must be publicly available to provide the possibility of independent judgment" (p. 37).

In one sense, by deferring to peer-review authorities, Osburn let (1989) himself, and other academic librarians, off the hook in terms of responsibility, whereas Berman's ideas strongly imply that academic librarians have a responsibility to look beyond peer-review decisions in the case of controversies. In Lang's reference to "One had to look elsewhere," the word *elsewhere* means other than, or beyond, the mainstream and peer-reviewed literature. However, elsewhere in this case does not necessarily mean that scholars have to look in places other than academic libraries. Lang himself has given unpublished documentation from some of his own "file" studies to libraries at Yale and Harvard (and perhaps other university and college libraries as well). It would seem that the donation of such documentation to libraries is in line with Lang's belief that libraries are above reproach.

Lang's file studies consist of compilations of discussions during scholarly debate, including letters to the editor and short articles that have been rejected by peer review authorities. His book *The File* (1981) is an example of an extensive file study that has been published (and it seems that other file studies might also be published). These file studies might provide excellent source material for courses in librarianship and information science, as they would help academic librarians understand problems of scholarly communication that can arise during academic controversies. The precise and extensive documentation found in these studies illustrates some of the activity and tactics that result in the silencing of scholars and their ideas.

A pertinent case involving responsibility and "elsewhere" took place recently. The so-called Dead Sea Scrolls have been in the hands of a group of establishment scholars for a long time. Publication of the texts was piecemeal and scanty, and drawn out over a long period of time. Some scholars who were not part of the "in" group had difficulty getting access to the source material. It seemed like another variation of the game of peer-review control over publication was being played out.

But then, as Baigent and Leigh (1993) pointed out, "the Huntington Library in California disclosed that it possessed a complete set of photographs of all unpublished scroll material" (p. 325). What is more, despite demands to give the photographs to the academic authorities in charge of the scrolls, and seemingly also despite legal threats, the library "announced its intention of making them accessible to any scholar who wished to see them" (p. 326). In effect, the library identified and made available some crucial documentation, despite peer-review authority protest. Interested scholars could go directly to the library (which would provide microfilm copies at a low price). Scholars had to look "elsewhere" for the material as far as the peer-reviewed mainstream literature was concerned, but they did not have to look "elsewhere" as far as a library was concerned, in order to obtain the scholarly material they were seeking.

In this case, the library took the lead in scholarly communication, with an expansive and generous sense of service to scholars that seems to be an embodiment of Anderson's beliefs. In a sense, the library became a colleague of scholars of religious history (and other interested scholars) by providing access to otherwise secret material. This is different from the normal service activity of acquiring and processing published scholarly material. A large part of the scroll material had not been published, and had not passed peer review yet. (In Osburn's [1989] view, would this material be included among the noise that academic libraries should not be concerned with?)

RESPONSIBILITY FOR RELIABILITY AND FOR CORRECTION OF ERROR

The concept of scholars and academic librarians as colleagues and partners in the search for truth was hinted at by Altick (1974). In his role as a scholar addressing a group of librarians, he said, "I as a pursuer of truth, you as the dedicated custodians of truth" (p. 4). One of Altick's main themes is that reference works are filled with error and should be corrected:

> The progress of knowledge consists in large part of proving received statements faulty, exploding myths, reordering the sequence of events, and thus giving the lie to reference books. ... Instances of the untrustworthiness of the books we rely upon every day of our professional lives could be cited almost without end. (pp. 15–16)

He then urged librarians and scholars to "maintain a spirit of permanent skepticism toward all the 'information' that is our common stock in trade" (p. 16).

The term "our common stock in trade" sounds much like a term colleagues would use in their conversation and professional dealings. (In this case, Altick, an English professor, was addressing a group of librarians.) At the same time, his reference to "untrustworthiness of the books we rely on" leads to the question of the role of librarians in the correction of error. The errors in question, for the most part, were not made by librarians but by scholars. It might be argued, in this case, that scholars, not librarians, have responsibility for the correction of all these errors that they (the scholars) themselves, along with their colleagues and academic predecessors, all made. Besides, librarians are already overloaded with their own work and beset with their own problems.

On the other hand, part of the librarians' work, especially reference work, is to give reliable and truthful information rather than false and misleading information. If reference librarians are informed of possible clamorous error published in a certain subject, what do these librarians do when users seek information on that subject.? Do they merely repeat the official published view, and wait for updated corrected versions of the mainstream peer-reviewed publications, or do they alert users to the possibility of clamorous error? How long might librarians have to wait to receive publications with the corrections? If there is "untrustworthiness" in relation to the contents of some works, is there necessarily trustworthiness in relation to the proclivity of authors, or their collegial colleagues, to publish admissions and corrections of their errors?

Regarding correction of error, Koshland (1988) once wrote in an editorial in *Science*:

> When mistakes do occur, whether by fraud, sloppiness, or honest error, it is essential that they be corrected as rapidly as possible, and retractions, however embarrassing, must be made. ... Today's scientists need to realize that errors must be handled more formally, and in full view of an anxious public. (p. 637)

Taking into consideration the coverage by *Science* of the *Cell*–Baltimore controversy, and also of the controversy relating to AIDS research, Koshland's words might be considered part of a classic rhetoric versus reality gap as discussed in chapter 3. Librarians might also point out that Koshland was speaking to scientists and editors, and perhaps also to investigative committees of institutions, but not necessarily to librarians.

There are indications, however, that librarians are becoming seriously involved in the process of correction of error, including the taking of a proactive stance in the dissemination of notices of correction of error. Duggar and a team of librarians from Louisiana State Medical Center (Duggar et el., 1995) wrote, "researchers who are simply unaware of retractions may be misled" (p. 18) and "medical librarians face a professional challenge to become involved in the scientific process by educating and informing the medical/scientific community about retractions" (p. 25). They described their library's methods of informing scholars of retractions: "Four departments cooperate to provide five access points to patrons" (p. 28). Moreover, an updated list is compiled of "all the retractions back to 1966. ... For ease of access, the list is kept at the circulation desk" (p. 30). In conclusion, the authors encouraged "other librarians to promote an awareness of retracted literature," and stated that "librarians have an important role in the removal of erroneous information from the medical literature" (p. 31).

The reference to "erroneous information" carries the problem beyond the scope of specific retractions. Some serious errors are not corrected by formal retractions. Many errors are so-called honest errors that elude detection for long periods of time. The same is true for errors caused by fraud or misconduct (however these terms are defined) in research. There is often strong resistance to allowing correction of error or to admitting that a prevailing paradigm in academia might be false. In the passage from the *Science* editorial cited earlier (Koshland, 1988) about mistakes "being corrected as soon as possible," it becomes obvious that retractions are only a part of the correction process in academia.

A recent article by Hernon and Altman (1995) addressed the problems of perpetuation of error in the scholarly literature in terms of "service quality" provided by academic librarians. They observed that "discredited works may remain within collections without any stigma attached to them" (p. 30) and they asked about the effect on service quality in such situations.

The study conducted by Hernon and Altman (1995) reveals that many librarians do not consider the correction of error their responsibility. Instead, the opinion is stated that scholars have the responsibility to decide among themselves what is accurate or inaccurate, and when their decisions are published, librarians will provide access to the publications containing these decisions. In this sense, service quality is technical and administrative, not expansive in the manner that Anderson described. Hernon and Altman affirmed that "service quality must consider, but not be confined to, the validity and reliability of information which a library provides" (p. 35).

If scholars were not silenced so often when they try to correct error, there would seem to be much merit in the view that librarians can let scholars take the responsibility for the correction of error. In any case, it would seem logical that original and primary responsibility for correction of error lies with the scholars who made the error, and then with the specialists in the field who detected the errors.

As can be seen from countless examples throughout history, there is strong resistance among academics to correction of error. Perhaps a case can be made that it is this very resistance that transfers some of the responsibility for correction of error onto academic librarians. The ball is thrown into their laps, or hit onto their side of the court, so to speak, when they find themselves in charge of the erroneous material amidst, on the one hand, some scholars who do not want the errors to be corrected, and, on the other hand, scholars and students (who did not make the errors) who are counting on the librarians to give them accurate, truthful, and reliable information. Along this line, Hernon and Altman (1995) noted that "one of the basic aims of research is to uncover error" (p. 28).

Their view about one of the researcher's basic aims might be the starting point for a hypothetical case study of the question of responsibility for correction of error on the part of academic librarians. In this hypothetical case, scholars involved in a research project, while working in the library, detect what they feel is serious error. At a certain point, they discuss the situation with the reference librarian, who has some specialized knowledge in the field. They ask the reference librarian about the existence of other possible material that might help confirm the error or explain it. The scholars then write an article that documents their case and submit it to a journal, only to have it rejected. They submit it to another journal. All the time they are continuing their research, and they inform the reference librarian about the peer-review rejection and the new submission.

At this point, in this hypothetical situation, another scholar starts researching, independently, the same subject, and goes to the reference librarian for assistance. If the reference librarian believes that librarians have no responsibility for the correction of error, the assistance given in this case might consist of providing the bibliographical references pertinent to the subject. If the bibliography contains erroneous material, it is up to the scholar to detect it.

Now suppose that after this, the mutual interest in the subject matter causes the paths of this scholar to cross with that of the scholars who detected the errors. The scholars inform the other scholar about the alleged serious error that they had detected, and relate that they had discussed these errors at length with the reference librarian. At this point, what opinion might this scholar have of the reference librarian who kept such vital information hidden?

If, on the other hand, the reference librarian felt some responsibility for correction of error, the scenario in this hypothetical case might be different. At the very least, the librarian might ask the scholars if they would want other scholars who are interested in the subject to contact them. The librarian might also suggest the names of other scholars who might be keenly interested and who might be able to provide further leads. And, based on knowledge of publications in the field, the librarian might give some useful suggestions about which journals might be inclined to publish the new research. The librarian might also alert other reference librarians in other libraries about the developments.

If nothing else, activities of this sort would help bring discussion of the subject out into the open, which would facilitate a type of network of scholarly discussion that could help counter the tendency toward isolating and silencing scholars in such situations. If strong and persistent peer-review rejection prevails, the librarians can say they did their part in bringing the material to the attention of scholars for critical analysis and debate.

ACADEMIC LIBRARIANS AND INTELLECTUAL FREEDOM ACTIVITY

The academic librarian's role does not have to end as it does in that hypothetical case study, however. Just as other librarians are interested in combatting intellectual suppression by means of a variety of intellectual freedom activities, academic librarians might be interested in cases of peer-review suppression that are based on double standards, toleration for falsification, and the protection of false paradigms. If this type of intellectual suppression is detected, librarians can take some steps that will aid scholars in their struggles to avoid being silenced.

One obvious step would be to form intellectual freedom (IF) groups that would document and evaluate cases that are brought to their attention. These groups could exist at various levels, ranging from individual libraries to geographical areas to professional organizations. In his "Ethical Bond" article, Swan (1992) envisioned that librarians and scholars "might well discover a healthy symbiosis that would promote, in collegial, nonintrusive, and efficient ways, a free and ethical environment for both inquiry and communication" (p. 11). In fact, an ethical bond between librarians and scholars would be the basis for such IF activity. These IF groups could become effective settings for such symbiosis, and for forums for the inquiry and communication to which Swan alluded.

Organization and activity could follow that of other IF groups within ALA, with special emphasis on specific cases of academic and peer review suppression. J Campanario (1996b) Nissani (1995) and others have documented numerous cases, from past centuries to the present, of peer-review suppression that resulted in long-term delay of correction of error and long-term delay of recognition of important discoveries. IF activity might have shortened the time necessary for the correction of error and for recognition of these discoveries.

Even if such activity did not result in definite resolution of cases, one of the most important functions would be to get the facts and issues out into the open. Peer-review tactics of double standards, secrecy, personal attacks, or false charges and claims are more likely to be successful and unnoticed by the larger academic community if the scholar whose work is being suppressed is isolated. The more an issue is out in the open, the more opportunity there will be for an increasingly larger group of scholars to evaluate the documentation relating to the issue.

One possible positive result of such IF activity could be improvement in peer review in general as well as in specific cases. Quality control, a rather frequent term used to describe the purpose of peer review, might extend to peer review itself in cases where suppression is suspected and detected. A major positive potential result could be that librarians, in a working out of an ethical bond that Swan (1992) envisioned, could have a role in helping to keep scientists and other scholars from being silenced.

Just so there is no misunderstanding about the scope of potential IF activity of this type by academic librarians, it should be pointed out that it would not necessarily involve second guessing of referees and editors on specific manuscripts they have rejected, or of erroneous manuscripts that they have accepted for publication. Multiple rejections do not mean by themselves that there is a case of intellectual suppression in the works. The manuscript might be of such poor quality, or so irrelevant and inappropriate for specific journals, that rejection decisions would be the most logical decisions.

On the other hand, academic librarians may be able to suspect, in a logical manner, a severe potential intellectual suppression case after only a single rejection, based on the subject matter, and based on the nature of the rejection. A challenge to a paradigm is obviously a likely candidate for suppression. So are manuscripts that purport to detect and correct serious errors in works in prestigious journals whose authors are famous and powerful persons in academia. The histories of science and other academic disciplines are filled with cases of suppression of challenges to paradigms that were believed to be true but turned out to be false. The *Cell*–Baltimore case illustrates how attempts to make corrections can be suppressed.

Another point that is important to keep in mind is that IF activity would not result in the suppression or censorship of the erroneous works that are being challenged. Instead, the main thrust of the activity would resemble that proposed by Berman, namely, to identify and make available the documentation in a manner as complete and accessible as possible. Such activity would not necessarily try to get editors to change their minds, nor would it try to bypass or substitute for peer review. Instead, it would supplement peer review.

If there is validity to a manuscript that peer-review authorities reject, the contents of the manuscript will most likely eventually appear somewhere in so-called minor publications or underground publications. (In some cases that Lang has become involved in, much pertinent documentation has been accumulated in the form of "file" studies.) If librarians place such material alongside the material that is being contested and challenged, scholars will be provided with a more complete documentation of the scholarly record. The truth will become easier to ascertain if as much documentation as possible is made available, instead of suppressing that which is believed to be false. By providing such access, academic librarians would not only be custodians of the truth, to repeat Altick's (1974) expression, but also illuminators of the truth as a result of IF activity. Without such additional material, it is possible, in some cases, that scholars will not even be aware that a challenge was made, in which case it would be virtually impossible to make a critical analysis of the evidence. Or, they may be aware that a challenge was made, but the material provided in the peer-reviewed literature may be so slanted that scholars do not get a clear idea of the real situation, as far as the scholarly record is concerned. In *Service Quality in Academic Libraries*, Hernon and Altman (1996) made some pertinent observations: "If the materials are not available ... then no higher order outcomes (such as the enhancement of learning, the facilitation of research, or the impact on intellects) will occur" (p. 6).

A question might be raised about whether academic librarians themselves feel they have responsibility for such an IF role. Another question is how the so-called electronic publishing era and the Internet will affect such a potential role for librarians, and also how it will affect the peer-review process itself. As Hernon and Altman (1995) observed, "The proliferation of electronic journals and computer networks affords more opportunity for misconduct" (p. 29). In terms of correction of error, will librarians and scholars be able to keep up with it all?

14

Silencing Scholars in the Electronic Age

In recent times, the proliferation of new journals in many disciplines has given a large number of scholars the chance to find a place for publication after they have received peer-review rejections from the older, traditional, and more prestigious journals. The electronic age, with electronic publishing and networking, will provide, at least in theory, the opportunity for all scholars to have their say on all matters about which they want to communicate their opinions and findings. It would seem, on the surface, that silencing of scholars will soon be a thing of the past. Peer review, under these circumstances, can be bypassed. Along this line, a recent article discussing electronic publishing (Reier, 1997) stated that "the Internet democratizes information," and, "without elitist editors to exclude material ... people can search for anything they want" (p. 21a).

In fact, Judson (1994) already wrote about the alleged "End of Peer Review:" He claimed that "the transformation brought in by electronic publishing ... will open up the processes by which scientists judge each other's work, making them less anonymous, capricious, rigid, and subject to abuse, and more thorough, responsible, and accountable" (p. 94). In effect, Judson envisioned the current peer-reviewed scholarly publishing system evolving into a continuous "open dialogue and collaboration among contributing scientists, editors, expert commentators, and readers" (p. 94). It would seem that Judson envisioned the traditional form of so-called invisible colleges being transformed into a system of electronic colleges.

POWER, AUTHORITY, AND ELECTRONIC PUBLISHING

The phrase "open dialogue and collaboration" in Judson's (1994) analysis sounds very much like the current rhetoric of academia with the present peer-review system. At this point, how can anyone be sure that there will not be a rhetoric versus reality gap in the electronic age as well? As long as peer-review authorities continue to control the vast lucrative sums of money for research grants, and continue to control, to one degree or another, promotion and tenure and prize decisions, how is it possible to be sure that paradigm dependency, paradigm protection, double standards, toleration of falsification, intimidation, retaliation, and fear to say what you believe will not continue to be factors leading to silencing of scholars in the electronic age?

A key issue is whether peer-review authorities will give up control of what specific research gets funded and of what material is taught in the classrooms as paradigms in academia. A related issue is whether any electronic publishing system will have a mechanism that can force the peer-review authorities to lose such control.

If a dissenting scholar in the past was regarded as something of a voice in the wilderness in terms of a challenge to a well-entrenched paradigm, many dissident scholars forming part of a computer network might be regarded as a chorus of discordant voices in a much larger and overcrowded intellectual wilderness. There does not seem to be any assurance that the impact of dissenting voices will necessarily be much different in the future than in the past. Also, if scholars are afraid to say what they believe when writing in journals, books, or when speaking during scholarly conferences or doing interviews, might they not have similar fears about expressing their ideas in electronic publications?

PROBLEMS OF QUALITY CONTROL

There is no question that the amount of information and the number of opinions and theories on record will increase greatly. How will all this information be processed and absorbed, and how will the processing affect impact? At present, the HIV–AIDS hypothesis is the paradigm in AIDS studies and AIDS research. It is taught in medical schools, vast sums of money for research grants are based on it, and the mass media report extensively on it as if it were proven fact. Serious challenges have been made, as discussed earlier, in a variety of publications and discussions, but the impact has not been strong enough to change official policy. If these challenges had been carried out by means of an elaborate and extensive electronic network and electronic publishing campaign, it does not seem that much would have changed at this point. Scholarly challenges carried out on the Internet or other forms of electronic communication might be regarded by peer-review authorities as the equivalent of ham radio operators trying to compete with major mass media networks for impact on public opinion.

In an open electronic publishing system that does not prohibit expression, there will be a huge swirling mass of information and ideas in many different fields. At a certain point, the sheer volume of material on a specific academic subject may make it a strenuous task to read and analyze all of the material on a topic in which a scholar is interested. In this case, questions of indexing and abstracting, bibliographical control, and quality control seem bound to remain, and also seem bound to increase in scope.

At present, there are notions of major (or mainstream, core, or primary) scholarly publications, as distinguished from so-called minor or fringe publications. As electronic publication advances, there might be attempts to set up two-tier or multiple-tier levels of scholarly information, with the academic professional societies and associations, comprised of leaders in their disciplines, giving the academic equivalent of a seal of approval for studies they like, and withholding approval from those they do not like. It seems that the NSF has already set up an electronic scholarly communication system with restrictions on the material that will be allowed to be discussed, and restrictions relating to which specific scholars will be allowed to have access to the material. Shapley (1997) reported that the Director of NSF "controls who uses" (p. 11) this system (which is called Very High Performance Backbone Network Service), and that the NSF has implemented an "'acceptable use' policy" that restricts "use to researchers whose projects have gone through a peer review" (p. 15).

CYBERSPACE CENSORS

In any case, for scholars conducting research amidst a rapidly swelling sea of information, it would seem that efficient indexing and abstracting would be of utmost importance. Rodney (1995) regarded the "lack of indexing" among the defects of electronic publishing. She also foresaw serious problems relating to intellectual freedom:

> If too many libraries embrace an electronic means of disseminating and preserving information, the average citizen's intellectual freedom and the right of access to information will be controlled because a small group of people will determine what is included on the internet. ... Those persons with the money will make the rules, and those who invest billions in the new digitized world will have control of access to knowledge and information, and limitation of intellectual freedom is boundless. (pp. 76–77)

It would seem logical and natural that the same types of material that were the targets for censorship and suppression during the preelectronic publishing age would remain targets for censorship and suppression during the electronic publishing age. In fact, there have already been some recent widely reported attempts at censorship of electronic publishing. Even before that, a warning about the potential for such censorship was made by a professor at California State University (in its Florence, Italy branch) several years ago (during a discussion of the Guido Riccio controversy). Electronic peer-review rejection might be called *peer blackout.*

A recent front page newspaper headline read "Germany Forces CompuServe to Censor Sex on the Internet." This article by Martin (1995) begins by stating "Germany has imposed strict censorship on the Internet ... to ban worldwide access to about 200 bulletin boards" (p. 1). In another instance, it appears that the German Communications Ministry is also intent on banning some material that authorities do not consider to be politically correct (James, 1996a). As might be expected, once a specific target for censorship is zeroed in on, calls for censorship of other subjects begin to be heard. Internet access providers have been asked to "refuse to carry messages that 'promote ... mayhem and violence,'" and it is reported that "efforts are growing to restrict certain types of information on computer networks" (Lewis, 1996, p. 2).

The "certain types of information" that are targets for censorship can include material that peer-review authorities do not like. According to a news item from Reuters (1996), Internet providers in Communist China have come under the control of some government organizations, including the Chinese Academy of Sciences. It would not seem unusual if academic learned societies and professional organizations in other countries were to seek to exert some form of peer-review influence over academic material transmitted via electronic publishing. (In addition to being blackballed and isolated, scholars might also become black-paged.)

Some recent legal action has shown that censorship of electronic communication can be far reaching, even if the specific target of censorship is a limited one. Andrews (1997) reported that the German government "indicted the head of CompuServe Corp.'s on-line computer service," with the accusation of "trafficking in pornography" (p. 13). The same company was also charged with failing "to block access to Internet sites offering Nazi and neo-Nazi material" (p. 13). This case was described as "a turning point in the debate over controlling pornography on the Internet" (p. 13). Furthermore, according to Andrews, some of the sites that were prohibited as a result of the German government's attempt to crack down on pornography actually "dealt with issues such as breast cancer and acquired immune deficiency syndrome and had nothing to do with pornography" (p. 13).

Censorship of electronic communication is not imposed only by governments. The providers of Internet services themselves might feel inclined to impose censorship on their clients in order to avoid the type of legal problems that CompuServe has been facing. In fact, Johnston (1997) revealed that one such provider, AOL Ltd., has revised and updated its contracts with subscribers. He observed that these new contracts forbid subscribers from "posting or transmitting any content that is 'unlawful, harmful, threatening, abusive, harassing, defamatory, vulgar, obscene, seditious, blasphemous, hateful, racially, ethnically or otherwise objectionable'" (p. 9). The vague nature of the wording in this case increases the possibility of a chilling factor that results in silence in the form of self-censorship. For example, the executives of AOL Ltd., the leaders of powerful institutions, and the leaders of governments and governmental agencies may have different views from the subscribers about which material is abusive, vulgar, or objectionable. (As discussed in Chapter 11, a passage from the Talmud did not seem objectionable to a professor at Chicago Theological Seminary, but it was considered objectionable by powerful leaders of that institution, with the result that the professor was silenced and punished.)

In addition to governments and Internet service providers, librarians can also restrict access to material in the electronic publishing system that is considered objectionable. Cohen (1997) described a situation in "Florida's Orange County Public Library System" in which a "Web filtering service" was put in place "so that patrons cannot view computer pornography" (p. 9). If academic authorities on specific campuses deemed certain material to be objectionable because it is politically incorrect, might they not try to employ similar filtering services to prevent access to such material on campus?

Electronic publishing can also lead to silencing of scholars in a paradoxical manner. Golden (1997) stated that during a renovation of the Main Library of the San Francisco Public Library "book space" ended up being "sacrificed for computer terminals" (p. 20). He related that as a result of this renovation, "More than 200,000 books ended up in the dump" (p. 20), including many books that were out of print and not easily accessible.

Golden's (1997) account deals with a situation in which the electronic publishing phenomenon crowds out printed books. In this case, there is not room for everything, and some material must be sacrificed. According to Lipetz (1991), peer-reviewed material might get crowded out, in the sense of being difficult to locate, as a result of electronic publishing. He concluded that electronic publishing will not bypass peer review, but instead cause a greater need for it. In effect, Lipetz viewed the situation as one in which there will be a greater need for quality control amid an information overload that could get out of control: "I shudder to think what modern technology could accomplish for us today if everything written were similarly accepted for publication without review" (p. 131). The result would be, according to Lipetz, "a deluge of publishable garbage" that would "shift the reviewing process from before-publishing stage to the after-publication stage" (p. 131). Lipetz expressed the hope that technology will help make the peer reviewer's work more efficient. (p. 132). One obvious potential way in which modern technology can help the peer reviewer is through the use of filters that eliminate the "garbage," thus making the search for material accepted by peer-review authorities easier for scholars. As far as impact is concerned relating to what material is taught in classrooms, and to which scholarly research is funded, it does not seem to make much difference whether peer-review authorities filter out unwanted material before the printed publication stage or after the electronically published stage.

Although the alleged deluge of garbage may signal a greater need than ever for peer review, Dalton (1995) suggested that the sheer volume of new information published electronically may be too great for peer review to keep up with. It would seem possible that at a certain point there will not be enough peer reviewers to go around to even read all of the works, much less make detailed analyses and recommendations for them. At the same time, electronic publishing will improve scholarly communication of the type known as invisible colleges. Scientists and other scholars, either on an individual basis or in groups, can discuss their findings with each other much more quickly, and in a much more efficient manner, before these ideas are formally presented to the larger academic or scientific communities.

Although much has been written about electronic publishing, it seems too early to state with any certainty how the electronic publishing phenomenon will bear on the silencing of scholars in the long run. Electronic systems have been described as "a crazy quilt of both utopian and Orwellian possibilities" (Corcoran, 1996, p. 10). The utopian aspect can apply to its expansive nature, and to its aid to scholarly communication of an invisible college nature, whereas filtering services are among the Orwellian possibilities. These apparent polar opposites of utopian efficiency and freedom of expression and Orwellian censorship can actually exist side by side in certain situations. For example, a scholar might publish, electronically, new findings and hypotheses that most likely would not have passed traditional peer review because they disagreed with a paradigm or part of a paradigm. Graduate students who are writing dissertations on the same subject might come across this new work and wish to include it as part of the dissertation. They discuss it with their professors and advisors, who advise against using the material, even hinting that inclusion of such material might result in failure. Wishing to get their degrees, the students omit the material.

Thus, in this hypothetical situation, scholars can bypass the peer-review system in an unbridled manner that prevents them from being silenced. At the same time, silence barriers can subsequently be created around the work that bypassed peer review, thus limiting its citation, diffusion, and impact in future publication and classroom discussion. It can be on (electronic) site, but still be kept out of mind.

It history and human nature are guides, it seems that the electronic publication revolution will develop and expand side by side with continuous attempts by authorities to silence unwanted ideas. These silencing attempts on the part of authorities will continue to face the "Eternal Spirit of the chainless Mind," which will incessantly try to penetrate, and eventually break down, whatever barriers are erected to silence scholars. If the adage that truth will eventually prevail has validity, the expansive and creative aspects of the electronic publishing phenomenon should be key factors in helping scholars to overcome silence barriers, to distinguish between truth and falsehood in the scholarly literature, and to discover new truths in their academic disciplines.

References

Abraham, D. (1984a). On Professor Feldman's insistence: Some closing remarks. *Central European History, 17*, 268–290.

Abraham, D. (1984b). A reply to Gerald Feldman. *Central European History, 17*, 178–244.

Abraham, D. (1985). Business wars: On Ulrich Noken's and my own contributions to Weimar scholarship. *Vierteljahrschrift fur Sozial-und Wirtschaftsgeschichte, 72*, 329–352.

Altick, R. (1974). *Librarianship and the pursuit of truth.* New Brunswick, NJ: Rutgers University, Graduate School of Library Science.

Altman, L. K. (1995, September 19). Experts blame drug firms for TB's global surge. *International Herald Tribune*, p. 3.

Andrews, E. L. (1997, April 17). CompuServe unit chief is indicted in Germany. *International Herald Tribune*, p. 13.

Aronson, N. (1986). Resistance to discovery: Vitamins, history, and careers. *Isis, 77*, 630–646.

Avella-Widham, G., Lutz, L., Mattejiet, R., & Mattejiet, U. (Eds.). (1977–1997). *Lexicon of the Middle Ages.* Munich: Artemis Verlag.

Bacci, P. (1927). Il Barna o Berna, pittore della Collegiata di San Gimignano è mai esistito? [Did Barna or Berna, painter of the San Gimignano Collegiata, ever exist?]. *La Balzana, 1*, 249–253.

Baigent, M., & Leigh, R. (1993). *The Dead Sea Scrolls deception.* London: Corgi Books.

Barbash, F. (1996, February 6). Publisher shelves a book. *International Herald Tribune*, p. 9.

Bartusiak, M. (1996, March 26). Books, *International Herald Tribune*, p. 12.

Barzanti, R. (1988, October 12) Esami e lettura per quella parete [Examination and a reading for that wall]. *N. C. Nuovo Corriere* (Siena), p. 15.

Beck, J. (1993). *Art restoration: The culture, the business and the scandal.* London: John Murray.

Beck, J. (1996, November 3). Letter to members of ArtWatch International, Inc.

Brandi, C. (1928). Barna e Giovanni d'Asciano [Barna and Giovanni d'Asciano.]. *La Balzana, 2*, 19–36.

Broad, W. (1980). Imbroglio at Yale (I): Emergence of a fraud. *Science, 210*, 38–41.

Brookesmith, P. (Ed.). (1984). *Thinking the unthinkable: Ideas which have upset conventional thought.* London: Orbis Publishing.

Bross, I. (1994). *Fifty years of folly and fraud "in the name of science."* Eggertsville, NY: Biomedical Metatechnology Press.

Buerkle, T. (1996, October 10). EU silenced early fears of mad cow health risk. *International Herald Tribune*, p. 1.

CAA News. (Newsletter of the College Art Association). (1996, November–December). CAA statements and guidelines, p. 3.

Caleca, A. (1976, November–December). Tre Polittici di Lippo Memmi, un ipotesi e la bottega di Simone e Lippo. I [Three polyptychs by Lippo Memmi, an hypothesis, and the workshop of Simone and Lippo]. *Critica d'Arte*, 49–59.

Campanario, J. M. (1995). On influential books and journal articles initially rejected because of negative referees' evaluations. *Science Communication, 65,* 304–325.

Campanario, J. M. (1996a). The competition for journal space among referees, editors, and other authors and its influence on journals' impact factors. *Journal of the American Society for Information Science, 47,* 184–192.

Campanario, J. M. (1996b). Have referees rejected some of the most-cited papers of all times? *Journal of the American Society for Information Science, 47,* 302–310.

Carvajal, D. (1996, May 8). U. S. holocaust debate is silenced. *International Herald Tribune*, p. 2.

Catt, I. (1978). The rise and fall of bodies of knowledge. *The Information Scientist, 12,* 137–144.

Chalmers, I. (1990). Underreporting research is scientific misconduct. *Journal of the American Medical Association, 263,* 1405–1408.

Cohen, R. (1997, May 8). See under "shush!": A library bans Internet smut. *International Herald Tribune*, p. 9.

College Art Association. (1995, January 24). A Code of ethics for art historians (Revised version).

Concordia University (Montreal, Canada), Board of Governors. *Action plan.*

Connor, S. (1995, March 24). World's first AIDS case was false. *The Independent*, p. 1.

Corcoran, E. (1996, July 2). Enter the swirling World Wide Web. *International Herald Tribune*, p. 1.

Cornog, M., & Perper, T. (1992, Fall). For sex, see librarian: Peanut butter. *Journal of Information Ethics, 1,* 5–12.

Crenshaw, C. (1992). *JFK conspiracy of silence.* New York: Penguin.

Croce, P. (1991). *Vivisection or science: A choice to make.* Rome: Buchverlag CIVIS.

Cude, W. (1987a). *The Ph.D. trap.* West Bay, Nova Scotia, Canada: Medicine Label Press.

Cude, W. (1987b, July 11). Tenured tyranny. *Globe and Mail*, p. C7.

Curtis, T. (1992, March 19). The origin of AIDS. *Rolling Stone*, 54–61, 106, 108.

Dalton, M. S. (1995). Refereeing of scholarly works for primary publishing. *Annual Review of Information Science and Technology, 30,* 213–250.

De Felice, L. (1991, March 28). Letter to the editor. *Nature*, p. 104.

de Grazia, A. (Ed.). (1978). *The Velikovsky affair.* London: Sphere Books.

de Grazia, A. (1984). *Cosmic heretics.* Princeton, NJ: Metron Publications.

De Marchi, L., & Franchi, F. (1996). *AIDS: La grande truffa* [AIDS: The great fraud]. Rome: Edizioni SEAM.

Diamond, S. (1992). *Compromised campus.* New York: Oxford University Press.

Di Trocchio, F. (1993). *Le bugie della scienza* [The lies of science]. Milan: Arnoldo Mondadori Editore.

Di Trocchio, F. (1997). *Il genio incompreso* [Misunderstood genius]. Milan: Arnoldo Mondadori Editore.

Duesberg, P. (1995). *Infectious AIDS: Have we been misled?* Berkeley, CA: North Atlantic Books.

Duesberg, P. (Ed.). (1996a). *AIDS: Virus—or drug induced?* Norwell, MA: Kluwer Academic.

Duesberg, P. (1996b). *Inventing the AIDS virus.* Washington, DC: Regnery Publishing.

Duggar, D., Christopher, K.A., Tucker, B.E., Jones, D.A., Watson, M., Puckett, M., & Wood, B. (1995, Spring). Promoting an awareness of retractions: The Louisiana State University Medical Center in Shreveport experience. *Medical References Services Quarterly, 14,* 17–32.

Dunn, E. (1993, April 4). A Light dusting or a good scrub? *Daily Telegraph,* p. 18.

Durbè, D. (Ed.). (1984). *Due pietre ritrovato di Amedeo Modigliani* [Two stone sculptures by Amedeo Modigliani are discovered]. San Giustino, Italy: Vimer, Srl.

Falcone, J. (1991). *Is knowledge constituted by power? The politics of knowledge in the art history community: A case study of "The Guidoriccio controversy."* Unpublished honors thesis in anthropology, Hamilton College, Clinton, NY.

Farias, V. (1989). *Heidegger and nazism.* Philadelphia: Temple University Press.

Feldman, G.D. (1984a). A collapse in Weimar scholarship. *Central European History, 17,* 159–177.

Feldman, G.D. (1984b). A response to David Abraham's "Reply." *Central European History, 17,* 245–267.

Fisher, M., Friedman, S.B., & Strauss, B. (1994). The effects of blinding on acceptance of research papers by peer review. *Journal of the American Medical Association, 272,* 143–146.

Fiske, E.B. (1986, September 21). Schmidt, inaugurated at Yale, appeals for campus freedom. *New York Times,* pp. 1, 40.

Fox, M.F., & Braxton, J.M. (1994). Misconduct and social control in science: Issues, problems, solutions. *The Journal of Higher Education,* 373–383.

Franklin, R. (1989). Foreword. In J. Swan & N. Peattie (Eds.), *The freedom to lie: A debate about democracy* (pp. xiii–xxi). Jefferson, NC: McFarland & Company.

Freuler, G. (1986). Lippo Memmi's New Testament cycle in the Collegiata in San Gimignano. *Arte Cristiana, 713,* 93–102.

Garattini, S., & van Bekkum, D.W. (Eds.). (1990). *The importance of animal experimentation for safety and biomedical research.* Dordrecht, The Netherlands: Kluwer Academic.

Gardner, J. (1989, July). Review of *Simone Martini. Atti del convegno.* [Florence: Centro Di, 1988]. *Burlington Magazine,* 487–490.

Gibbs, W.W. (1995, August). Lost science in the third world. *Scientific American,* p. 92.

Golden, T. (1997, January 28). A book is a book is a book? Not in the '90s. *International Herald Tribune,* p. 20.

Goldhagen, D. (1996). *Hitler's willing executioners.* New York: Knopf.

Grant, D. (1965). *A short history of opera.* New York: Columbia University Press.

Gratzer, W. (1996, July 4). Cases of conviction. *Nature, 382,* 35–36.

Gray, P. (1996, February 5). Attention name droppers. *Time,* p. 77.

Greenberg, D. (1987, October 15). Rockefeller U. faculty cool to President Baltimore. *Science and Government Report,* 5–6.

Greenberg, D. (1989, October 1). NIH enlarging panel for reopened Baltimore case. *Science and Government Report,* 4–5.

Greenberg, D. (1990, November 1). Copyright-suit winner faces misconduct charge. *Science and Government Report,* 4–6.

Greenhouse, L. (1988, April 23–24). After 45 years, a doctoral degree in persistence. *International Herald Tribune*, p. 1.

Hammerschmidt, D.E., & Gross, A.G. (1995, October). The problem of biomedical fraud: A model for retrospective and prospective action. *Journal of Scholarly Publishing, 27*, 3–11.

Hanchette, J., & Brewer, N. (1996, December 3). Gulf War vets' doctors say VA tried to fire them. *USA Today*, p. 3A.

Hannah, C. (1986). Who listens when women speak? The struggle for feminist critique in universities. In B. Martin, C. M. A. Baker, C. Manwell, & C. Pugh (Eds.), *Intellectual suppression* (pp. 200–212). London: Angus & Robertson.

Harvard University Gazette. (1982, January 29). Medical school dean releases report on falsification of research data. pp. 1, 12.

Hellmich, N. (1996, May 1). Health risks of being obese affect millions. *USA Today*, pp. 1A–2A.

Hentoff, N. (1986a, July 29). How Yale punishes bad thoughts. *Village Voice*, p. 27.

Hentoff, N. (1986b, August 5). Terrorists of the mind. *Village Voice*, p. 29.

Hernon, P., & Altman, E. (1995, January). Misconduct in academic research: Its implication for the service quality provided by university libraries. *The Journal of Academic Librarianship*, 27–37.

Hernon, P., & Altman, E. (1996). *Service quality in academic libraries.* Norwood, NJ: Ablex.

Hillman, H. (1991). Resistance to the spread of unpopular academic findings and views in liberal societies, including a personal case. *Accountability in Research, 1*, 259–272.

Hillman, H. (1995). Honest research. *Science and Engineering Ethics, 1*, 49–58.

Hillman, H. (1996). "What price intellectual honesty?" asks a neurologist. In B. Martin (Ed.), *Confronting the experts* (pp. 99–130). Albany: State University of New York Press.

Hillman, H. (1997). Parafraud in biology. *Science and Engineering Ethics, 3*, 121–136.

Hollis, B. (1987, December 14). I turned in my mentor. *The Scientist*, 11–12.

Horrobin, D. (1990). The philosophical basis of peer review and the suppression of innovation. *Journal of the American Medical Association, 263*, 1438–1441.

Horton, R. (1996, May 23). Truth and heresy about AIDS. *New York Review*, 14–20.

Jacobstein, J. (1987, December 14). I am not optimistic. *The Scientist*, 11–12.

James, B. (1996A, January 27–28). Bonn orders German cyberspace off-limits to a neo-nazi. *International Herald Tribune*, p. 4.

James, B. (1996B, March 20). New tuberculosis threat. *International Herald Tribune*, p. 5.

Jannella, C. (1989). *Simone Martini.* Florence, Italy: Scala.

Johnson, D. (1994, May 12). Sexual harassment chilling academic discourse. *International Herald Tribune*, pp. 1, 3.

Johnston, C. (1997, April 26–27). AOL users in Britain warned of surveillance. *International Herald Tribune*, p. 9.

Judson, H. (1994). Structural transformations of the sciences and the end of peer review. *Journal of the American Medical Association, 272*, 92–94.

Kaplan, G. (1986, November–December). Editorial. *The SAANZ Women's Section Newsletter*, p. 2.

Kasperson, R.E., & Kasperson, J.X. (1991). Hidden hazards. In D.G. Mayo & R.D. Hollander (Eds.), *Acceptable evidence* (pp. 9–28). New York: Oxford University Press.

Kimball, R. (1990). *Tenured radicals.* New York: Harper & Row.

Koshland, D. (1988). The price of progress [Editorial]. *Science, 241*, 637.

Krug, J., & Levinson, A. (1991, January). *Memorandum,* pp. 1–6.

Kuhn, T. (1970). *The structure of scientific revolutions.* Chicago: University of Chicago Press.

Kupfer, M. (1996, June). The lost wheel map of Ambrogio Lorenzetti. *Art Bulletin,* 286–310.

Kupferberg, H. (1975). *Opera.* New York: Newsweek Books.

Ladd, E., & Lipset, S. (1977). *The 1977 survey of the American professoriate.* (Questionnaire).

LaFollette, M. (1992). *Stealing into print: Fraud, plagiarism, and misconduct in scientific publishing.* Berkeley: University of California Press.

Lang, S. (1981). *The file.* New York: Springer-Verlag.

Lang, S. (1988, February 3). Academic, journalistic, and political problems [Paid advertisement]. *The Chronicle of Higher Education,* p. B4.

Lang, S. (1992, March 30). *The three laws of sociodynamics.* (Unpublished. Mathematics Department, Yale University).

Lang, S. (1993). Questions of scientific responsibility: The Baltimore case. *Ethics and Behavior, 3,* 3–72.

Lang, S. (1994, Fall). HIV and AIDS: Questions of scientific and journalistic responsibility. *Yale Scientific, 68,* 8–23.

Lang, S. (1995, Winter). HIV and AIDS, Part II: To fund or not to fund? That is the question. To inform or not to inform? That is another question. *Yale Scientific, 69,* 15–21.

Lauritsen, J. (1993). *Poison by prescription: The AZT story.* New York: Pagan Press.

Leslie, L.Z. (1989). Manuscript review: A view from below. *Scholarly Publishing, 20,* 123–128.

Levin, R.C. (1996, December). Preparing for Yale's fourth century. *Yale Alumni Magazine,* 24–31.

Limbaugh, R. (1993). *See, I told you so.* New York: Pocket Books.

Lipetz, B.A. (1991). Implications of new technology for the reviewing process. *Information Processing and Management, 27,* 129–133.

Mallory, M., & Moran, G. (1987, March). The border of "Guido Riccio" [letter to the editor]. *Burlington Magazine,* p. 187.

Mallory, M., & Moran, G. (1989, September–October). Guidoriccio: Una Storia Infinita. [Guidoriccio: A story that never ends]. *Donchisciotte,* p. 24.

Mallory, M., & Moran, G. (1994, October). Scholarly search for the truth, and problems associated with indexing/abstracting. *The Indexer, 19,* 99–101.

Mallory, M., & Moran, G. (1996). The Guido Riccio controversy in art history. In B. Martin (Ed.), *Confronting the experts* (pp. 131–154). Albany: State University of New York Press.

Manwell, C., & Baker, C.M.A. (1986a). Evaluation of performance in academic and scientific institutions. In B. Martin, C. M. A. Baker, C. Manwell, & C. Pugh (Eds.), *Inetellectual suppression* (pp. 264–300). London: Angus & Robertson.

Manwell, C., & Baker, C.M.A. (1986b). Paralysis of the conscience. In B. Martin, C. M. A. Baker, C. Manwell, & C. Pugh (Eds.), *Intellectual suppression* (pp. 129–150). London: Angus & Robertson.

Margolis, H. (1993). *Paradigms and barriers: How habits of mind govern scientific beliefs.* Chicago: University of Chicago Press.

Marshall, E. (1990, July 6). Science beyond the pale. *Science, 249,* 14–16.

Martin, B. (1986a). Archives of suppression. In B. Martin, C.M.A. Baker, C. Manwell, & C. Pugh (Eds.), *Intellectual suppression* (pp. 164–181). London: Angus & Robertson.

Martin, B. (1986b). Elites and suppression. In B. Martin, C.M.A. Baker, C. Manwell, & C. Pugh (Eds.), *Intellectual suppression* (pp. 185–199). London: Angus & Robertson.

Martin, B. (1986c). Mutagens and managers. In B. Martin, C.M.A. Baker, C. Manwell, & C. Pugh (Eds.), *Intellectual suppression* (pp. 123–129). London: Angus & Robertson.

Martin, B. (1992, June). Scientific fraud and the power structure of science. *Prometheus, 10*, 83–98.

Martin, B. (Ed.). (1996). *Confronting the experts*. Albany: State University of New York Press.

Martin, M. (1995, December 29). Germany forces CompuServe to censor sex on the Internet. *International Herald Tribune*, pp. 1, 10.

Martindale, A. (1986, April). The problem of "Guidoriccio." *Burlington Magazine*, 259–273.

McQueen, M. (1988, December 2). Dartmouth editor charges persecution. *USA Today*, p. 1.

Mead, M. (1928). *Coming of age in Samoa*. New York: William Morrow.

Menuhin, Y. (1981). *Violin*. New York: Norton.

Mervis, J. (1989, November 27). NIH disarray stymies *Cell* paper investigation. *The Scientist*, pp. 1, 4.

Moran, G. (1976, January). Is the name Barna an incorrect transcription of the name Bartolo? *Paragone, 311*, 76–80.

Moran, G. (1977, November). An investigation regarding the equestrian portrait of Guidoriccio da Fogliano in the Siena Palazzo Pubblico. *Paragone, 333*, 81–88.

Moran, G. (1991). Scholarly communication, peer review, and reference librarian ethics: A Case study of the *Lexicon of the Middle Ages*. *The Reference Librarian, 33*, 159–172.

Moran, G., & Mallory, M. (1988). "Selective" card cataloging (or in-house screening of periodical indexing) of art history articles in authors' files, and the potential effects of this "selectivity" on the bibliographical entries relating to specific art historical problems: A case study. In *Art periodicals: Papers of the 2nd European Conference of the Art Libraries of IFLA (pp. 123–132)*.. Amsterdam: Overleg Kunsthistorische Bibliotheken in Nederland.

Moran, G., & Mallory, M. (1991A, Spring). The Guido Riccio controversy and resistance to critical thinking. *Syracuse Scholar*, 38–63.

Moran, G., & Mallory, M. (1991B, Fall). Some ethical considerations regarding scholarly communication. *Library Trends, 40*,(2), 338–356.

Morton, H.C., Price, A.J., Rosenberg, J., Styles, D., Tenopir, C., Hagen, B., & Mayers, J. (1988). *Writings on scholarly communication*. Lanham, MD: University Press of America.

Morton, H.C., & Price, A.J. (1989). *The ACLS survey of scholars*. Lanham, MD: University Press of America.

Mumby, K. (1992). Personal communication to friends and supporters.

Nigg, H.N., & Radulescu, G. (1994, July 14). Scientific misconduct in environmental science and toxicology. *Journal of the American Medical Association, 272*, 168–170.

Nissani, M. (1989). An experimental paradigm for the study of conceptual conservatism and change. *Psychological Reports, 65*, 19–24.

Nissani, M. (1994). Conceptual conservatism: An understated variable in human affairs. *The Social Science Journal, 31*, 307–318.

Nissani, M. (1995). The plight of the obscure innovator in science: A few reflections on Campanario's note. *Social Studies of Science, 25*, 165–183.

Noble, W. (1990). *Bookbanning in America*. Middlebury, VT: Paul S. Eriksson.

Osburn, C. (1989). The structuring of the scholarly communication system. *College & Research Libraries, 50*, 277–287.

Pacey, P. (1992). Editorial. *Art Libraries Journal, 17*, 3–4.

Pascal, L. (1991). *What happens when science goes bad: The corruption of science and the origin of AIDS: A case study in spontaneous generation* (Working Paper No. 9).

Wollongong, Australia: University of Wollongong Science and Technology Analysis Research Programme.

Pell, E. (1984). *The big chill*. Boston: Beacon Press.

Peters, D., & Ceci, S. (1982). Peer review practices of psychological journals: The fate of published articles, submitted again. *Behavioral and Brain Sciences, 5*, 187–195.

Prattico, F. (1996, October 4). Perchè perdiamo la guerra con l'AIDS? [Why are we losing the war against AIDS?]. *La Repubblica*, p. 42.

Pugh, C. (1986). In the twilight zone: Academia and human rights. In B. Martin, C. M. A. Baker, C. Manwell, & C. Pugh (Eds.), *Intellectual suppression*. London: Angus & Robertson.

Raeburn, P. (1987, August 30). Study finds reluctance to expose scientific fraud. *The Champaign-Urbana News Gazette*, p. A-7.

Ragionieri, G. (1985). *Simone o non Simone* [Simone or not Simone]. Florence, Italy: la Casa Usher.

Ratner, H. (1988). Stalking the Salk. *Child and Family, 20*, 328–333.

Reier, S. (1997, March 14). Internet arrives at a crossroads. *International Herald Tribune*, p. 21a.

Relyea, H.C. (1994). *Silencing science: National security controls and scientific communication*. Norwood, NJ: Ablex.

Remus, W. (1980, April). Why academic journals are unreadable: The referees' crucial role. *Interfaces, 10*, 87–90.

Rennie, D., & Flanagin, A. (1995). Peer review in Prague [Editorial]. *Journal of the American Medical Association, 274*, p. 986-7.

Reuters. (1996, February 6). China sets more rules to regulate internet. *International Herald Tribune*, p. 15.

Roberts, S. (1996, September 21–22). Despite HIV, Morrison seeks "one last fight." *International Herald Tribune*, p. 19.

Rodney, M. (1995, Summer). Subtle censors: Collection development in academic libraries. *North Carolina Libraries, 53*, 74–77.

Rosand, D. (1979, Summer). The elusive Michelangelo. *Art News, 78*, 48–51.

Rose, L. (1978, Winter). "Just plainly wrong": A critque of Peter Huber. *Kronos, 4*, 33–69.

Ruegg, W. (1986, Winter). The academic ethos. *Minerva, 24*, 393–412.

Ruesch, H. (1989). *1000 doctors (and many more) against vivisection*. Massagno, Switzerland: Buchverlag CIVIS Publications.

Ruesch, H. (1991). *Slaughter of the innocent*. New York: Civitas Publications. (Original work published 1978).

Ruesch, H. (1992). *Naked empress*. Klosters, Switzerland: CIVIS Publications.

Ruesch, H. (1993, Spring-Summer). To our readers. *International Foundation Report, 14*, 16.

Ruesch, H. (1995, Summer). Revisionist history sees Pasteur as liar who stole rival's ideas. *International Foundation Report, 18*, 1–3.

Sarasohn, J. (1993). *Science on trial: The whistle-blower, the accused, and the Nobel Laureate*. New York: St. Martin's.

Schaller, B.R., & Schaller, C.V.C. (1995, November). Alumni notes. *Yale Alumni Magazine*, p. 68.

Schmaus, W. (1987, September). *An analysis of fraud and misconduct in science*. Paper presented at the AAAS–ABA National Conference of Lawyers and Scientists Workshop on Scientific Fraud and Misconduct, "The Woods," Hedgesville, WV.

Schneider, H.G. (1989). The threat to authority in the revolution of chemistry. *History of Universities, 8*, 137–50.

Schrecker, E. (1986). *No ivory tower: McCarthyism and the universities.* New York: Oxford University Press.

Serebnick, J. (1991, Fall). Identifying unethical practices in journal publishing. *Library Trends, 40,*(2), 357–372.

Shapley, D. (1997, January 28). A new, faster Internet takes shape in America. *International Herald Tribune,* pp. 11, 15.

Sharma, D. (1996). Confronting the nuclear power structure in India. In B. Martin (Ed.), *Confronting the Experts* (pp. 155–174). Albany: State University of New York Press.

Sharp, D. (1990). What can and should be done to reduce publication bias? *Journal of the American Medical Association, 263,* 1390–1391.

Sprague, R. (1987, December 14). I trusted the research system. *The Scientist, 1,* 11–12.

Springell, P. (1986). For the freedom to comment by scientists. In B. Martin, C. M. A. Baker, C. Manwell, & C. Pugh (Eds.), *Intellectual suppression* (pp.74–79). London: Angus & Robertson.

Strohman, R. (1995). Preface. In P. Duesberg, *Infectious AIDS: Have we been misled?* (pp. vii–xiv). Berkeley, CA: North Atlantic Books.

Swan, J. (1991, Fall). Ethics inside and out: The case of *Guidoriccio. Library Trends, 40,*(2), 258–274.

Swan, J. (1992, April 13). Scientists and librarians: An ethical bond must unite them. *The Scientist,* p. 11.

Swan, J. (1994, Spring). Sharing and stealing: Persistent ambiguities. *Journal of Information Ethics, 3,* 42–47.

Swan, J., & Peattie, N. (1989). *The freedom to lie: A debate about democracy.* Jefferson, NC: McFarland & Company.

USA Today. (1993, November 18). Keep our speech free. (Editorial), p. 8A.

USA Today. (1995, October 3). Costly treatment. p. 9A.

Varaut, J.M. (1990). Experimentation and the law. In S. Garattini & D.W. Van Bekkum (Eds.), *The importance of animal experimentation for safety and biomedical research* (pp. 35–38). Dordrecht, The Netherlands: Kluwer Academic.

Velikovsky, I. (1978). *Ages in chaos.* London: Abacus.

Velikovsky, I. (1980). *Worlds in collision.* Bungay (Suffolk), England: Abacus.

Venturi, A. (1907). *Storia dell' arte Italiana* [History of Italian art]. Milan: Hoepli Editore Libraio della Real Casa.

Wade, N. (1995, January 8). Contrarians at the gate. *The New York Times Magazine,* pp. 14–15.

Walker, M. (1994). *Dirty medicine.* London: Slingshot.

Wall Street Journal. (1986, September 23). Yale's beastly behavior. (Editorial).

Weller, A. (1990). Editorial peer review in US medical journals. *Journal of the American Medical Association, 263,* 1344–1347.

Wenneras, C., & Wold, A. (1997, May 22). Nepotism and sexism in peer-review. *Nature, 387,* 341–343.

Williams, D. (1996, May 8). Italy peers reluctantly into 2 faces of its wartime past. *International Herald Tribune,* p. 6.

Windom, R.E. (1988, April 12). Testimony before the U.S. House of Representatives Energy and Commerce Subcommittee on Oversight and Investigations, Washington, DC.

Woodward, C.V. (1975). *Report of the committee on freedom of speech at Yale.* Yale University.

Woolf, P. (1986). Testimony prepared for the U.S. House of Representatives Task Force on Science Policy of the Committee on Science and Technology. Washington, DC.

Yale Weekly Bulletin and Calendar. (1982, September 13–20). Yale policy statement on collaborative research.

Zeri, F. (1988, October 26). No, non è di Simone questo brutto Guidoriccio [No, this ugly Guidoriccio is not by Simone] (in *Giotto e i maestri del Trecento*). *la Repubblica* (Supplement), pp. 49–52, 57.

Zimmerman, D. (1995, June 1). Gallo leaving NCI, speaks his mind. *Probe, 4*, 1, 4–5.

Author Index

Subject Index